language for everybody

WHAT IT IS AND HOW TO MASTER IT

ILLUSTRATED

MARIO PEI

"The person who speaks, easily and correctly, the standard speech of the broad language community to which he belongs will normally find himself better off all around. He will be able to express his ideas and personality and get what he wants. He will be able to make friends and influence people. He will find that his opinions carry weight with the men and women he associates with. He will also find that he has greater understanding of others, their ideas, and their problems."

—DR. MARIO PEI
Professor of Romance Philology
Columbia University

•   •   •

what this book is about

The person who owns and operates a piece of machinery usually likes to know how it works. The automobile driver, even though he may not be mechanically inclined, takes an interest in the repairs that are made by his mechanic. He wants to know about the parts that have to be adjusted or replaced, the operation of various gadgets, the way in which twenty thousand parts, more or less, collaborate in achieving his goal, which is transportation.

The normal person, young or old, has a similar interest in the marvelous machine that enables him to accomplish an even more important objective—communication with his fellowman.

That machine is language—spoken, written, gestural, symbolic. It is language that permits a person to place his thoughts at the disposal of another. Language precedes, accompanies, and follows practically all human endeavor. Without language, ninety-nine percent of human activity would cease.

The more we know about an automobile, the better we can take care of it, the better we can use it, the farther and faster we can travel in it. And so with language. What is it? What are its parts? How did it begin and how was it made? What makes it go, and how can we improve it so that it will carry us farther, faster, and more comfortably on the journey of communication?

I have written this book to answer these questions simply and helpfully. I have written it as an introduction to language, much as an automotive engineer might take you on a tour that would give you a comprehensive view of how an automobile comes into being. If I may carry the metaphor further, I have planned a tour that will take you to the iron mines of language, through the steel refineries and casting plants, and into the factories, where the parts are made and assembled. I try to tell in a few words what the parts are, and I conduct you to the cutaways, in which you can see the interior machinery in motion. Finally, I take you in a finished car to the proving grounds, where we see what the car can do under all kinds of conditions, and finally to the highway where other cars of all makes and models are streaming past. The car is yours to join with the stream and, whenever you wish, to turn off into the less traveled roads and lanes.

I have written this book—or tour—in six parts, and although the parts follow a definite order of development, you may open to any one of them, depending upon your immediate interest and the completeness of your linguistic knowledge at this moment.

Part I, "Language in Your Daily Life," tries to show how language—spoken and written—lies at the very heart of our thinking, our communications, our actions. I suggest that the role of the individual as a working, studying, playing creature is determined to an enormous degree by his practical awareness of language use. This role can be vastly bettered by a greater knowledge of one's own language, as well as the languages of countries other than one's own. In Part I, I also survey the distribution of world languages today.

Part II, "Language in the Laboratory," seeks to answer the question, what *is* language? How do we make and articulate language sounds? What takes place in us when we respond to words uttered by others? How are words changed in size and shape, from moment to moment, and how are they moved around so that they will take on this or that meaning? How do stress, accent, intonation alter the sense of what we put into words? Finally, what are the language laws to which we must adhere if we are to communicate most effectively, and what are the latest scientific aids to language learning?

Part III, "History of Language," goes back into our linguistic ancestry and shows why our language is what it is today. Our language, and all languages, have grown from many and various beginnings. Language, because it is the intimate expression of living beings, is itself a living thing; like all living things, it is the product of many forebears, it grows and develops, it assumes individuality and maturity. The history of language is deeply woven into the history of man. In languages, as in people and nations, there have been growth, unification, subdivision; there have been wars, conquests, mergers. There have, in a sense, been linguistic nations, provinces, expeditions, migrations, cities, highways, resorts. Changes have come with time, geography, climate, natural resources. Languages have been shaped by many factors: commercial, cultural, religious, military. And we today are heirs to these rich and variegated processes.

Part IV, "Sociological Implications of Language," has to do with language's role as a social factor. As with races of men, language has its majorities and minorities. It has had many rises and falls, and these are often associated with the rises and falls of peoples. Language has its national and international aspects; it has a "Department of State," which administers relations among the various tongues. This part looks into the present and future of languages and suggests what we can do about it.

Part V, "Languages in Comparison," is just that. Here I have some things to say about the great language families and the smaller ones, the parentages and offspring, the cousinships and intermarriages. Sometimes family resemblances are strong, sometimes subtle; often they are deceiving. Here we meet some of our relatives for the first time and compare notes.

Part VI, "Some Practical Language Hints," is intended to start you on the road to language improvement and language learning. It does not pretend to be exhaustive, but only to point the way. To start in the right direction is important, because by doing so we reach our goal much faster and we avoid getting lost and discouraged. I offer here some suggestions on how to identify foreign languages and names; how to sharpen the tool of our own language; how to go about learning another language in the easiest and most useful way, whether it is the written or the spoken version that we wish to master.

MARIO PEI

Columbia University
September, 1956

contents

what this book is about, *v*

1 LANGUAGE IN YOUR DAILY LIFE

how language—and languages—can help you, 3
language study: old and new emphasis, 9
language: physical, social, or cultural phenomenon?, 18
english, 26
modern foreign languages, 33
classical languages, 42
cultural aspects of language: dialect, 51
cultural aspects of language: slang, cant, jargon, 59

2 LANGUAGE IN THE LABORATORY

physical and physiological aspects of language,   69
language sounds,   77
language forms,   84
the word,   92
accent, intonation, and the syllable,   97
some laws of language,   107
scientific aids to language learning,   114

3 HISTORY OF LANGUAGE

language and the world's past,   121
evolution of language,   129
arteries of language,   136
when two languages meet,   146
language and colonialism,   153
trade and military influences on language,   161
when language migrates,   169
liturgical languages,   177

4 SOCIOLOGICAL IMPLICATIONS OF LANGUAGE

language cycles and zones,   189
the language community,   196
language minorities,   205
language as the standard bearer of culture,   211
geography of language,   219
what makes a language important?,   225
international aspects of language,   231
language and the world's future,   236

5 LANGUAGES IN COMPARISON

how language affiliations are determined, 247
language families, 254
similarities and otherwise, 267
some typical language structures, 273

6 SOME PRACTICAL LANGUAGE HINTS

what language is that?, 289
how to learn a spoken language, 300
how to learn a written language, 309
how to improve your own language, 319

SELECTIVE BIBLIOGRAPHY 327

INDEX 331

a note on how to use this book

In addition to the basic text, there are in this book a number of line drawings as well as "illustrative" examples which are set in type. These examples appear at appropriate places throughout the text and are distinguishable from the text by being set in slightly smaller type. Also, they are separated from the text by a line at the beginning and end of each example. Some examples extend for two or more pages but in every case can be differentiated from the text, as explained.

1

LANGUAGE IN YOUR DAILY LIFE

how language—and languages— can help you

A well-known linguist advises you to "leave your language alone"; that is, speak naturally, even if incorrectly, letting the chips fall where they may. Go ahead and use "ain't," "it's me," "who did you see?," "I laid on the bed," he advocates. Another distinguished authority in the field suggests that it would be a splendid thing if no more spelling were taught for half a century, and people were allowed to spell as they please; at the end of that period, he adds, the chances are we would have worked out a new system of spelling that would reflect the pronunciation.

Statements like these are spectacular, and they sound good on the surface. They encourage the tendency, inborn in each of us, to follow the line of least resistance and avoid work and effort.

Also, they have in them a grain of sense. Consider, for example, the different sorts of car driving you see on the road; some are glaringly bad and lead to crashes; but certainly, within the range of safety, there is room for various ways of holding the steering wheel, applying the brakes, making a turn. Not all good golf players hold their clubs in precisely the same fashion; one man who could never break ninety as long as he held his club in the way taught him by the pro found himself down in the low eighties as soon as he threw instruction overboard and handled the club in the way that was most natural for him. Some people pound the typewriter with two fingers of each hand and their eyes on the keyboard, and are almost as speedy and accurate as devotees of the touch system.

However, there are limits to the effectiveness of doing as you please. This is particularly true in language. Even the man who wants you to "leave your language alone" admits that if you use "ain't" and "I done it" in the "best" circles, you won't get invited to tea again. As for the matter of spelling, we may get away with "thru" and "nite," but phonetic spellings like "natcherly," "watchagonnado," and "I should of done it" will mark you as an illiterate.

Rightly or wrongly, most people consider language as an index of culture, breeding, upbringing, personality, sometimes even of intelligence, decency, and integrity. Under the circumstances, it is unwise, not to say harmful, to pay no heed to your language. The present status of the language being what it is, the use of wrong words and forms, or the inability to produce the right ones, may do as much damage to your chances of getting ahead (and along) as using a knife on your peas or slurping your soup.

Language is something more than a system of communications; it is also a social convention which one must observe, under penalty of being misjudged. Ignorance or improper use of language can easily interfere with your success and advancement. It can take money out of your pocket.

Conversely, the proper use of the proper language in the environment for which it is designed can lead to success in both business and social relations. For this, there is a well-grounded psychological reason.

Language is a set of rules tacitly agreed to and accepted by common consent of all the speakers. There is no intrinsic connection between the *object* "hat" and the *word* "hat" save that the word has been set apart by the English-speaking community to serve as the *symbol* of the object. A French-speaking community will use not "hat" but *chapeau* to represent the object we call a hat. The validity of the language symbol for the object is subjective and unstable, in precisely the same way that a dollar bill, or a pound note, is a subjective and unstable token of purchasing power, and not at all identical with the things it can buy.

If you find yourself alone in a desert you will quickly realize that the value of such dollar bills as you may have in your pocket shrinks to nil, and that a slab of bacon or a canteen of water is infinitely more valuable than a handful of hundred-dollar notes. You will also find that your language equipment is of no particular value, since there is no one to use it on.

But human beings normally do not live alone in deserts. They live in communities of their fellowmen, and in such communities symbol values come into play. The dollar bill has no value in itself; it is only a piece of paper. But it is everywhere accepted as a *symbol* of purchasing power. In the same way, language becomes of value because it is accepted as the symbol of thought, the medium by which thought is transferred from one person to another.

It is at this point that the symbol comes in for close scrutiny. Why is a forged dollar bill not accepted, while one produced by the government presses is? Intrinsically, the privately produced dollar note is just as valuable (or valueless) as the good note. But the community has decided that only such dollar bills as bear the authentic imprint of the U. S. government shall be valid as media of exchange and symbols of metal currency. This is because we know the government has the silver with which to redeem the paper note.

In language, the community has decided that certain words and forms are valid as symbols of thought and shall be accepted by all members of the community, while others, for one reason or another (not necessarily a logical one), are not valid. Those not valid may serve the purpose of temporary exchange of meaning in a limited way, just as some forms of scrip served the purposes of money in small communities during the depression days, or in certain army units during the occupation of foreign lands. Their use, however, is limited, while the fully standard forms have universal currency throughout the entire speech community.

The type of language you ought to strive to write and speak should therefore be the one that has the widest, not the narrowest, currency, that is universally accepted and understood wherever there are English speakers. You should not be content with a kind of language that is restricted to one locality, or one social class.

To discover what is universally current throughout the speech community calls for some effort. Through ignorance, you may sometimes delude yourself into believing that the local or class speech form you happen to be using is standard when as a matter of fact it is not. If you are wrong and don't know it, there is no way of correcting your error. But if you are wrong and are aware of the fact, you can do something about it.

The question is not so much one of striving to achieve "correctness" in accordance with some arbitrary or antiquated model, but of striving to come as close as possible to the general usage of the community. To speak without gross and glaring localisms, and with a minimum of class features, slang, and jargon, is desirable. This can only be achieved by watching your language, not by "leaving it alone."

The person who speaks, easily and correctly, the standard speech of the broad language community to which he belongs will normally find himself better off all around. He will be able to express his ideas and personality and get what he wants. He will be able to make friends and influence people. He will find that his opinions carry greater weight with the men and women he associates with. He will also find that he has greater understanding of others, their ideas, and their problems.

In addition to the comparison between authentic U. S. currency and scrip or forged notes, another comparison is possible, between an authentic dollar bill and an authentic British pound note. Both are fully valid and fully accepted in their own areas. But the areas don't coincide. Dollar, pound, franc, mark, lira, ruble, yen are all legitimate forms of currency, but you cannot translate one into purchasing power in the area of another without going through the process of exchange.

Something quite similar happens in the case of foreign languages as compared with your own native tongue. The other languages are valid media of thought transfer in their respective countries, just as yours is valid in your land. The process by which you get your linguistic money exchanged in the foreign area is to have translators and interpreters at your disposal to convey your thoughts to the local people and get theirs in return. But just as you may also provide yourself, before you set forth on your travels, with amounts of foreign money, you may, in like manner, provide yourself with greater or smaller amounts of foreign languages, which will save you the trouble of stopping at the local exchange office or securing the services of a translator or interpreter.

Materially speaking, a knowledge of foreign languages makes your traveling easier and more comfortable and allows you to carry on your activities in the foreign country as naturally as you would in your own.

On another plane, a knowledge of foreign languages gives you a keener insight into the world-wide human mind, permits you to compare ways of expression and modes of thought, gives you a greater understanding of other peoples, and makes for far more pleasant and friendly relations, and this is true whether you travel or not. A good deal of the antipathy and intolerance existing in the world today hinges upon lack of linguistic understanding.

It is therefore desirable to know, as well as possible, both your own language and the languages of other groups. Language, once it is gained, can be put to work for you. It can help you in your business or occupation, in your social life, in your travels, in your enjoyment of the world in general. It expands your horizons, and makes accessible to you the treasuries of world thought, both in your own chosen line of endeavor and in that broad field of leisure which modern technology has put within reach of practically all men.

Some major shifts have taken place recently in connection with points of view concerning language and languages. As is usual in these cases, not all change is necessarily progress.

Down to the early decades of the present century, it was customary to view language as something almost fixed and immutable. Grammar, which might be described as a language's body of laws, was set, and any deviation from it was counted as an error. It was granted that vocabulary might change, but only slowly and after the fullest deliberation by "authority." Literary norms and stylistic standards, ranging from Chaucer to Dickens, formed, as it were, a linguistic constitution. The language came to be viewed and taught prescriptively: this was right, that was wrong, and no two ways about it.

If it is any consolation to English speakers, precisely the same situation prevailed in other languages. French, German, Italian, Spanish all were presented by the grammarians to their speakers in the same fashion. In addition, a hierarchy of languages had been set up by both statesmen and scholars in the course of the centuries that followed the period of exploration and colonization of new continents. The only languages that really counted were the western European ones, with their classical ancestors, Greek and Latin. A curious reflection of this point of view is to be seen in the fact that anyone attempting to construct an artificial language, like Volapük, Esperanto, or Interlingua, would inevitably make both his grammar and his vocabulary a combination of western European tongues plus

Greek and Latin; it was assumed that the earth's other nations would be only too happy to bow to the superiority of western civilization.

The revolution in language that has been in progress since the end of World War I has several different facets. For what concerns the national language (specifically English, in our case), it has become more and more universally recognized that language is not static but dynamic; that it is not in a state of immobility but in a state of constant change and flux. The principle of change is universal in language (see page 108), and recognition of this fact has given rise to what might be termed a principle of relativity in language matters, replacing the rigidity of the past. This in turn has led to greater tolerance (perhaps too much) toward substandard, semiliterate forms. "Errors" in grammar and spelling, deviations both of a local variety (dialects) and of a class variety (slang) are no longer frowned upon or deemed uncouth. It will be noted that this new view of language closely parallels the movement of "democracy" in the political, social, and economic spheres, the granting of "equality" to all, even to those who are not ready for it, and the philosophy of self-expression regardless of whose toes you are stepping on. To this extent, it may be argued that the current attitude toward language is a fairly good index of man's present environment. Whether all this is, in the long run, good or bad, only time and history can decide. There is the possibility that it is intrinsically neither good nor bad but merely historical. There is also the possibility that the historical pendulum, having swung too far in one direction, will begin to swing in the opposite direction, as has so often occurred in the past.

At any rate, the standard language, formerly viewed as the prerogative of the few, has now become the possession of the many. Our most widely accepted grammars now endeavor to be descriptive rather than prescriptive; that is, to set down the language as it is actually spoken and written by the majority of its speakers rather than the way it was ideally conceived by the grammarians and schoolmasters of the past. To cite one example: in a grammar of 1900, a phrase like "It is me" would be set down as a gross error; in a grammar of today, it would be stated that while "It is I" is still used by a great many people, "It is me" is currently used by the majority, including such great names as Churchill; the reader is left to make his own choice. In present-day dictionaries, not merely colloquialisms but vulgarisms and slang terms are listed, not to encourage their use but to acquaint the reader with their meanings.

While we may deplore certain phases of the "new freedom" in matters of language, the attitude of the modern grammarians seems in the main more reasonable and, above all, more historical than that of their predecessors. It is far more in accord with the historical facts of language as we know them, which indicate that language is constantly changing and that the illiterate form of one period becomes the elegant form of the next.

At the same time, there is no point to pushing language change too far and too fast. Progress, to be progress, must show some semblance of order. This is particularly true in language, where the transfer of meaning requires that there be general acceptance of innovations, under penalty of seeing your unified language break up into mutually incomprehensible dialects and even separate languages, as the Latin of the Roman Empire gave rise to the Romance languages.

ARCHAIC AND OBSOLETE

maze (to make dizzy)
refect (to refresh with food or drink)
deadly (fatally, mortally)
deathsman (executioner)
dere, dear (hard, severe, glorious)
meanly (moderately)
mazard (cup, bowl, head)
hungerly (hungry looking)

OBSOLETE SLANG

Hungarian (thievish beggar)

DIALECTAL

reedbird (Southern), bobolink
reedmace (English), cattail
pliskie (Scottish), trick
hurdies (Scottish), derrière

COLLOQUIAL

sticks (the)
bamboozle
maze (I'm in a)
mean (person)
hunk
hunch
hurray
wryneck

SLANG

yegg (gunman)
to pluck someone (to fleece)
hunky-dory (O. K., shipshape)
measly (very few, small, piddling)
mooch (to beg, cajole)
moonshine (homemade liquor)
dead-pan (serious-faced)
boob (fool)
crackajack (wonderful)
dandy (*adj.*, excellent)
plug-ugly (rough, rowdy person)

NOTE: "Wryneck" for "stiff neck" is antiquated. The last four words in the slang list are beginning to be out of fashion, "boob" being replaced by "dope," "jerk," "schmo," etc., "crackajack" and "dandy" by "swell," "plug-ugly" by "tough guy." The dictionary omits "moolah" for "money," and over-looks the use of "dead-pan" as a verb ("he deadpanned"). "Dead beat" is "sponger" in slang, but "worn out" in colloquial. "Plug" has the slang meanings of "to hit hard," "to shoot" ("I plugged him with my gun"); "to work hard" ("Keep plugging at it"); "inferior" ("He's just a plug"); and the colloquial meaning of "bombastic publicity" ("He gave me a nice plug in his radio program.").

The words above appear in the dictionary count described on page 62.

When we come to foreign languages, the new approach is even more radical. Prior to World War I, it was assumed that only an intellectual élite would be interested in foreign languages, for purposes of general culture rather than for travel or business. As a result, the languages were presented primarily in their written form, so that the learner would be enabled to read them. Relatively little attention, save in special cases, was given to the spoken form of the foreign language; it was assumed that if anyone was interested in that, he would either secure private instruction or go to reside in the foreign country.

Coupled with this attitude was the same type of perfectionism in grammar that appeared in the study of the native language. Perusal of Regents or college-entrance examinations in foreign languages dating back to the 1910s or 1920s shows a highly impractical, ridiculous insistence upon minor, picayune points of grammar that seldom show up in actual speech, like the use of *ce dont* in French. This was coupled with a strong preference for literary as against everyday words. You would find "sunset" and "heroism" but not "beefsteak" or "washroom" in your lesson vocabulary.

The modern approach views language as primarily a spoken activity, and the stress is on speaking and understanding rather than on reading, writing, or the niceties of grammar. It is also frankly practical and materialistic, to the extent that it envisages the use of foreign languages for purposes of warfare, business, or travel rather than for the reading of literature or the composing of graceful diplomatic notes. Many of the more advanced teachers of foreign languages avoid the written form of the language altogether until the elements of the spoken tongue have been assimilated by ear, as we shall see later. They also make use of all sorts of visual and auditory aids, favoring a technique of listening and repeating, either with native speakers or with recordings (see pages 114-118).

Here again we may note a reflection of prevailing philosophies. The modern experts view foreign languages, like good English, as accessible to all, not as the prerogative of a few. Present-day trends are openly practical and utilitarian, and so is our view of language methods and purposes.

Here again a warning note may be sounded, lest we go overboard on the port side of the ship while trying to avoid going overboard on the starboard side. Getting rid of the worship of the past participle and its rules for agreement may be an advantage, but not if we replace it with the cult of the native-speaker accent, which may vary from locality to locality and from class to class. We may understand and make ourselves understood in a foreign tongue even if we make a few grammatical errors; but the same holds true even if we don't pronounce French quite like a Parisian, or Spanish quite like a Castilian.

The written language, particularly in these days of widespread literacy, ought not to be neglected. Even on the practical side, the written form of a foreign language is

indispensable; in it are couched not only works of literature but popular magazines, daily newspapers, road signs,
essential directions and warnings, even restaurant menus.
People who do not care to travel may nevertheless want to
learn a foreign language, primarily in its written form,
not only for literary enjoyment but for business and professional purposes. An importer may want to read a foreign
catalogue, or a doctor a medical tract in German.

Still another shift in points of view about language applies to the relative importance of the languages themselves. Where, at the beginning of the century, only a
handful of languages were considered important or significant, it is now recognized that a far larger group must
be reckoned with in the world of today and tomorrow.
Latin, Greek, French, Spanish, German, Italian, English
are no longer the only languages we need to consider. The
swift march of events since the outbreak of World War II
indicates that many large groups not only of Europe and
America but also of Asia and Africa, which were formerly
inarticulate in world affairs, have come of age and are demanding to be heard. Languages like Russian, Portuguese,
Chinese, Japanese, Hindustani, Indonesian, Arabic have
come to the fore, along with many tongues of smaller
groups, like the Koreans and Vietnamese, with which we
have to have dealings of one sort or another. Some of
these tongues show a structure radically different from
that of the western languages with which we are most
familiar.

Here again we have extremists who advocate that the
same treatment be accorded to Melanesian Pidgin, Haitian
Creole, or the language of an obscure group in the Amazon
jungles that is accorded to the great tongues of civilization,

ESSENTIAL WARNING SIGNS

ENGLISH	GERMAN	FRENCH	SPANISH	ITALIAN	RUSSIAN
Entrance	Eingang	Entrée	Entrada	Entrata	ВХОД (vkhod)
Danger!	Gefahr!	Danger!	¡Peligro!	Pericolo!	ОПАСНОСТЬ! (opasnost')
Stop!	Halt!	Arrêtez!	¡Pare!	Ferma!	ОСТАНОВКА (ostanovka)
No Smoking!	Rauchen verboten!	Défense de fumer!	¡Prohibido fumar!	Proibito fumare!	КУРИТЬ ВОСПРЕЩАЕТСЯ! (kurit' vospreshchayetsya)
Keep Right!	Rechts fahren!	Tenez la droite!	¡Guardar la derecha!	Tenere la destra!	ДЕРЖИСЬ НАПРАВО (derzhis' napravo)

whether western or Oriental. This is perhaps a question of primary interest to linguistic specialists, but again it is a reflection of current philosophical trends of the equalitarian variety.

For what concerns the average individual, the changes in viewpoint that we have been discussing all have their practical applications. First, in connection with English, you must decide whether you want to use a type of language that can be easily understood throughout the entire English-speaking world and is readily accessible to all classes, or a particularized form of language suitable to one locality and one social class.

Secondly, when it comes to foreign languages, you are faced with a choice both of language and of approach. The tongue or tongues you choose should logically be the ones most likely to be of service to you in whatever line of activity you wish to follow. If you expect to be an oil engineer in Arabia, it is probable that Arabic will be more useful to you than Russian or Chinese; but if you have in mind an extended tour of Italy, Italian will serve you better than French or German.

If you do not have any foreign adventure in mind, or if your future course is such that it will be served equally well by any one of three or four languages, then perhaps you should fall back on your own likes and dislikes or on what you may judge to be most useful in a general way. In this connection, the so-called "dead" languages, Latin and Greek, which contribute so much to a proper understanding of living English, emphatically ought not to be left out of account.

When it comes to how to study a language, individual needs and tastes again come into play. If you wish to ac-

quire a speaking and understanding knowledge for purposes of travel and touring, you will do well to follow the
spoken-language technique of listening to and repeating
phrases and sentences. If you want to read French and German medical tracts, on the other hand, the acquisition of a
native-speaker accent is largely a waste of time, and you
will do well to settle for one of the old-style reading courses,
with particular stress on your own field of special activity.
If you just "like French," there is no reason why a combination of methods and techniques cannot be worked out.
This is precisely what is done in most of our language
schools, where a balanced diet of reading, writing, speaking, and understanding is supplied to the ones who want it.

language: physical, social,
or cultural phenomenon?

It has become fashionable to classify fields of
learning into one of three major sections: physical science,
social science, and something rather vaguely described as
the humanities.
This division is supposed to correspond to something
that occurs in nature. The physical sciences take care of all
that is not man-made, including man himself. The social
sciences deal with man's behavior in his relations with his

fellowmen. The humanities cover those aspects of man's activity which are individual and creative.

Naturally enough, there is plenty of overlapping. It is easy to describe physics, chemistry, astronomy, geology as clear-cut physical sciences; government, economics, sociology, history fall naturally into the social-science division; philosophy, literature, art, music are in the humanities group. Doubts begin to arise in fields like anthropology, which deals with man, a physical being, but also with his customs and institutions, which are social. Architecture is a branch of the physical sciences for what concerns its engineering features and the measurement and use of structural materials, but its esthetic features require that it be also included in the humanities.

As for language, there is no topic that lends itself to so many and so varied classifications. To the extent that language is produced by the human speech organs, it is biological and physiological; to the extent that it consists of sound waves which travel through the air until they strike the ear of the hearer, it lies within the domain of physics. Language and its study may therefore legitimately be described as a physical science.

But language is also the tool and medium of philosophy and literature, which have to be expressed in terms of language. This "tool" aspect has in the past struck the imagination so forcibly that language is traditionally linked with literature in most high-school and college curricula. It would indeed be difficult to conceive of literary values that could or would make use of any medium other than language.

Not only literature, but also other humanistic subjects are normally expressed in linguistic terms. The tool aspect of language extends to all activities of the human being, including his handling of the physical and social sciences. Practically everything has to be transmitted from one individual to another in terms of language. It is therefore perhaps unfair to single out the transmission of literary values and leave out of account the transmission of economic, social, or physical values as they might appear in a business document, a legal charter, or a scientific paper.

More fundamental, however, is the fact that language is all-pervasive. It accompanies practically every activity of man when that activity involves the participation of others. Man works in silence only when he works alone, and not always then. The instant his activity requires the cooperation of others, language comes into play, in spoken, written, perhaps gestural or symbolic form. Even if there is no immediate exchange of language, the activity carried on in common is normally based upon a previous linguistic understanding. Language pervades the fields of religion, government, the law, commerce and finance, international relations, science and technology, amusements, military affairs. Everything we do that involves others requires language as a tool. The present-day trend is therefore to consider language as a social science *par excellence,* even though its physical and humanistic aspects may not be neglected. This view is strengthened by the fact that language not merely conveys thought but has something to do with the shaping of thought (see pages 214 and 215).

Language may thus be viewed as something primarily physical, primarily esthetic, primarily sociological, or as a combination of all three. Practical aspects of these different points of view concerning language appear in the various schools of language learning.

Those who consider the physical and physiological aspects of language paramount normally favor the type of language learning that is most closely linked with the mechanical operation of the speech organs and the physical laws of sound; that is, the memory and mimicry technique whereby spoken phrases and sentences are acquired and recognized in a series of automatic reflexes.

The school that is primarily concerned with language as a tool for literary creation and a vehicle for literary values tends to favor precision in grammar and vocabulary and elegant expression in writing; its ideal method remains the somewhat outdated reading-and-grammar approach.

Those who believe in language as primarily a social science connected with all phases of human behavior tend to be all-embracing in their approach to the problem of language learning; they accept and use both of the previous techniques, further extending them to cover all branches of activity. To these people, language never appears in a vacuum but is always placed in a framework of human relations.

Should we consider as language only that form of communication of thought which is produced by the vocal organs, then transmitted by air waves and received by the human ear? Or should the term "language" be extended to anything that serves the purpose of transferring meaning, so as to include, first and foremost, writing; secondly, meaningful gesture; lastly, the numerous symbolic systems that embrace the drumbeats of the African natives, the smoke signals of the American Indians, the knotted ropes of the Incas, the notched twigs of certain Australian tribes, as well as fully modern devices such as traffic lights, semaphores, and even directional signs, like the arrows that mark a one-way street?

Picture message: Eskimo: "No eating is in the tent":

Egyptian hieroglyphic: combination of picture message and
sound message:

Amûn $\left\{ \begin{array}{l} \text{(} \quad = \quad m) \\ \text{(} \quad = \quad n) \end{array} \right.$

Egyptian hieroglyphic: sound message—cartouche of Pharaoh
Pepi I (sixth dynasty):

$\left(\begin{array}{l} = \quad p) \\ = \quad y) \end{array} \right.$

Semitic transition from picture writing to sound writing:

, originally representing head of ox, and standing for the
word for ox, *alef* in Semitic, gets to be used with the value of
the first sound in the word *alef*, and becomes Hebrew א and
Greek and Latin A.

, originally representing a house, and standing for the
word for house, *beth* in Semitic, gets to be used with the value
of the first sound in the word *beth*, and becomes Hebrew ב
and Greek and Latin B.

人 , pronounced *jên*, is originally the picture of a man, and stands not for the sound *jên*, but for the idea of "man." (This permits the Japanese, whose spoken word for "man" is *hito*, to use the same written symbol.)

国 , pronounced *kuo*, means "kingdom," "country."

中 , pronounced *chung*, means "center," "middle," "inside."

英 , pronounced *ying*, means "superior"; by reason of the similarity of the spoken sound to the first syllable of "English" and "England," it also has those meanings.

中 *chung*	}	"middle kingdom," "China"
国 *kuo*		
英 *ying*	}	"England-country-man," "Englishman"
国 *kuo*		
人 *jên*		

The word "language" issues from the Latin *lingua*, 'tongue." The original idea, therefore, bears upon the human speech organs, with stress upon one organ, the tongue, which happens to display the greatest flexibility when speech is produced. Some people consequently regard anything that does not involve the speech organs as beyond their scope. Others, however, are fascinated by the semantic aspects of language, that is, language's role as a meaning carrier, and since many things besides speech carry meaning, these people extend "language" to cover not merely everything that relates to word meanings, word relationships, word connotations and colorations but also gestures, symbols, and meaningful signs of all descriptions. Many of the meaning-carrying systems are separate fields of science (pasimology, for instance, is the scientific study of gestures).

Without delving too deeply into what might be styled "speechless" methods of communication, it may safely be stated that writing, the most widespread of the substitutes for speech, is so closely linked with speech itself as to fall under the heading of "language" in the acceptance of the majority.

The point to be held in mind in this connection is that writing is only a symbol of speech and is not speech itself. Since spoken words are themselves symbols of thoughts and objects, writing is only a symbol of a symbol, just as a check is a symbol of money, which in turn is a symbol of purchasing power.

The link between writing and speech may be close and intimate, as when writing attempts to reproduce symbolically, by means of an alphabet, each and every sound produced in the spoken language; or it may be quite remote, even avoiding any direct tie with the spoken sounds, as happens in the picture-writing of the ancient Egyptians and the modern Chinese. It is an interesting fact, however, that while writing systems usually start out by symbolizing objects and thoughts rather than sounds, they often veer from picture writing to sound writing. This attraction exerted by the spoken sounds upon the written symbols is perhaps a tacit avowal of the superiority of the spoken over the written language. Another such indication is supplied by the fact that the normal individual learns to speak and understand long before he learns to read and write. A third element of proof appears in the fact that all human groups, without exception, possess speech, but not all possess writing.

It therefore seems reasonable to view language as primarily speech—that is to say, audible sounds produced by the human vocal apparatus and transmitted by sound waves to the ears of other human beings. But in order to be language, these human sounds must be based upon a previous understanding among their users that they carry certain definite meanings. Otherwise, they will be mere noises.

english

Of primary interest to us as speakers of English is our own language. We may look at it as it is—from the standpoint of its structure and vocabulary. Or we may look at it with reference to where it is used, and how many use it, in comparison with other languages.

Leaving the first of these aspects for later discussion, it will be well to note that among the world's numerous languages English is second in number of speakers, being outstripped only by Chinese. It can safely be asserted that no fewer than 250 million people throughout the world have English as their mother tongue. Since the total population of the globe is estimated at about two and a half billion, this means that one person out of every ten in the world is a native speaker of English.

Mere numbers, however, do not tell the whole story. There are two other factors that are linguistically important. One is the distribution of a language's speakers across the globe, the other is the stage of material, intellectual, and spiritual civilization that has been achieved by those speakers.

Distributionally speaking, English is perhaps the most fortunate of the world's languages. There is no major area of the earth that holds no English speakers. The North American continent has the greatest concentration, with between 160 and 170 million in the United States and another 15 million in the Dominion of Canada. Europe has at least 50 million native speakers of English, located in the British Isles. Australia and New Zealand furnish the third largest body of native English speakers, with well over 10 million for the two countries combined. The last large body of native English speakers is in the Union of South Africa, and numbers about two million.

Scattered groups are located in American and British possessions and former possessions—Hawaii, Alaska, the Philippines, Puerto Rico, the Canal Zone; British Honduras, British Guiana, Bermuda, the Bahamas, Jamaica, and other British Antillean islands; African regions linked with the British Crown (Somaliland, Kenya, Tanganyika, Rhodesia, Southwest Africa, Nigeria, the Gold Coast, etc.); Asiatic lands like Malaya and Hong Kong, Mediterranean strongholds like Gibraltar, Malta, and Cyprus, and Pacific islands far too numerous to mention.

But the 250 million, more or less, who have English as their native and first tongue are far from telling the entire story. English is so widespread among native speakers of other languages that it has been suggested that no fewer than 600 million people, or roughly one out of every four on earth, can be reached with it.

There may be some exaggeration in this figure, but there is also considerable truth. To begin with, English is the most widely taught foreign language in the schools of practically all non-English-speaking lands that do not lie behind the Iron Curtain. At least five million continental Europeans speak it fluently; so do another five million Spanish and Portuguese speakers in South and Central America, Mexico, and the Caribbean islands. In Asia, English is widely known and used in populous countries that were once British possessions and even now retain vague links with the British Commonwealth of Nations. India, Pakistan, Burma, Ceylon contain vast numbers of English speakers (India, in fact, claims to be the third English-speaking land on earth, with at least 25 million English-

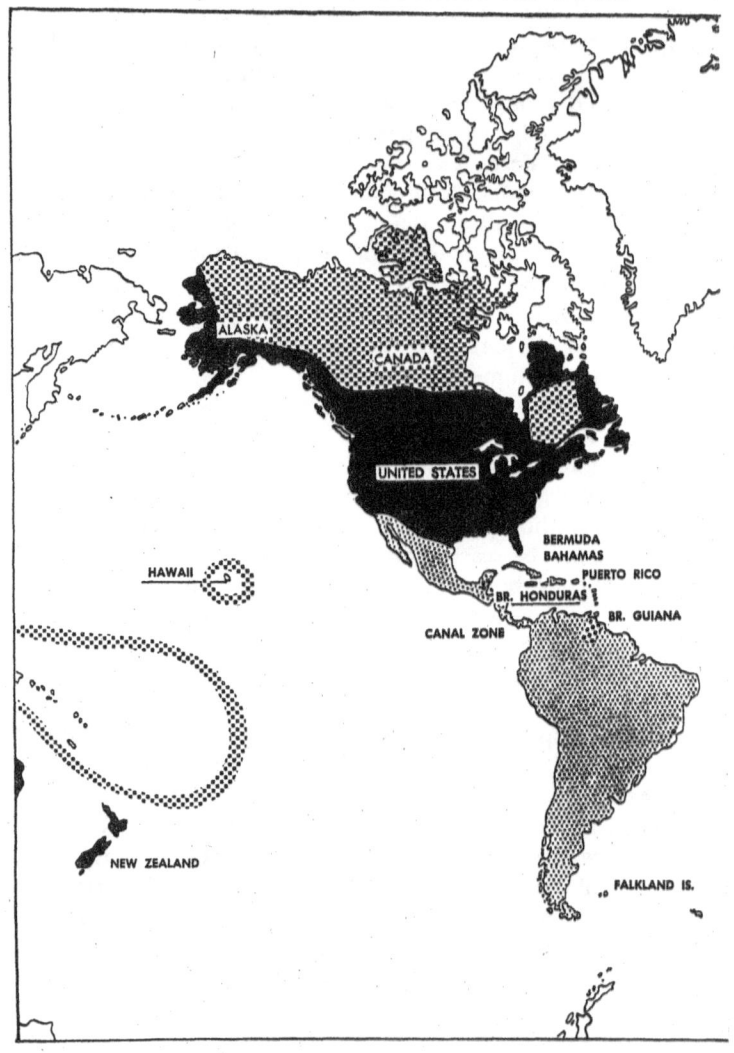

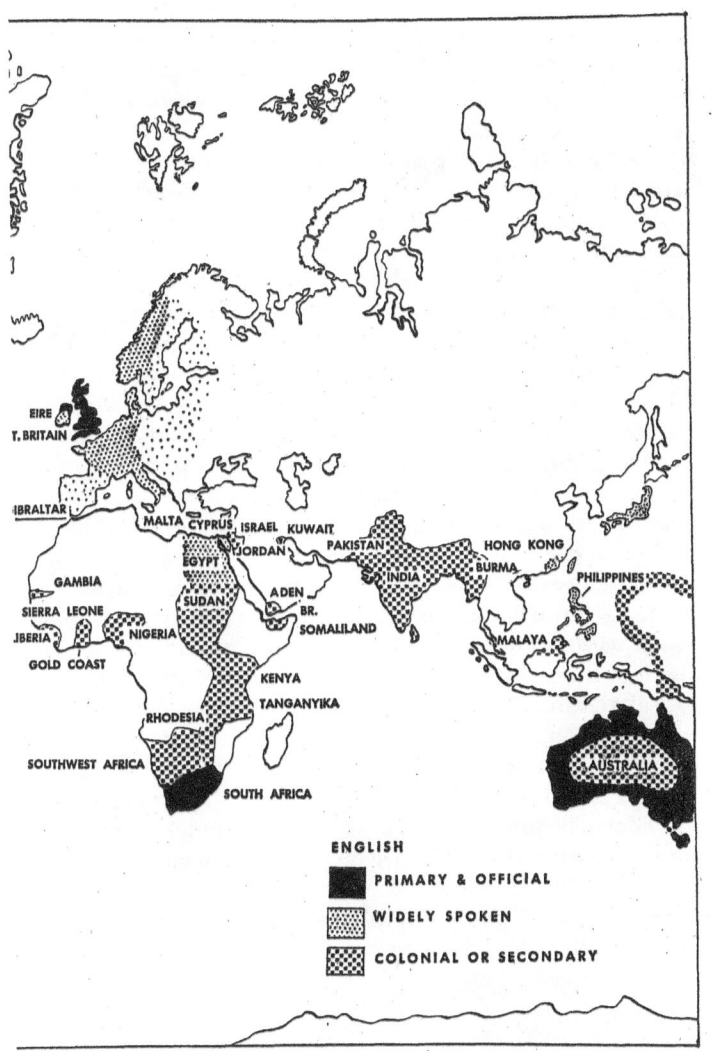

EIRE
T. BRITAIN
IBRALTAR
MALTA CYPRUS ISRAEL KUWAIT
JORDAN   PAKISTAN
EGYPT   HONG KONG
GAMBIA   ADEN   INDIA   BURMA
SIERRA LEONE   BR.   PHILIPPINES
IBERIA   NIGERIA   SOMALILAND
GOLD COAST   MALAYA
SUDAN
KENYA
TANGANYIKA
RHODESIA
SOUTHWEST AFRICA   AUSTRALIA
SOUTH AFRICA

ENGLISH

█ PRIMARY & OFFICIAL

▒ WIDELY SPOKEN

▦ COLONIAL OR SECONDARY

speaking Indians). The distributional and cultural influence of English over the lands of Asia and Africa was spectacularly shown at the Bandung Conference, in April, 1955, where English was used as the primary official language. In Africa, countries now fully independent, like Egypt and Liberia, hold large numbers of English speakers. Where English did not succeed in implanting itself as a second language for colonial populations, it did the next best thing and created picturesque Pidgin forms. Some of these, like the West African Pidgin, have remained on a purely oral level, while others, like the Pidgin of Melanesia, have practically attained the proportions of an international and even written *lingua franca* for natives speaking a multitude of mutually incomprehensible tongues.

In part, this triumph of English throughout the world has been due to the force of exploration, colonization, and expansion displayed by English speakers in the course of the past four centuries. In part, it is due to the leadership achieved in recent times by the major English-speaking nations in the fields of trade, industry, finance, science and general culture. The spreading of British and American products throughout the globe, the fact that the Anglo-Saxon nations are far ahead of all others in industrial production, international banking, and scientific and technological research, have undoubtedly had a great deal to do with the acceptance of English in countries where it is not the native speech. Let us also remember, however, that the English language has been spread in no small part through the efforts of missionaries, both Catholic and Protestant, who have carried the Gospel of Christ to lands where it was formerly unknown. In recent times, too, there has been the spreading of English and American literature, drama, and spoken films to countries that did not know them previously.

This geographical picture of the English language would be incomplete without some reference to the dialectal varieties of English that have arisen, either on the original English-speaking soil of Britain or in the far-flung countries to which English has been carried. It is a surprising thing about the English language that despite its extended positions it shows far less in the way of local divergences than do other languages which appear in much more concentrated form on the map. This is perhaps due to the fact that the expansion of English has taken place in relatively modern times, when systems of travel and communication were well on the way to being established. This meant that the conditions of geographic and cultural isolation that favor the breaking up of a language into widely divergent dialects no longer existed. Other factors, too, must be taken into account: an established cultural tradition, a written form, and a consciousness of linguistic unity.

In spite of this fundamental unity of the English language, there is to be observed a definite cleavage between the language of the United States and Canada on the one hand, that of Britain and other British Dominions and possessions on the other. Further cleavages are to be noted within each of the two main groups.

American English shows three broad divisions, an Eastern, a Southern, and a Midwestern (or General American), with the numerical odds favoring the last. In addition, purely local speech forms appear in the great cities or in semi-isolated communities, such as the so-called Brooklynese (actually a speech form common to certain classes of all of New York's boroughs) or the picturesque talk of the Ozark mountaineers.

For what concerns British English, the local differences are far more deep-rooted and pronounced. At least twenty-five clearly defined local dialects have been noted in the

IMMIGRANT: Is enough he's making after all a living!
BIG-CITY NATIVE WITH IMMIGRANT TOUCH: So what he's my
boss? It gives him a right he should talk that way?
NEW YORK: Let's adjoin to the adjerning room.
OZARK: That pesky, rambunctious, no 'count skonk!
SOUTHERN: You-all goin' to carry me somewheh?
BRITISH (SOMERSET): Doan 'ee worry! We got they in the bag!
SOUTH AFRICAN: Are you going with at schimmel day?
AUSTRALIAN: I went on a larrikin, got shikkered, and smooged
a sheila.

DAUGHTER: Cornwall *dafter;* Cumberland *dowter;* Norfolk
darter.
MOTHER: Cumberland *mudder;* Devonshire *meuther;* Northumberland *muthor.*
HEART: Devonshire *hort;* Lancashire *hert;* Northumberland
hairt.
CROWN: Cumberland *crwoun;* Lancashire *creawn;* Northumberland *croon;* Yorkshire *crahn.*

British Isles, including Irish, Scots, and Welsh versions of English. Australia and New Zealand hold most of their local features in common with the Cockney of London, but both have developed striking localisms. The same is true of South African English, which has been subjected to the influence of Afrikaans (the variety of Dutch used by the Boers) and of various native languages.

modern foreign languages

It has been estimated by reputable experts that the total number of languages in spoken use today, exclusive of dialects, is 2796.

This startling total includes over one thousand languages of American Indian groups, five hundred languages of African Negro tribes, and another five hundred, more or less, spoken by small and obscure groups of Asia and the Pacific islands.

Languages with a million or more speakers probably do not exceed two hundred. Of these, many are remote and little known. The number of languages that are likely to be significant to the average individual is no greater than a hundred.

Even among these, the number of speakers, distribution, and practical and cultural importance vary widely. Some are of importance almost exclusively because of the number of their speakers. Others, with fewer speakers, show features of distribution which render them worthy of attention. These may be combined with commercial or cultural traits, occasionally with diplomatic or strategic importance.

All these features are irrelevant to the linguist, who views each language as a separate and equal problem. But they cannot be irrelevant to the average man, who is faced with a choice. The number of languages he can pursue is limited, often to a single one beside his own. To make an intelligent and advantageous choice, he must know something about the world's chief languages, where they are spoken, by how many and what kind of people, what use he can make of each of them in connection with his own personal career and problems.

One important reason for a student's dissatisfaction with foreign-language study is that he has made the wrong choice and finds himself learning one language when he would actually like to learn another. This, of course, hinges largely upon personal situations. But it also hinges in part on widespread ignorance concerning the comparative aspects of the languages available for study.

The most objective factor connected with languages is the *number* of their speakers. Here, the approximate figures speak for themselves:

Chinese	500,000,000	French	80,000,000
English	250,000,000	Indonesian	80,000,000
Hindustani	160,000,000	Portuguese	60,000,000
Russian	150,000,000	Bengali	60,000,000
Spanish	120,000,000	Italian	60,000,000
German	100,000,000	Arabic	50,000,000
Japanese	100,000,000		

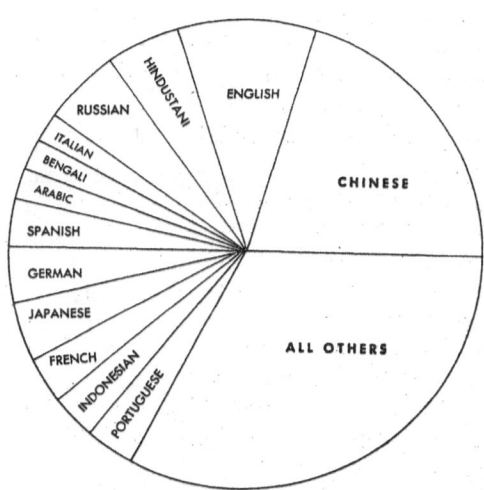

NUMERICAL DISTRIBUTION OF WORLD'S LEADING THIRTEEN LANGUAGES

	MILLIONS OF SPEAKERS		MILLIONS OF SPEAKERS
Chinese (all dialects)	500	Japanese	100
English	250	French	80
Hindustani	160	Indonesian	80
Russian (including		Portuguese	60
Ukrainian and		Italian	60
Byelorussian)	150	Bengali	60
Spanish	120	Arabic	50
German	100	All others	830
		Total	2600

It is a striking fact that these thirteen languages are the only ones to attain the fifty-million total. Others lag far behind.

Mere numbers are far from telling the entire story. *Distribution* of a language is of tremendous importance in making that language of practical use to its learner. A language widely spoken in numerous parts of the globe is more likely to be encountered by the tourist, soldier, or businessman (the scientist or missionary normally has a very specific problem in connection with a specific area).

English is the most widely distributed of the world's languages. Hard on its heels comes French. French is found in Europe in France, Belgium, and Switzerland, where it is both native (the language of the people) and official (the language of the government). It is also found in all other European countries, even those behind the Iron Curtain, for it has always been viewed as the language of diplomacy, elegance, culture and refinement. In the Western Hemisphere, French is to be found as a native and official language in eastern Canada, Haiti, and various French possessions (French Guiana, Martinique, Guadeloupe, etc.). In Africa, French is official in Morocco, Tunisia, Algeria, French West Africa and Equatorial Africa and Madagascar. It survives as a colonial language in Indochina and in numerous parts of the Pacific and Indian Oceans. In many of the lands of Latin America, Asia, and Africa, French is viewed as it is in Europe, as the language of culture and refinement (though English tends to displace it in that function). The over-all result is that French has an international importance that far outstrips what would be warranted by the number of its native speakers.

Third in distributional strength, but in a lop-sided sort of way, is Spanish, which dominates the linguistic scene in the Western Hemisphere south of the Rio Grande but is otherwise restricted to Spain and the few Spanish African colonies that are left. A reflection of the former colonial importance of Spanish is to be seen in the Philippines, where part of the population still uses a Spanish imparted in the days before the Spanish-American War.

Russian is the major tongue of the Soviet Union, and its use is rapidly spreading in the European Soviet satellites. It is a landlocked language, restricted to eastern Europe and northern Asia, but it covers one sixth of the land surface of the earth.

German is the key language of central Europe, covering Germany, Austria, and Switzerland and extending widely into neighboring countries. Some of these were at one time wholly or partly under German or Austro-Hungarian dominance (Czechoslovakia, Hungary, Yugoslavia, Poland); others enjoyed and continue to enjoy extensive trade relations with Germany (Holland, Denmark, Norway, Sweden). To a slightly lesser degree than French, German is viewed as a cultural tongue, particularly for what concerns various branches of science. German overseas possessions were lost as a result of World War I, but traces of the language survive in parts of Africa and in some Pacific Islands. The migration of millions of Germans to North and South America has led to the continued use of German as a traditional tongue in many communities of the United States, Argentina, Brazil, and Chile.

Portuguese appears not only in European Portugal but in South American Brazil, a country larger than the continental United States. Brazil's population of about fifty million constitutes nearly half the total of all South America. There are also flourishing Portuguese colonies in Africa, India, and the Pacific.

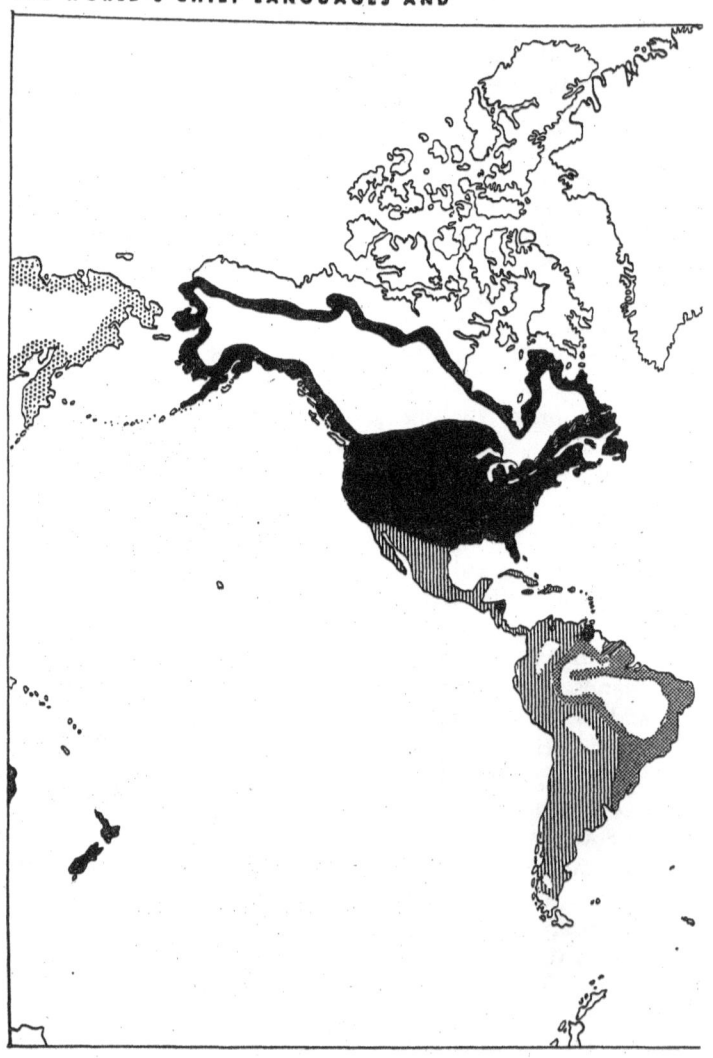

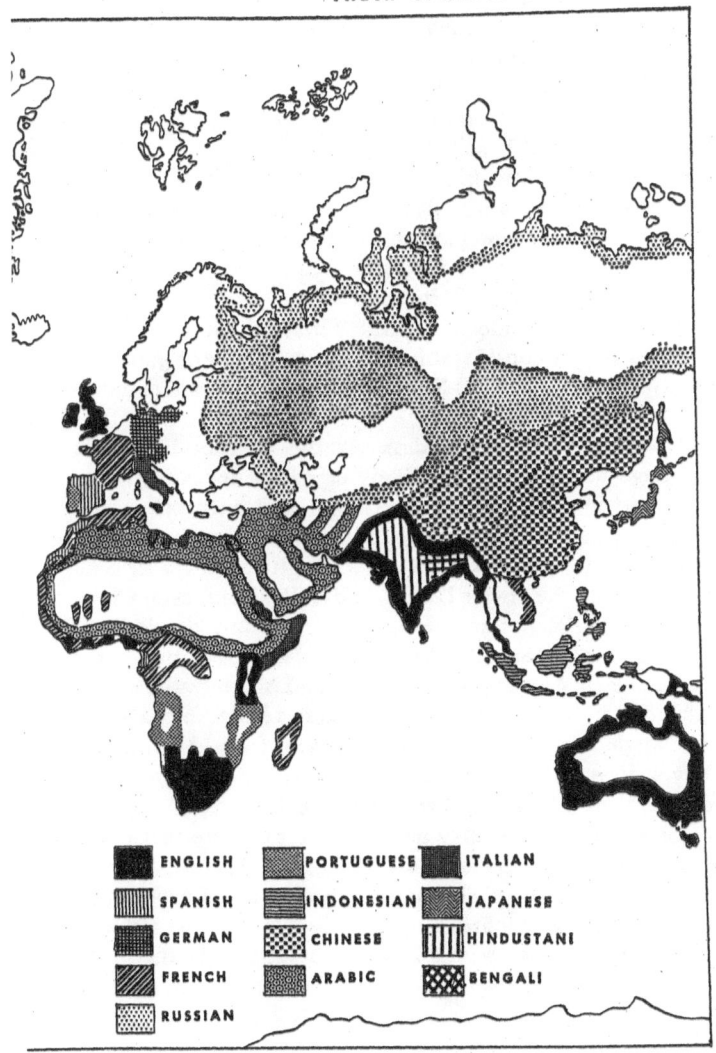

ENGLISH	PORTUGUESE	ITALIAN
SPANISH	INDONESIAN	JAPANESE
GERMAN	CHINESE	HINDUSTANI
FRENCH	ARABIC	BENGALI
RUSSIAN		

Italian is widespread throughout the Mediterranean area and survives to some degree in former Italian colonies such as Libya, Ethiopia, and Eritrea. The emigration of millions of Italians to North and South America has resulted in Italian-speaking communities in the United States, Argentina, Brazil, and Uruguay.

Of the remaining big languages (Hindustani, Chinese, Japanese, Indonesian, Bengali, Arabic), it may be said that they are for the most part confined to the country where they are both native and official. Chinese emigrants have carried some form of Chinese to other Far Eastern lands, such as Malaya, Indochina, and Thailand, to which they have moved in considerable numbers. Traces of Japanese survive in lands, such as Korea, once under Japanese domination.

Among the thirteen leaders, Arabic, the non-European language with the smallest body of native speakers, is the one enjoying greatest distributional and cultural power. As the carrier of Islamic thought, it affects perhaps three hundred million speakers of other tongues, located in Iran, Afghanistan, the Soviet Union, India, Pakistan, even China and Indonesia, not to mention Turkey and the Balkans and regions of central Africa which have been under the influence of Moslem missionaries and slave traders. The territory in which its native speakers reside embraces all of North Africa north of the Sahara, from Morocco to Egypt, its original homeland of Arabia, and the Arab states of the Near East (Iraq, Syria, Jordan, Lebanon).

Geographically, it may be interesting to note that of the thirteen leading languages seven (English, French, Spanish, Portuguese, Italian, German/ Russian) are European in origin, but that the first four have become Euro-American, while the last has become Eurasiatic. Of the six that originate in Asia (Chinese, Japanese, Indonesian, Hindustani, Bengali, Arabic) the last has become Afro-Asiatic. These changes have been effected by processes of emigration, conquest and colonization that will be discussed in Part III.

Hindustani, numerically the third of the world's languages, is a combination of Urdu, the official language of Pakistan, and Hindi, the leading tongue of India (the two languages diverge radically in written form, but come close in speech). Bengali, despite its numbers, is a secondary language of East Pakistan and northeastern India. Both Hindustani and Bengali belong to the same big family of languages (see pages 254 ff) that embraces the seven great European tongues, but Chinese, Japanese, Indonesian, and Arabic are each representative of a separate language family.

As an individual in search of one or more foreign languages, you will find it expedient to restrict your choice to one or more of the twelve great languages which, together with English, are used by well over two thirds of the world's inhabitants. Barring special circumstances dictating the choice of a lesser language (you might, for instance, be placed in charge of your firm's Swedish office, in which case Swedish, the language of about eight million people, might prove more useful than any of the larger ones), it may be said that it is essential for the well-rounded modern man to have some measure of command over at least one of the world's leading languages in addition to his own.

Which one or ones you choose depends upon your needs and tastes. The American educational system generally makes provision for at least three (French, Spanish, and German; this choice is in part a throwback to an earlier international situation). The other languages are widely available, particularly in the colleges and universities, with preference for Italian, Russian, Portuguese, Japanese, Chinese, and Arabic, in the order listed (only a few of the major universities have courses in Hindustani, Bengali, or Indonesian).

German and the Romance languages (French, Spanish, Italian, Portuguese) are easier for English speakers to learn by reason of language-family connection and similarity of vocabulary. They are also more closely connected with our own culture, and have made and received greater contributions to and from our own language.

One essential thing to be held in mind is that each and every one of these languages, and of the thousands of others besides, is to its own speakers precisely what English is to you—a normal, regular, unconscious means of communication with their fellow speakers. It is emphatically not, from the viewpoint of its speakers, an intellectual exercise or a school chore. Endeavor, if possible, to acquire the same point of view toward the language you are learning as you have toward English.

classical languages

In addition to the modern spoken tongues, other languages, no longer popularly spoken, claim our attention. The term "classical" is applied to those tongues which, once widely used, are now quiescent but continue to carry literary, philosophical, scientific, and etymological values.

The two languages most widely studied as classical are Latin and Greek, but other tongues could fit the definition. Hebrew and Aramaic, which carry the significant message of the Old Testament and have contributed a good deal to our English vocabulary, particularly in the religious sphere; Sanskrit, the sacred language of ancient India and the oldest of the Indo-European languages (see page 254) on record; possibly even Akkadian, the language of the Babylonians and Assyrians, and the ancient Egyptian of the hieroglyphic inscriptions, could be termed classical tongues.

It is a significant fact that while classical languages are usually viewed as dead and unspoken today, the degree of their deadness, like that of the virus in polio vaccines, is a matter of controversy. Hebrew, for instance, is fully alive and spoken today in Israel, though the ancient Biblical tongue has received numerous additions from modern languages to make it suitable for a twentieth-century civilization. Greek is in spoken use today in Greece, though not quite in the form it had in ancient Athens. Latin is still a spoken language among the priests of the Catholic Church, and is occasionally used in lectures and written documents. Furthermore, some of these languages may be legitimately said to live on in their descendants. Anglo-Saxon is continued in modern English, Latin in the Romance tongues.

By common consent throughout the western world, the ancient languages most widely considered for present-day study are Latin, Greek, and, more remotely, Hebrew. For this there are good reasons. Latin, in addition to being the direct ancestor of French, Spanish, Italian, and Portuguese, has contributed so much to the vocabulary and syntax of other modern western languages, particularly English, that it is almost impossible to gain an intelligent control of any of those languages without it. Greek, on the other hand, supplies major portions of our scientific and technical vocabulary. Often scientific terms which are puzzling in their English form become crystal-clear when they are analyzed into their Greek components. ("Microscope," for example, is "small-see," while "telescope" is "distance-see.") This situation is not at all peculiar to English but applies to all western languages. So widespread is Latin and Greek participation in the terminology of the more scientific, literary, and intellectual segment of European vocabularies that many people think this Graeco-Latin complex will form the nucleus of the international language of the future.

The Latin-Greek role in the formation of modern languages is not, however, merely a matter of vocabulary contributions. The civilization of the Greeks and Romans forms the basis of our common western culture. Views of life and habits of thought that Westerners today hold in common have been inherited from Greece and Rome, having been blended with a new religious element stemming from the Hebraic culture of the Jews and early Christians. Our philosophy of religion, government, human relations, science, and progress rests firmly upon this classical foundation, which has a continuous history extending from antiquity to our own day.

During the Middle Ages and the Renaissance, Latin was the common language of scholarship and international intercourse in western Europe, while Greek performed a similar function in the Balkans and Asia Minor. With the fall of Constantinople to the Turks in 1453, Greek was reintroduced by refugee scholars to western Europe, and the two languages were used side by side until the final emergence of the modern tongues as languages of written and official as well as spoken communication relegated them to the position of cultural tongues.

Today, Latin is fully available in the American educational system, and it is the language selected by many as their first choice when they venture outside the field of their native English. Greek, once widespread, is now less generally available. The study of Hebrew, once the pursuit of Biblical scholars, has a new vogue in connection with the rebirth of a national Jewish state in Israel.

From the point of view of the individual seeking to expand his knowledge of languages, the claims of the classical tongues deserve serious consideration.

The practical, spoken-language use of Hebrew is limited to the relatively small population of Israel, which is less than two million. The classical Greek taught in the schools has strong points of contact with the modern Greek used by about eight million inhabitants of Greece, and a transfer from the one to the other is not too difficult. Latin, outside of its use in the Catholic Church, has no immediate speaking population.

There is, however, a powerful transfer value that attaches to each of these tongues. Hebrew unlocks the gates to the Semitic languages, and one who knows Hebrew finds Arabic relatively easy. A good foundation in Latin acts as a key to the entire Romance group of modern languages and gives us a sharper understanding of English. Both Latin and Greek give an insight into the basic structure and vocabulary of the entire Indo-European language family (see page 254), of which they are typical. Since some of the languages of the family, notably Russian and the other

Slavic tongues, have remained very close to the original Indo-European structure, a knowledge of the grammatical make-up and terminology of either Greek or Latin renders the study of those modern tongues far easier than it would otherwise be.

The claim is sometimes advanced that the study of Greek and Latin has a disciplinary value in the formation of logical habits of thought and the ability to think things through. This justification for their study is strongly countered by some people, who hold that such logical habits of thinking may be built up by any pursuit that calls for the exercise of the intellect (crossword puzzles or the solving of riddles, for instance). Whatever the rightness of their position may be, it is undeniable that the study of Latin and Greek will at least bring to light, as a by-product, the mental processes of the ancients and their ways of thinking about human problems, which are often applicable today. It is also undeniable that the study of these languages carries as another by-product an insight into ancient history, and a realization that many of the problems that beset humanity today are far from new, and that they have been met and solved before. The ways in which they have been solved, the errors that were made and not repaired, the consequences of those errors, often carry a mighty lesson which the people of today might do well to learn.

There is no doubt, however, that the greatest practical value of the classical languages lies in their clarification of our own tongue. If we examine at random a page of the English dictionary, we will find that over fifty per cent of our words come from Latin or Greek sources, and that the original meaning of the Greek and Latin roots casts a powerful searchlight upon both the meaning and the possible uses of our own words. People going in for scientific pursuits, in the fields of medicine, engineering, technology, chemistry, biology, astronomy, geology, and as many others as you may care to mention, will find their problems of terminology and its understanding and application enormously simplified if they have, as part of their training, a working knowledge of Latin or Greek, or both.

LATIN AND GREEK ROOTS APPEARING IN SUBWAY SIGNS AND ADVERTISEMENTS

KEY: Above each English word appears the language from which it is derived, in accordance with the following scheme: AS—Anglo-Saxon; Sc—Scandinavian; LF—Latin-French; F—French; L—Latin; G—Greek; GL—Greek-Latin; GLF—Greek-Latin-French; CLF—Celtic-Latin-French. Where the English word goes back to a Latin or Greek source, the Latin or Greek form from which it is derived is given beneath the English word.

LF	AS	LF	Sc	AS	AS	LF	AS	AS	LF	AS
Notice:	all	persons	are	forbidden	to	enter	upon	or	cross	the
notitia		*persona*				*intrare*			*crux*	

F
tracks.

AS	AS	AS	LF	AS	AS	LF	AS	AS	LF	AS
Spitting	on	the	platforms	or	other	parts	of	this	station	is
			•platta-forma			*pars*			*statio*	

AS Sc AS
un-law-ful.

LF	Sc	LF	AS	LF
Offenders	are	liable	to	arrest.
offendere		*ligare*		*ad-restare*

* Hypothetical form.

```
L       LF        L       L
```
Port authority bus   terminal.
portus auctoritas omnibus terminalis


```
AS  LF AS GLF  AS   GLF   AS    L
```
In case of air raid, tune your radio.
    casus   *aer*   *tonos*   *radius*


```
   LF      Sc   AS    LF      CLF  AS    F      AS  AS  AS
```
Vacation loans on signature, car or furniture; fast one-day
 vacatio   *signum*   *carrus*

```
   LF
```
service.
servitium


```
AS   AS   AS     AS    AS     G         AS    Sc  LF
```
A drink that thousands of sophisticated drinkers are just
                           sophos   *justus*

```
   LF
```
discovering.
dis-cooperire


```
 F   AS    GLF       L    LF
```
Try the economy family size.
     oikonomia familia assidere


```
GLF    AS    LF     GLF       AS    AS    AS  AS  AS
```
Glamor girl, nurse, diplomat, business man, teacher—a good
gramma   *nutricia* *diploma*

```
AS   AS   AS AS AS  AS
```
wife must be all of these.


```
LF      G     AS     G        AS     LF
```
Just phone your telephone business office.
justus phone   *telos-phone*   *officium*

LF	L	LF	AS	AS	GL

Modern refrigerators use so little electricity!
modernus   *frigus*   *uti*   *elektron*

Out of a total of 96 words, 49 are Anglo-Saxon, 5 are Scandinavian, 22 are Latin-French, 3 are French, 7 are Latin, 3 are Greek, 1 is Greek-Latin, 5 are Greek-Latin-French, 1 is Celtic-Latin-French. Greek and Latin roots account for 39 of the 96 words, or over 40%, with 9 originating in Greek, 30 in Latin. If repetitions of the same word are not counted, Latin and Greek roots account for 38 out of 81 words, or over 46% of the total.

NOTES ON DERIVATIONS

In the preceding table, Anglo-Saxon accounts for most of the basic words of high frequency (*all, to, on, upon, or, the, of, this, is, in, your, a, that, be, these, so*). Further, it takes in frequent nouns, adjectives, and verbs (*forbid, spit, other, fast, one, day, drink, thousand, man, teach, good, wife, must, little*). It supplies many of the common prefixes and suffixes (the *un-* and *-ful* of *unlawful,* the *-er* of *drinker* and *teacher,* the *-ness* of *business*). *Girl* does not appear until the Middle English period (*maid* and *maiden* are the old Anglo-Saxon terms), but it seems to have grown up on British soil. *Raid* is a Scottish adaptation of *road.*

Scandinavian, through the Danish invasions, contributes *are, law,* and *loan.* Other important Scandinavian contributions not appearing in our passages are *they, their, them, take, husband,* etc. (see page 152).

Among the words of Latin origin, "car" comes from *carrus,*

which the Romans borrowed from the Celtic-speaking Gauls. "Bus" is an abbreviation of *omnibus*, which in Latin means "for everybody." Some of the Latin roots do not appear in classical dictionaries, but seem to have existed in the speech of the common people; the *platta of *platform* is an instance of this Vulgar Latin. *Persona* was built up in Latin from *personat*, "sounds through," referring to the mask worn by Roman actors. The -*ure* of "signature" and "furniture" comes from Latin -*ura* through French.

Among the Greek roots, *sophos* means "wise," *sophia* "wisdom," and the root appears in many words ending in -*sophy* ("philosophy," "theosophy"). "Glamor" is a peculiar Scottish adaptation of English "grammar" to signify "witchcraft," on the theory that anyone skilled in reading and writing was a magician. The original Greek root, *gram-* or *graph-*, appears in all sorts of words that convey the meaning of "write." "Diploma" has the original meaning of "folded twice," as was done with any important document. The Greek *elektron*, from which we get "electricity," meant "amber," by rubbing which a shock may be obtained. "Economy" comes from *oikia*, "house," and *nomos*, "law" (the art of running a well-ordered household).

cultural aspects of language: dialect

Two important factors affecting language in its relation to the individual are localism and class difference in speech.

Both may be said to stratify language, or divide it into layers. But while the stratification of dialect is horizontal, the combined effects of slang, cant, and jargon (see next chapter) are vertically felt. The two stratifications seldom occur in isolation, but normally are intermixed. The person who speaks a local dialect will generally mix it with nationwide slang or with the jargon of his trade or profession.

We have already outlined (see page 31) the broad dialect areas of the United States (Eastern, Southern, and Midwestern, or General American). These classifications are based largely on the way the speakers treat the sounds of their language, although the use of certain individual words and, occasionally, of grammatical forms and constructions also enters the picture. Some years ago, a noted linguist used to carry on a radio program entitled "Where Are You From?" Faced with a panel of persons unknown to him, he would ask each of them to read a printed list of words. From the way in which each person pronounced these key words, the linguist was able to place him as coming from a locality east or west, north or south, of a certain line. This was because differences in pronunciation tend to follow definite frontiers, almost as precise as state or national boundaries. The course of the frontier dividing two pronunciations of the same word, or the use of two different words in the same meaning, is plotted, and the resulting line on the map is called an isogloss. No two isoglosses coincide all along the way, but a mean or average course can be plotted for a number of pronunciation or vocabulary differences. This resultant bundle of isoglosses supplies us with the basis for the division of language into dialects.

A few of the key words used will illustrate the point. East of a line running roughly along the crest of the Alleghenies, people make a precise difference in the pronunciation of "marry," "Mary," and "merry"; west of the line, all three words are pronounced exactly alike. The trained linguist, noting the way his speaker pronounced these three words, was able to place him at once as coming from east or west of the Alleghenies. Another isogloss, perhaps that of "greasy" with a hard or soft s, would place the speaker north or south of a certain line (in the case of "greasy," the line runs between Trenton and Philadelphia). Additional words would then circumscribe the speaker more and more (a difference in the pronunciation of the o in "dog" and "log," or "wahsh" vs. "wush," or "egg" vs. "aigg," for instance), until finally the linguist was able to pronounce confidently that his subject came from somewhere within a dozen miles of Richmond, Va., or from the central part of Iowa. In the majority of cases he would be absolutely right. It sounded miraculous, but it wasn't.

Provision would of course have to be made for "mixed patterns," where a subject born and bred in one locality had spent long years in another area and had unconsciously given up some of his native characteristics in favor of the ones of his new locality. But, as a rule, the expert could even pick out accurately a mixture of two or three patterns.

At no time did the radio program make use of preferences for individual words to designate certain objects, but this would have been quite possible. Such special words as

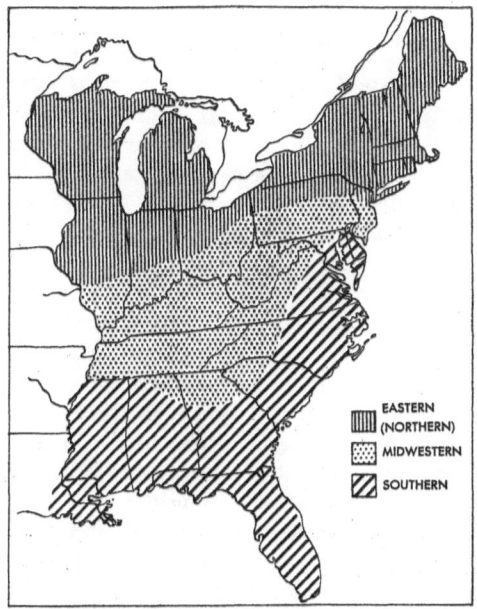

EASTERN
(NORTHERN)

MIDWESTERN

SOUTHERN

MAJOR AMERICAN DIALECTS EAST OF THE MISSISSIPPI

Three main currents of American English came from New England, Pennsylvania, and the eastern coast of the Southern States. The Alleghenies prevented straight westward expansion from Virginia and the Carolinas, with the result that the Pennsylvania stream dips southward, forming the basis of Midwestern or General American. No comprehensive study has been made of the area west of the Mississippi, but it is believed that such a study would indicate farther northward and southward expansion of the Midwestern stream.

"bag," "sack," and "poke" (preferred respectively by the East, the Midwest, and the South), or the "pavement" and "hoagy" of Philadelphia vs. the "sidewalk" and "hero sandwich" of New York, or the "tonic" of parts of New England vs. the "soft drink" of other regions (some regions of the South regularly use "dope" where the North uses "coke") are just as characteristic, though not as regular in their occurrence, as variations in the pronunciation of the same word.

Dialect appears in all languages that have any territorial extent worth speaking of. In many of the world's greater languages, they are far deeper, more extensive, and more easily discernible than they are in English. In the English of Britain they are far more extensive than in the English of America. In some countries, like Italy, there is such a perceptible difference in intonation among the various regions that even though a speaker uses the grammatical form of the standard national language, his region of origin can be determined without any difficulty. In other countries, like China, the dialects are so widely divergent that they constitute to all intents and purposes separate languages, being mutually incomprehensible.

Local dialects may be survivals of ancient language differences. The divergence between the northern and the southern British dialects, for instance, is said to arise from the fact that in the north the original invaders were Angles, whose speech differed slightly from that of the Saxons who settled the south, and that later on the northern provinces of England received an influx of Danes who gave up their Scandinavian language in favor of English, but still retained some Danish words and habits of pronunciation. In America, the divergences among the three major groups of English speakers are largely accounted for by the fact

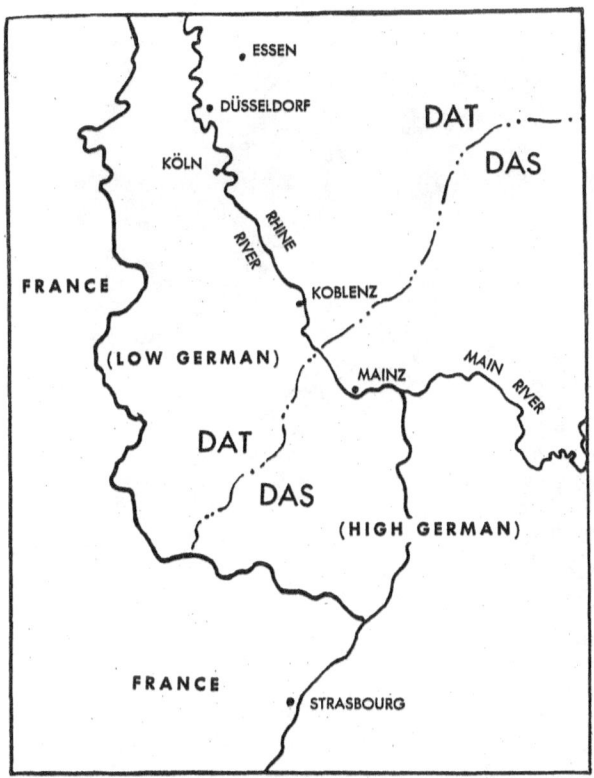

ISOGLOSS OF PRONUNCIATION OF GERMAN "DAS" IN SOUTHWESTERN GERMANY

South and east of the line that crosses the Rhine, the High German pronunciation (*das*) prevails. North and west of the line, the popular speech pronounces *dat,* in Low German fashion. This isogloss, combined with several others running in the same general direction, though not coinciding, establishes a rough border line between High and Low German.

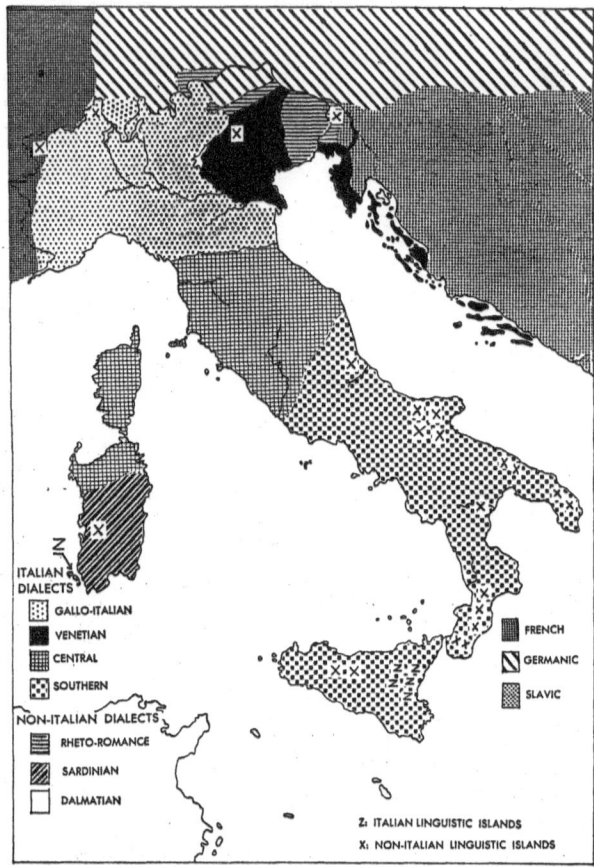

ITALIAN DIALECTS

- GALLO-ITALIAN
- VENETIAN
- CENTRAL
- SOUTHERN

NON-ITALIAN DIALECTS

- RHETO-ROMANCE
- SARDINIAN
- DALMATIAN

- FRENCH
- GERMANIC
- SLAVIC

Z: ITALIAN LINGUISTIC ISLANDS
X: NON-ITALIAN LINGUISTIC ISLANDS

PRESENT-DAY DIALECTS OF ITALY

True Italian dialects are subdivided into four main groups: Gallo-Italian in the northwest (Piedmont, Lombardy, Liguria, Emilia); Venetian, which appears also along the coastlines of

Istria and Dalmatia and in the Adriatic islands; central (Tuscany, Umbria, Marche, Latium), including Corsican and the two north Sardinian dialects, Sassarese and Gallurese; and southern (Campania, Abruzzi, Lucania, Puglia, Calabria, Sicily). Groups described as Romance but not Italian are Romansh (or Rhetian, or Rheto-Romance, or Ladin) of Friuli and the Trentino, whose affiliations lie with the Engadine and Grisons dialects of Switzerland; central and southern Sardinian (Logudorese, Campidanese), most conservative and closest to Latin of all Romance varieties; and the extinct Dalmatian, once spoken along the eastern Adriatic coast, whose last survivor was the dialect of the island of Veglia, extinct since the beginning of this century.

Italian linguistic islands, marked by Z, consist mainly of Gallo-Italian speakers who moved to Sicily during the Middle Ages. Non-Italian linguistic islands, marked by X, consist of Greek, Albanian, and Serbian refugees who moved to southern Italy and Sicily to escape the Turks; Catalan speakers in Alghero, Sardinia; German, French, and Slavic speakers in the extreme north, northwest, and northeast. Italian dialects spill over the political border into France, around Nice, and into Switzerland (Canton Ticino), as well as into territory recently ceded to Yugoslavia.

---

that they came at different periods from different areas of England, whose speech peculiarities they retained.

It has been observed, however, that even where the original language seems to have been identical, dialectal differences occur in the course of centuries. This phenomenon is accounted for by the fact that an innovation will spring up in one part of the common language area but for one reason or other be rejected by other parts, which go on using their old speech or establish innovations of their own. The principle involved (and it is universal) is that language is never static, but dynamic, and subject to change and diversification.

From the standpoint of the individual and his self-interest, the question might here be raised whether it is desirable to retain, in your speech, features that are definitely dialectal and mark you as coming from a certain area, or whether it is better consciously to seek standardization, give up localisms of pronunciation and vocabulary, and try to achieve a form of speech that will be equally valid throughout the major area where the language is spoken. This question, of course, must be answered in accordance with your own tastes, preferences, and business or social interests. It is quite conceivable that in some areas or activities you may find it preferable to rely upon a local form of speech, and not make yourself glaringly different from the people around you by using a national standard which is not accepted or liked by those around you. This situation, however, particularly in modern times, tends to become more and more exceptional.

Modern means of communication, such as the radio, television, and the spoken film; modern means of transportation, such as the automobile and the railroad; and modern universal and compulsory education all tend to unify the language and impose a national standard. In the case of two or more countries using the same official language, as Britain and America, there is a tendency toward individuality in spelling, pronunciation, and the use of words, but even here the trend is toward unification and blending. High standards of material civilization oppose the conservation and spreading of dialects and favor uniformity. Variety, the spice of life, is picturesque and soul-satisfying to the ego, but standardization is more convenient.

cultural aspects of language:
slang, cant, jargon

These three terms are occasionally used interchangeably, but they should not be. Slang is best defined as a substandard form of speech that is generally intelligible to the entire population, or at any rate to the majority of the speakers, whether they choose to use it or not. Jargon is that form of speech (often merely a segment of the vocabulary) which is used in a certain trade, calling, or profession, but does not otherwise differ from the standard language. Cant is a special variety of jargon used by the criminal or underworld classes and designed, more or less deliberately, to be intelligible only to them.

Confusion arises from the fact that the three forms often overlap and run into one another. It is a common enough phenomenon for an originally underworld term to get into the general popular slang, and thereafter be used or at least understood by the whole community. The same applies to selected portions of individual professional or trade jargons, which for one reason or another get to enjoy publicity and popularity. Examples of both could be multiplied, but "grand," as applied to a thousand dollars, and "gat" (or "rod" or "persuader"), as applied to a revolver, will suffice as examples of underworld terms. For professional jargon we may select the psychologist's "id" (popularized also by crossword puzzles) or the medical "polio" (for "poliomyelitis") or radio's "mike" for "microphone."

These forms of language have seemingly always existed, and in all languages. A slang use of *kapala*, "pot," for "head," is to be found in Sanskrit, earliest of all Indo-

European languages on record. The Romans used so much slang that many linguists claim that the Romance languages are the descendants not of the classical Latin we study in school but of the slang Latin used by the crowds in the market place and the soldiers in the camps. Certainly the survival in the Romance languages of slangy Latin words like *caballus* for "horse," *testa* for "head," *bellus* for "beautiful," *cantare* for "to sing," instead of the more elegant and literary *equus, caput, pulcher,* and *canere,* would seem to indicate that this is partly true. (Note, however, that the high-falutin words appear in the more literary portion of the modern vocabularies: "equine," "capital," "pulchritude," Italian *canoro.*)

The cant of thieves and criminals appears in abundance in ancient and medieval works, such as those of Plautus, a Roman writer of popular comedies, and Villon, a fifteenth-century French poet, whose *argot* or *jobelyn* (both words mean "cant") is so thickly scattered through his writings that parts of them cannot be deciphered today.

As for jargon, that too has always existed. The Egyptian priests of the cult of Isis and Osiris made use of words that the mass of the worshipers did not know; Sumerian and Babylonian workers in clay, Greek weavers, Roman gladiators, medieval armor makers, sailors of all periods and nationalities, physicians and astrologers, artists and artisans, all have had their specialized vocabularies reserved for the trade.

Today, all languages have a more or less extensive range of slang words, forms, and expressions, looked upon askance or with downright disapproval by the purists, but widely used by the general population. Slang tends to legitimize itself, as was the case with the Roman slang terms cited above, becoming part of the standard language and losing all slang connotations. Our present-day vocabularies and dictionaries, freed of the old purist influences, generally give a broad cross section of slang terms, vulgarisms, and colloquialisms (the differences among these classifications are of degree, not of kind), and they are kept in until they either achieve legitimacy or die a natural death, which happens frequently, because the death rate among them is abnormally high.

For every slang term that survives and gets into the standard language, there are tens of others that wither away and become as dead as the song hits of yesteryear (con-

---

INTERACTION OF SLANG AND DIALECT

Pure nationwide slang: I ain't got none!
　　　　　　　　Jeet? No, joo?
Big-city slang: Getting gout!
　　　　　　　Hey, youse guys!
　　　　　　　So long, toots, I gotta blow now!
Slang, touch of dialect: Dey're a bunch o' joiks!
　　　　　　　　　Them's them!
Big-city dialect,
touch of slang: An' I don't never git no breaks!
　　　　　　　I'm gonna take de goil to Pros-separk (Prospect Park); she's an inside dame all week, a seketerry at the liberry.
Dialect, touch of slang: I ain't hear'n tell of it.
　　　　　　　　　If I'd a knowed it was you, I'd a retch out an' wove.
Pure dialect: I was sittin' on a stoop at Toity-toid Street an' Foist Avenoo.
　　　　　The score is nary-nary in the ninth, with us'uns to bat.
　　　　　He-brutes is ornery critters!

DIALECTALIZED SLANG

American: I'm in a jam!   *British:* I have a sticky wicket!
American: Wallop the guy!   *British:* Biff the bloke!
American: Scram!   *British:* 'op it!   *Australian:* Imshi!
Midwest American: You bet! (for "you're welcome");
  South African: Inkosi! (for "Thanks").
American: Attaboy!   *New Zealand:* Kapai!
American: Yoohoo!   *Australian:* Cooee!

"Hump" and "plum," in addition to their legitimate meanings, are slangily used in various parts of the English-speaking world. But slang "hump," which in America means "to exert," has in Britain the meaning of "a fit of blues," while in Australia it means "a long tramp with a bundle" (somewhat like our "hike") or "to carry a bundle." "Plum," which in U. S. slang is used in the sense of a "juicy plum" (government or other soft job) or in "plum crazy," means in Britain the sum of £100,000 or its possessor.

SAMPLE DICTIONARY COUNT

Out of 315 words appearing on five pages selected at random in Webster's *New Collegiate Dictionary,* 1951 edition (pages 212, 403, 547, 649, 710), 45, or 14%, are slang, colloquial, dialectal, archaic, or obsolete. Slang words are 13, or 4%; colloquial words are 8, or 2½%; dialectal words are 10, or 3%; archaic words are 9, or 3%; obsolete words are 5, or 1½%. Slang and colloquial words together account for 6½% of the total, archaic and obsolete words together for 4½% of the total.

sider, for instance, the fate that befell the "twenty-three skidoo" or the "finale hopper" of our youth).

Slang is attributed on the one hand to the individual's desire for linguistic creation, on the other to the readiness on the part of the masses to accept any innovation that sounds expressive, cute, new, or picturesque. But this seems to be the origin of many legitimate words (witness "microphone," "dianetics," etc.), so that there may be said to be no intrinsic difference between language and slang, save in the way the innovation is viewed at a given period and in a given area. The innovator must have some form of prestige among his immediate hearers for his innovation to be accepted and acquire currency. An innovation created by Churchill or Eisenhower would normally stand a better chance of spreading than one perpetrated by Joe Doakes, but the overwhelming majority of cases on record are of anonymous origin, which perhaps only proves the numerical superiority of the Joe Doakeses over the Churchills and Eisenhowers. In modern times, many slang innovations can be traced to writers, newspaper columnists, screen, stage, radio, and TV personalities, but most of the slang continues to be supplied by "anonymous" soldiers, teen-agers, and men in the street (when we say "anonymous," we mean that these people are known in their immediate circle, but unknown to the general public, and by the time their creation gets out, the name of the creator is lost in the shuffle).

The jargons of the trades and professions often have the characteristics of a limited slang, but are even more often made up of words without which a particular trade or profession would find it difficult to function. Modern times have seen the multiplication of activities and fields of knowledge, and this has been attended by a multiplication of terms. More than half the words in any modern civilized language are of a technical nature and are known and used only by the people directly concerned. To the outsider they are fully as bewildering as if they were foreign. Each calling has its own specialized vocabulary, which may range from a few dozen terms in the case of bellhops and soda jerks (note that these now universal slang terms originated as jargon forms in the respective callings) to countless thousands in such highly specialized fields as medicine and chemistry.

Some of the jargons may be described, at least in part, as class languages, because they carry with them the implication of an intellectual superiority which may be real or fancied. This is the case with the Gobbledegook (or Officialese or Federal Prose) used by administrative bureaucrats, the overcultivated language employed by many art and music fanciers, the literary style affected by certain poets and prose authors, even the purely social language adopted in some suburban milieus. Jargon, however, while it employs its own more or less extensive terminology, is forced to rely overwhelmingly upon the standard language for its sounds, its grammar, and most of its vocabulary. This is true in lesser measure of slang, very little of dialect.

In connection with slang, cant, and jargon, you are faced with the same problem that confronts you in the field of dialect. Shall you or shall you not use slang? It is doubtful if you will care for cant, save to the extent that it will enable you to recognize terms encountered in reading detective fiction; but what about jargon, some variety of which you are bound to possess, in accordance with your calling? Shall it be severely restricted to trade and professional use, or be allowed to spill over into ordinary conversation and to tinge it all with shoptalk?

SOCIAL STRATIFICATION OF LANGUAGE, WITH INFLUENCES FROM DIALECTS AND OCCUPATIONAL JARGONS

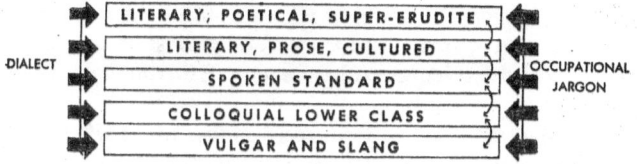

Super-erudite: "Those individuals do not possess any."
Cultured: "Those men haven't any."
Spoken standard: "Those men haven't got any."
Lower-class colloquial: "Those guys haven't (ain't) got any."
Slang: "Dem guys ain't got none."

From top to bottom level, every word changes. There is constant interchange among the levels, and all are affected by influences from local dialects and occupational jargons. Scots-dialect forms, for example, enter the poetry of Burns and the prose of Scott, while "dem" for "them" reflects New York dialect influence.

Here again, circumstances must dictate behavior. It is probably impossible to avoid slang altogether, for it is too firmly ingrained in the consciousness of English speakers. Besides, considering what has been said about the origin of slang and its normal historical course, it is hardly desirable to do so. You may find yourself avoiding a word or form which may well become part of the regular language of tomorrow.

The watchword in connection with both slang and jargon would seem to be moderation. If you fill your conversation with slang, you will hardly be able to avoid giving the impression that you are uncultured, ignorant, illiterate (exception is made, of course, for those who use slang as a profession, as on the stage, or who are so skilled and versed in its use that it turns into a social or professional asset, as happened with George Ade, Damon Runyon, and Dizzy Dean).

For what concerns jargon, by all means use it where and when necessary. But remember also that there is nothing so tiresome to the uninitiate as to have to listen to something they do not understand and should not, in justice, be expected to understand. Double-talk may be amusing for a time, but it quickly turns boresome, and jargon, to the one who is outside the field, is nothing but double-talk. This goes, too, for ultra-refined, ultra-intellectual, ultra-literary and ultra-artistic forms when they creep into normal language.

On the other hand, remember that we may always expect both slang and jargon to be with us (for cant, it may be hoped that if a crimeless society is ever achieved, it may disappear). It is right and proper that this should be so, because slang is part of the creative process of language change, while jargon is the mark and index of man's legitimate and beneficial activity in all specialized fields, whether manual or intellectual.

2

LANGUAGE IN THE LABORATORY

physical and physiological aspects
of language

Reduced to its simplest mechanical level, spoken language consists of a series of sound waves sent out by the human vocal apparatus. These sound waves travel through the air and strike the ear of another person. This, of course, is not the complete definition of language, for it leaves out the semantic aspect. As the definition stands, it could apply to any sort of noise you make with your mouth which is heard by someone else.

That language may be distinguished from mere man-produced noise it is required further that the sounds carry a significant message which will mean roughly the same thing to the hearer as to the speaker. This can be achieved only through previous agreement, which involves the brains of the two individuals concerned. If I say "book," having in mind the object which the sounds of "book" symbolize to me, and my hearer does not have the same set of symbols, but accepts for the object something like *livre, kniga,* or *hon,* the message is not completed, and no true language results.

Granting, however, that my hearer and I, belonging to the same speech community, agree in recognizing the sequence of sounds in the word "book" as symbolical of the same object, we may then pass on to the purely mechanical process by which the transfer of meaning is effected.

My lungs, mouth, lips, tongue, and palate, acting upon a command received from the brain, get themselves into a series of preordained positions whereby the air vibrations corresponding to the sounds of "book" are set up in the air. These vibrations, which move out from my mouth in waves, reach the ear of my listener in the same sequence in which they are produced, and set up in his hearing apparatus a series of responses coinciding with his own acceptance of the sounds of "book." This series is mechanically transmitted to his brain and arouses there an image corresponding, more or less closely, to the one originally conceived by my brain and in accordance with which I set my own organs of sound symbolism in motion.

The process is a complicated one, though it is over in far less time than it takes to describe it. The first portion of it is psychological and involves a conscious desire on my part to convey the notion of "book" to my hearer. To do this, my brain cells must pick out of their pigeonholes, of which the brain has billions, first the appropriate oral symbol, the word "book," which lies in the back of my consciousness. Then they must resolve it into its audible com-

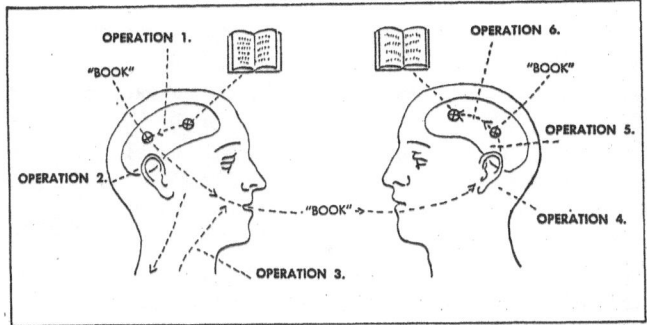

COMPLETE SPEECH PROCESS

Speaker gets concept of "book" from brain cell, transfers to speech center (operation 1), where concept is exchanged for sound symbol. Speech center sends order to utter "book" to speech organs (operation 2). The word is uttered by the speech organs (operation 3). It is transmitted by air waves to the listener's ear (operation 4), which refers it to the speech center of the listener's brain (operation 5). It is then referred to the decoding center (operation 6), where the word symbol gives rise to the concept of "book" in the listener's brain.

ponents, the sounds of "book" (this process is not too unlike the one whereby a printer, setting up a line by hand, picks the individual characters out of their cases and sets them in order). Now comes the physiological response to the impulse from the brain. There are three separate sounds in b-oo-k, and each one involves not one but several speech organs at once. The lungs, acting as a bellows, set up a stream of air which begins to travel up the windpipe. At the glottis, or Adam's apple, the breath stream causes two cartilages called vocal cords to vibrate even while it travels on toward the lips, which I have protruded and pursed, but am holding tightly closed. The instant I release them, the combination of breath stream rushing through the suddenly formed opening of the lips and the vibration of the vocal cords far below sets up air waves of the type and frequency of the sound "b." Immediately thereafter, with the vibration of the vocal cords still continuing, I draw back my tongue, hold the lips open, and allow the air stream to vibrate in the resonant chamber of the mouth. The air vibrations set up by this process correspond to the sound of short "oo," which follows the "b" in concentric waves into the outer air. Next, I quickly halt the vibration of the vocal cords, bring the back part of my tongue into contact with my soft palate so as to form a complete obstruction, then suddenly release this, while at the same time I draw back my lips, which had been left protruding by the preceding two sounds. Now the sequence of "b," "oo," and "k," transformed from a mental concept into a succession of lung-and-mouth movements, and then into a series of wavelike vibrations in the outer air, strikes in quick succession the ear of my listener, setting up in his eardrum vibrations which he has been trained to associate with the sounds in question. The vibrations are transmitted to his brain, which quickly assembles them as sound symbols to be accepted in the sequence in which they were produced and transmitted. The brain cells now act as a decoding agency and pick out of the mental code book the relationship between the series of three sounds and the object which my listener and I have agreed to call "book." At this point the transfer of meaning is completed and there is established between me and my hearer an exchange of spoken language, though of a very simple and rudimentary kind.

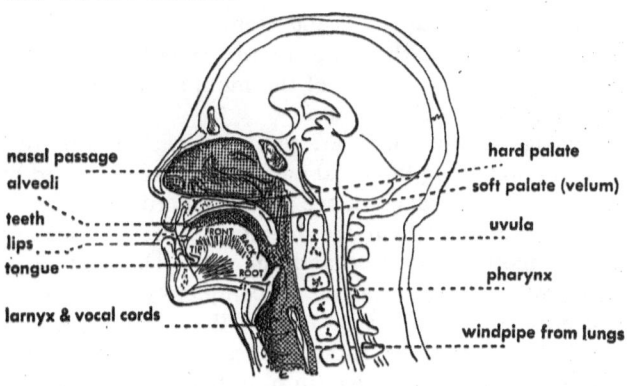

nasal passage

alveoli

teeth

lips

tongue

larnyx & vocal cords

hard palate

soft palate (velum)

uvula

pharynx

windpipe from lungs

Naturally enough, the mere exchange of the word "book" is a very unsatisfactory piece of information, but since it is normally accompanied by other words ("I have a" or "please give me the"), we need not worry about that.

The sound waves set up in the outer air are not intrinsically different from any other sound waves. They can be precisely measured by instruments, and their wave length, pitch and intensity determined. It is interesting to note that while vibrations within the range of 30 to 30,000 per second may be described as sound, the range used in language normally is much smaller. All this is physics.

The process whereby human-language sounds are produced pertains not to the realm of physics, but to that of physiology. The organs involved are the lungs, which merely serve to set up the breath stream utilized for speech; the windpipe, through which the air stream passes; the glottis, which contains the vocal cords, then the mouth itself, with its upper surface (uvula, soft palate, hard palate) and its lower surface (back and front of the tongue); the teeth and lips; and the nose, to the extent that certain sounds call for the shutting of the mouth passage and the escape of air through the nose.

Language sounds which are produced with a minimum of obstruction along the vocal passage and accompanied by vibration of the vocal cords are usually described as vowels. Differences among them are due to the size and shape I give my mouth resonator and the way I hold my lips. Consonants involve a partial or complete closure of the passage somewhere along its length. If the closure is complete and followed by sudden release, the consonant is called a plosive or occlusive (in *p, b, t, d, k, g* we note this complete closure followed by sudden release). But the process may or may not be accompanied by vibration of the vocal cords. If the vibration is there, we have voiced or sonant occlusives (*b, d, g*); if it is not there, we have unvoiced or surd occlusives (*p, t, k*). If the closure and release come at the lips, we have labials (*p, b*); if they involve the teeth, we have dentals (*t, d*); but note that in some languages, including English, the tip of the tongue may make contact not with the back of the teeth, but with the ridges of the upper gums, or alveoli, in which case the sound is more technically described as alveolar, though the term "dental" is often popularly used; if the point of closure and release is the soft palate or velum, and contact with it is made by the back of the tongue, we have velars, sometimes called gutturals (*k, g*).

Notice at this point that the six consonant sounds we have been discussing (*p, b, t, d, k, g*) can be described completely and accurately by referring to the fact that they are produced by closure and release (that is, by calling them plosives or occlusives); by stating whether they are

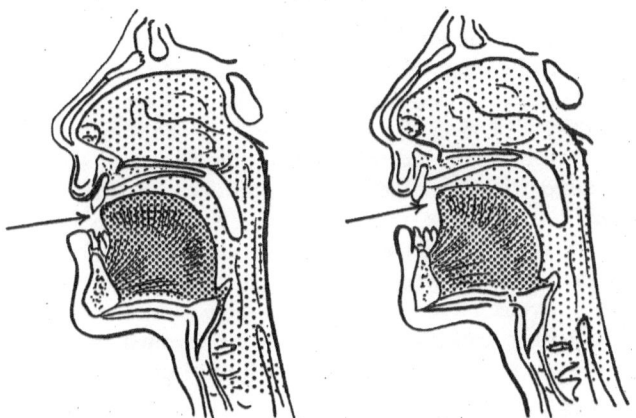

DIFFERENT POINTS OF ARTICULATION OF FRENCH AND ENGLISH "T"

Frenchman pronounces *t*:
Tip of tongue touches back of upper teeth.

Englishman pronounces *t*:
Tip of tongue touches ridge of upper gum (alveolus) above upper teeth.

---

or are not accompanied by vibration of the vocal cords (that is, by calling them voiced or unvoiced); and by stating their point of articulation (if the lips are involved, they are labials; if the teeth or gum ridges come into play, they are dentals or alveolars; if the back palate is the point of contact, they are velars or gutturals). The scientific description or definition of the sound of *b* is "voiced labial plosive"; for the sound of *k* we would use "unvoiced velar plosive"; and so on down the line.

If we now examine sounds like those of *f, v,* hard or soft *th,* we find that instead of complete closure and release, we have a partial closure, through which the breath stream forces its way. These are spirant or fricative sounds, so called because the sound can be indefinitely prolonged and is attended by friction (whereas the sound of the plosive is over as soon as release occurs). *F* and hard *th* are unaccompanied by vibration of the vocal cords, hence they are unvoiced fricatives; *v* and soft *th* have the vibration, so they are voiced fricatives. *F* and *v* are produced by letting the lower lip and upper teeth supply the point of friction, so they are labio-dental fricatives; the two *th*-sounds involve only the teeth and tongue, so they are dental fricatives.

M, n, ng are nasals, since they involve complete closure of the mouth and the escape of the air through the nose. *L* and *r* are sometimes described as liquids or sonants (the latter term, however, is applied also to the nasals, since they all involve a vowel-like resonance); perhaps a better term for them would be linguals, since they involve certain positions of the tongue, which is the main factor in their production. All are voiced. The unvoiced sibilant *s* and the voiced sibilant *z* really fall in with the fricative classification, as they both involve prolonged friction. The more usual sounds of *y* and *w* (*boy, year; bow, wear*) are described as semivowels or semiconsonants; they are glide sounds before or after pure vowels and resemble vowels for what concerns mouth position, but have a function similar to that of consonants. The sounds normally represented in English spelling by *sh* and its voiced counterpart (the *s* of *measure* or *pleasure*) are palatal fricatives. Preceded by the sounds of *t* and *d*, they produce mixed sounds that begin as plosives and end as fricatives, represented in writing by *ch* and *j* (or the "soft" *g* of *general*). To such mixtures, the term "affricate" is often applied.

So far, we have been describing language sounds from the point of view of the producer. What of the recipient?

As the sound waves strike the eardrum and are relayed for decoding to the listener's brain, they may be distorted by imperfect utterance, or by a disturbance in the air through which they travel, or by a faulty receiving apparatus, so that there may be wide rifts between what the speaker produces and what the listener hears. Yet there is usually complete understanding if speaker and listener belong to the same speech community.

There is no question that sounds are distorted and modified in their travels and that reception is generally defective. In a conversation over the telephone, it is quite normal for the hearer to "hear," in the true sense of the word, only about half of the sounds produced by the speaker, and to have to supply the rest out of his own experience and knowledge of the context; that is why, when you spell out proper names for the operator, you say "*t* for 'Thomas,' *m* for 'Mary' "; in the sound group that makes up "Thomas" or "Mary," the other sounds serve as a check and identification for the initial *t* and *m*; but if you isolate the *t* or *m* from its sound context, it can easily be confused with other sounds.

This "law of imperfection" in the transmission of sounds accounts for many things and has many applications. It explains, for example, why a two-year-old who is learning to speak will find it difficult to imitate all the language sounds he hears and will often substitute one for another. His difficulties are partly due to unfamiliarity with the mouth positions required by certain sounds, but they are also due in part to imperfect reception. More clear-cut is the evidence of your own reproduction of a sentence spoken in a foreign tongue. Even though none of the sounds used in that tongue may be strange to you, you will nevertheless find yourself confusing *n*'s and *m*'s, *t*'s and *d*'s, *p*'s and *k*'s. This does not happen when you are asked to repeat a sentence in a tongue you are thoroughly familiar with, because even if you fail to catch some of the sounds, you are able to supply them from your own consciousness of what the context should be.

This "law of imperfection" also accounts in large part for the changes that occur historically in the sound scheme of any given language. There is imperfect reception of a sound or sounds produced by the older generation of speakers on the part of the new generation, and the substitution of a "wrong" for a "right" sound takes place. The two sounds may coexist for years and even centuries side by side, both being accepted by the speakers, until the older one finally gives way and the new one alone survives.

English once had a sound, still represented in writing by the combination *gh*, which was very similar to that heard in modern German *ach*. This sound has utterly disappeared from the standard language, being, however, retained in individual dialects, such as the Scots (often, in learning German, you are told to pronounce the German *ch* in certain positions "as in Scottish *loch*"). In Old English, or Anglo-Saxon, there was a sound, represented in writing by *y*, which was very similar to that of French *u* today; for French *u*, you are told to purse the lips as though you were going to say *oo*, then try to say *ee*. For two pronunciations surviving side by side, we have only to recall the two current ones for "tomato" and "either."

Considering all the possible shifts in the position of the vocal organs that could conceivably be made, the number of language sounds that could actually be produced by those organs probably runs in the thousands. Out of this vast range, each language picks out a very limited number (normally somewhere between twenty and sixty) and discards all other possibilities. No language (in fact, no dialect) makes use of precisely the same sound scheme that is used by another.

This leads to another principle of language learning, that of sound substitution. As you learn a foreign language with its strange sound scheme, you unconsciously tend to substitute for the foreign sounds, which are not intrinsically difficult but merely unfamiliar to you, the nearest sounds from your own language scheme. This, of course, gives you a foreign accent. This principle, which seems to work almost universally for adult learners, has no validity whatsoever in the case of children up to the age of ten or thereabouts. The child's language habits are not set, those of the adult are.

The sound scheme of modern English (remembering that there are dialectal variations) involves between twelve and fourteen pure vowel sounds, plus a number of diphthongs (two different vowel sounds coming in close succession and often represented in writing by a single letter, like the *i* of "bide" or the *o* of "bode"), plus twenty-two pure consonant sounds—a moderate but adequate sound equipment.

It may be remarked at this point that the written alphabet as we use it in English is a very unsatisfactory representative of the sound scheme of the language. It often employs two or more letters to indicate what is a single speech sound (*th* is a case in point) or a single letter to represent a succession of two or more sounds (the *i* of "side" or the *u* of "use").

It is a curious thing that no two speakers of a language pronounce what is supposed to be the same sound in precisely the identical fashion. This is due to individual differences in the structure of the speech organs and even in their use (you may, for example, pronounce the *th* of "this" either by placing the tip of your tongue against the back of the upper teeth, or against the back of the lower teeth, or against the back of both rows of teeth, or actually between the teeth). These individual variations are taken in their stride by the listeners, who are thoroughly accustomed to them. There comes a point, however, where this tolerance ceases, and the speaker who goes beyond the bounds of tolerance is set down as a foreigner trying to speak the language, or a jokester trying to be funny, or a rugged individualist bordering on the crackpot.

Consider, for instance, what happens when a foreigner says "I leave in this house" when he means "I live in this house." He is overstepping the boundary of the English speaker's consciousness of the permissible range of the *ee* sound, and carrying it over into the territory of the short *i* sound. In another language (Spanish, for instance) there would be no such boundary, and the speaker, depending on his emotion or emphasis, might pronounce *vivo* with the sound of "leave" (a more normal pronunciation), but also with something close to the short *i* sound of "live." In Spanish, this would cause no confusion of meaning; in English, it does.

Speech sounds, which are objective, physical realities, definitely measurable by precision instruments, are linked, therefore, with the speaker's consciousness of such sounds, which is not always so precise or objective. The line of demarcation is set by the meaning which the sound carries to the hearer. A bundle of sounds which the speakers of the language agree to recognize as within the range of a single sound (because the use of one or another of the sounds makes no difference in the meaning) is technically known as a phoneme. In English, the *ee* sound of "leave" and the short *i* sound of "live" constitute two different phonemes; in Spanish, they are a single phoneme, since the substitution of one for the other makes no difference in the meaning.

In English, the sound of *p* in "pit" is accompanied by a rather energetic puff of breath, almost as though it were spelled *p-h-it*; in "spit," there is no such puff of breath. The two sounds of *p* differ considerably, and in some languages, such as Chinese or Hindustani, they would constitute separate phonemes and could lead to confusion of meaning if one were employed for the other. In English, they are never in opposition, because it is an unwritten convention among English speakers that an initial *p* shall have the puff, but a *p* following an *s* shall not. Hence, in English the two sounds of *p*, despite their real difference, are regarded as a single phoneme. Substitution of one for the other is possible (if you are emotionally disturbed, you may come out with "I'll sp-h-it in your eye!"; if you are feeling very weak, you may come out with "pit" without the puff); but the basic meaning won't change.

The phoneme has a special application in the learning of a foreign language. By setting forth the phonemic make-up of the language and carefully outlining the boundaries of each phoneme, a far better pronunciation of the language is achieved. Foreigners learning English by this method are drilled on the significant differences of English phonemes; Spanish speakers, for example, whose normal tendency would be to confuse *ee* and short *i* sounds, are given such thorough drilling in the differences of production and meaning of these sounds that they will never again say "I leave in this house" or "I am living for Cuba tomorrow."

ILLUSTRATION OF ENGLISH VOWEL PHONEMES

	Front				*Back*		
SHORT	bit	bet	bat	the	hot	but	good
LONG	beat	there	girl	father	bought	boot

NOTE: While there is general agreement about the English consonant phonemes, there is great difference of opinion about the vowels. This is caused in part by the fact that different dialects of English use different vowel schemes. A British phonetician gives the pure vowel phonemes as twelve in number. An American phonetician lists nine basic vowels, plus eleven in which the basic vowel sound is said to be followed by H, Y, or W (for example, the vowel sound of "boot," which we prefer to describe as a pure vowel, is given by him as *uw* (buwt); that is, the vowel sound of "good" followed by a *w*-sound.

The most common diphthongs (combinations of two successive vowel sounds pronounced in one breath group) are illustrated by:

bite   bait   bout   boat   boy   cue

CHART OF ENGLISH CONSONANT PHONEMES

		La-bial	Labio-Den-tal	Den-tal	Alveolar	Pala-tal	Velar	Glot-tal	Liquid or Lingual
PLOSIVE	*Unvoiced*	p			t	ch	k		
	Voiced	b			d	j	g		
FRICATIVE	*Unvoiced*		f	*th*ing	s	sh		h	
	Voiced		v	*th*is	z	measure			l,r
NASAL	*Voiced*	m			n		ng		
SEMI-VOWEL		w				y			

CHART OF HAWAIIAN PHONEMES

CONSONANTS: h, k, l, m, n, p, w
VOWELS: a, e, i, o, u (as pronounced in "father," "bet," "machine," "or," "food")

Because of the lack of the sounds b, d, f, g, j, r, s, t, v, the Hawaiian rendering of "Merry Christmas" is *Meli Kaliki-maka;* "February" comes out as *Pepeluali,* and "October" as *Okakopa.* Hawaiian admits no consonant groups, and all syllables must end in vowels. Note the substitution of *l* for *r,* of *k* for *t* and *s,* of *p* for *b* and *f,* and the placing of a vowel after each consonant.

What difference does it make whether you say "The man runs" or "The men run"? The basic concept is the same: one or more human beings are involved in a certain type of activity. The meaningful difference between the two simple statements is that one involves a single man, the other more than one. In the terms of our grammar-school days, one involves a singular, the other a plural, subject.

The notion of plurality instead of singularity is achieved in two ways, both of which involve language sounds: changing the *a* of "man" to the *e* of "men" and leaving out the *-s* of "runs." Both these changes affect the structure of the words in which they appear; both are morphological (the *morph-* part of this word comes from a Greek word meaning "shape," "form," or "structure").

If we now take a sentence like "Paul sees John" and change it around to "John sees Paul," we have a difference in concept even more radical than the one above. The one who does the action in one case receives it in the other, and vice versa. Yet we have made no change in form in any of the words, so there is no morphology involved. We have changed the position or order of the words. The change we have made is syntactical ("syntax" and "syntactical" also come from the Greek, where the original word means "arrangement," "order").

Morphology and syntax taken together, the change in the form of words and the change in the arrangement or order of words, constitute a language's grammar. Without these two devices we would have at our command only sounds and individual words, which would permit us to transfer a certain amount of meaning, but in a very imperfect and unsatisfactory way and without any precision. Grammar is therefore a powerful aid to expression of clear thoughts.

Every language has grammar of one fashion or another. In the modern understanding, the grammar of the language is not something set up to force you to express yourself in a certain manner. It is merely the sum total of all the devices you and all other speakers of the language are already using to make your meaning clearer. Hence it should be regarded not with veneration or fear but with interest and curiosity.

Every language has a grammar, just as every language has sounds. The sounds of no two languages coincide. Neither do the grammars. Morphology and syntax, the two devices that constitute grammar, may be mixed in very different doses. Some languages rely almost exclusively upon morphology, endings like the -s of "runs," internal changes like the one whereby "man" changes into "men," prefixes like the "under" in "understand," which gives the compounded word a meaning that one would never guess from either of its component parts. Others rely almost exclusively on syntax and word order, as when we get completely different meanings from "I see it through" and "I see through it." English, like most languages, has a combination of both.

There was a time when morphology played a far bigger role in English than it does today. In Anglo-Saxon, nouns had entire series of endings and internal vowel changes that indicated not merely number, or the difference between singular and plural, but also gender (masculine, feminine or neuter) and case (whether the noun was the subject, the object, the possessor, etc.). Adjectives like "white" or

COMPARISON OF ANGLO-SAXON AND MODERN ENGLISH ENDINGS

NOUN

	SINGULAR		PLURAL	
	A-S	*Eng.*	*A-S*	*Eng.*
Nom.	stān	stone	stān-as	stone-s
Gēn.	stān-es	stone-'s	stān-a	stone-s'
Dat.	stān-e	stone	stān-um	stone-s
Acc.	stān	stone	stān-as	stone-s

ADJECTIVE (STRONG DECLENSION)

	SINGULAR				PLURAL			
	A-S			*Eng.*	*A-S*			*Eng.*
	MASC.	FEM.	NEUT.		MASC.	FEM.	NEUT.	
Nom.	gōd	gōd	gōd	good	gōd-e	gōd-a	gōd	good
Gēn.	gōd-es	gōd-re	gōd-es	good	gōd-ra	gōd-ra	gōd-ra	good
Dat.	gōd-um	gōd-re	gōd-um	good	gōd-um	gōd-um	gōd-um	good
Acc.	gōd-ne	gōd-e	gōd	good	gōd-e	gōd-a	gōd	good

VERB

Infinitive—A-S drīf-an   *Past Participle—A-S* ge-drif-en
        Eng. drive   *Eng.* driv-en

	PRESENT		PAST	
	A-S	*Eng.*	*A-S*	*Eng.*
Sg. 1	drīf-e	drive	drāf	drove
Sg. 2	drīf-st	(driv-est)	drif-e	(drov-est)
Sg. 3	drīf-ð	(driv-eth)	drāf	drove
		driv-es		

Pl. 1	drīf-að	drive	drif-on	drove
Pl. 2	drīf-að	drive	drif-on	drove
Pl. 3	drīf-að	drive	drif-on	drove

PERSONAL PRONOUNS

	SINGULAR		PLURAL	
	A-S	*Eng.*	*A-S*	*Eng.*
Nom.	ic	I	wē	we
Gen.	mīn	my, mine	ūser	our, ours
Dat.	mē	me	ūs	us
Acc.	mē	me	ūs	us
Nom.	hē	he		
Gen.	his	his		
Dat.	him	him		
Acc.	hine	him		

"good" had similar endings; even our little article "the" had a set of endings. Verbs showed by their endings or internal vowel changes all those differences which today are indicated by using with them "I," "you," "he," "we," "they," as well as many more. Many languages in spoken use today still do this.

English, however, has rather ruthlessly cut down its morphological equipment, and apparently without ill effects. What we have today is an -*s* ending which we normally use to indicate that a noun is plural ("kings") and a verb third person singular ("runs"), a -*d* or -*ed* which marks the past and past participle of many verbs, an -*ing* that marks the present participle. There is an *'s* (or merely an apostrophe) that marks possession. We also have, however, a variety of vowel changes both in nouns and in verbs ("foot-feet," "mouse-mice," "take-took," "see-saw") and an -*en* ending that crops up occasionally in nouns and verbs ("ox-oxen," "child-children," "take-taken"). In personal pronouns, we have inherited a clear-cut distinction between the subject, the object, and the possessor form ("I-me-my" or "mine"; "he-him-his"; "we-us-our" or "ours"; "they-them-their" or "theirs"); but even this breaks down in the case of "you," which is used for both subject and object, and of "her," which is both object and possessor.

By way of contrast, English relies very largely on word order to clarify its meanings. In addition to the general rule that the doer of the action (subject) shall come before the action word (verb) and the latter in turn be followed by the recipient of the action (object), we have other word-order conventions. Articles ("the," "a," "an") and adjectives ("white," "good") normally come before nouns ("the good man"). Prepositions, like "to," "of," "for," "with," "by," come before the noun or phrase to which they refer ("with the good man"). Occasionally word order is made to take the place even of prepositions; we may say, for instance, "I gave the book to the man" or "I gave the man the book."

Once in a while, English combines morphology and syntax to achieve the same result. The forms "he" and "him" are morphologically distinct; the first is used as subject, the second as object. Yet, when it comes to their position in the sentence, we follow the same syntactical rule that is applied in the case of nouns, where there is no distinction of form. We say "I see him" and "he sees me." "I" and "he" already indicate by their distinctive form that they are subjects; but, in addition, we place them in the subject position, much like a man who wears both suspenders and a belt.

One of the first things that have to be learned by the person who sets out to acquire a foreign language is that in both morphology and syntax he must expect to find differences between his native and his new language. In the matter of syntax, for instance, both English and French will arrange "I see the man" in the same order. But where English says "I see him," French puts it "I him see." Chinese, which has no morphology and does everything by syntax, lacks the distinction between "he" and "him" and consequently says "I see he," while for "he sees me" the order is reversed: "he see I." Both English and French say "I have seen your brother" in the same order, but German puts it: "I have your brother seen." German, in addition, would put an ending on the word "your" that would mark "your brother" as object, thus combining word order and morphology to achieve a single purpose.

In the case of verbs—words that denote action or state—some languages indicate practically everything morphologically, by endings. The Latin equivalent for "I shall love" is *amabo*, where the basic meaning "love" is conveyed by *ama-*, the idea that the action will take place in the future is indicated by *-b-*, and the fact that "I" will perform the action (first person singular) is shown by the *-o* at the end of the word. English, instead, uses three separate words arranged in a certain order: a subject pronoun "I," a helping verb or auxiliary "shall," which by itself would not mean too much, but which conveys the idea of futurity when used with any other verb, and the basic "love." German handles this situation as English does (*ich werde lieben*), Spanish as Latin (*amaré*), while French has an interesting combination of both (*j'aimerai*); here *aim-* con-

veys the basic notion, -er- the infinitive idea, transferred to
the future by being compounded with *ai,* but the "I" is indicated twice, by the ending -*ai,* and also by the subject
pronoun *j'* (for *je*), which has the precise meaning of "I."
Chinese, which uses no endings whatsoever and has no
auxiliaries like our "shall," "will," "have," gets around it
by saying "I bright day love" ("bright day" is the optimis-
tic Chinese way of expressing "tomorrow").

Another point that strikes the learner of a foreign language is the difference in what various languages consider
essential, at least to the extent that a distinction has to be
made in speech or writing. In English, some nouns, by
their meaning, are masculine and represented by "he,"
others are feminine ("she"), others are neuter ("it"). But
the nouns themselves seldom carry any ending that is dis-
tinctively masculine, feminine, or neuter (where this happens, as in "chorine" or "majorette," the ending is generally borrowed from another language, usually French), and
the articles and adjectives that precede them never do. In
a language like Spanish, the indication of gender not only
is usually given by the ending of the noun but has to be
repeated in all accompanying words (*el muchacho alto,*
"the tall boy"; *la muchacha alta,* "the tall girl"). Some languages, like Hungarian, on the other hand, disregard the
gender concept to the extent not only of not having any
distinctive endings, but even of having no separate words
for "he," "she," and "it."

The main grammatical concepts we recognize in English, to the extent that we make some provision for them by
a variation of form or by accompanying them with another
word, are: gender (masculine, feminine, neuter: "he,"
"she," "it"); number (singular, plural: "box," "boxes,"
"he," "they"); case (subject, possessor, object: "he," "his,"

ENGLISH: The father saw the good boy and said to him: "Go home."

LATIN: Pater bonum puerum vidit et ei dixit: Domum redi. (Father good boy saw and to-him said: Home back-go.)

FRENCH: Le père a vu le bon garçon et lui a dit: Rentre à la maison. (The father has seen the good boy and to-him has said: Go-back to the house.)

ENGLISH: I don't know where you bought your hat.

GERMAN: Ich weiss nicht, wo Sie Ihren Hut gekauft haben. (I know not, where you your hat bought have.)

ENGLISH: How long have you been waiting?

GERMAN: Wie lange warten Sie schon? (How long wait you already?)

FRENCH: Depuis combien de temps attendez-vous? (Since how-much of time wait you?)

SPANISH: ¿Cuánto tiempo hace que usted espera? (How-much time makes that you wait?)

ITALIAN: Da quanto tempo aspetta? (Since how-much time wait-you?)

RUSSIAN: Skol'ko vremeni Vy zhdyote? (How-much of-time you wait?)

"him"); person (first, or speaker; second, or person spoken to; third, or person spoken of: "I," "you," "he"); tense (time of action: present, past, future, etc.: "I see," "I saw," "I shall see"); voice (subject does or receives the action: "I see," "I am seen"). In addition, we divide up words into separate classes called parts of speech, according to their form or use; but this is a complicated matter, and will be discussed in the next chapter.

Note at this point that these grammatical concepts appear in other languages in varying degrees, or may not appear at all and may be replaced by other concepts which the speakers consider essential. Of this we have seen samples; but we shall see many more.

the word

The word might be described as the minimal, or individual, unit of meaning, were it not for the fact that in a single word, as we have seen, there are often assembled several meaning units. It is true that the combination is generally of one primary, or basic, and one or more secondary units, as when we say "birds" and have a primary meaning, "bird," combined with a symbol of plurality, -s. Even in "bird" it might be argued that we have the basic meaning plus a minus feature, the lack of a plural sign, and that since this minus feature conveys the notion of singularity, it is something that exists, and is significant, like the zero in 10, which by itself equals nothing.

Some people view words as primarily written-language conventions, that permit convenient spacing in writing; these people claim that the real language unit, at least in spoken language, is the sentence, which conveys an entire thought. The objective existence of the word, however, seems to be proved by the fact that you can lift it out of its context and use it in another context. To a limited degree, the same may be said of significant endings and even of internal changes within words. Linguists often get around this problem by speaking of morphemes (independent units of form, like the -s of "birds," which convey significant accessory notions) and semantemes (units of meaning).

Words are divided up into classes according to their form, behavior, and uses. We generally speak of a noun as the name of a thing ("wall"), quality ("goodness"), or person ("John"). Adjectives are those words which modify or describe nouns ("good," "white"). Pronouns are words which stands for nouns ("I" might be said to stand for my name; "it" can refer to "wall"; "yours" can take the place of "your book"). Articles are little handles that we use on nouns, often to indicate that they have been mentioned already ("the"), or that they have not ("a," "an"). Verbs are action words or indicate states ("go," "speak," "stand," "have," "be," "become," "live"). Adverbs answer questions like "when?", "how?" and generally appear in connection with verbs or adjectives ("*When* did he go?" "He went *yesterday*"; "*How* tall is he?" "*Very* tall?"). Prepositions are little words like "of," "to," "with," which come before nouns and show how they fit into the rest of the sentence. Conjunctions serve to connect either words or parts of sentences ("and," "if," "but"). Interjections are pure exclamations, which normally convey a message all by themselves and very often indicate an emotional state ("Ah!", "Golly!").

These nine classes of words are known as parts of speech, and the theory is that every word in the language will fit into one or another of the nine pigeonholes. But there are some catches:

1. Many words fit into two or more pigeonholes; if I say "the white man," I am using "white" to describe man, so it is an adjective; but if I speak of "the whites and the Negroes," I am using "white" as a noun, and even giving it an -s in the plural, something I cannot do when I use it as an adjective. In "Mail this letter," "Put this letter in the mail," "Put this letter in the mailbox," I am using the word "mail" first as a verb, then as a noun, lastly as an adjective (which has been combined with the noun to form with it a single word).

2. This kind of word grouping works out only moderately well for English, as we see from the confusing examples above. In some languages it works out much better, because nouns, adjectives, verbs have very special endings used only with that class of word. In Italian, for example, the verb "mail" is *impostare*, the noun "mail" is *posta*, the adjective "mail" is *postale*; obviously no confusion is possible there. But there are other languages where the distinction among parts of speech appears less than in English, or does not appear at all. In Chinese, the same word, *ta*, may be a noun ("bigness"), an adjective ("big"), a verb ("enlarge"), and a few other things besides; Chinese does not classify its words as we do, but simply makes a distinction between "full" words, which have a complete meaning

ARTICLES: the, a, an
NOUNS: man, man's, men, men's
ADJECTIVES: clear, clearer, clearest
VERBS: love, loves, loving, loved; see, sees, saw, seeing, seen
PRONOUNS: I, my (mine), me; who, whose, whom; this, these; what
ADVERBS: clearly, fast, where
PREPOSITIONS: with, by, from, in, to
CONJUNCTIONS: and, but, if, that
INTERJECTIONS: ah!, golly!, ouch!

"PARTS OF SPEECH" AS RECOGNIZED BY SOME CHINESE GRAMMARIANS

FULL WORDS $\begin{cases} \text{Living (verbs)} \\ \text{Dead (nouns and adjectives)} \end{cases}$
EMPTY WORDS—Particles, abstract words

---

in themselves, and "empty" words, which have to be used in connection with other words to acquire a specific meaning.

3. Even in languages that divide up their words pretty much as we do, there is no general agreement. Russian and Latin have no articles, no words corresponding to our "the" or "a." *Liber* in Latin and *kniga* in Russian may mean "book," "a book," "the book." Do languages miss what they don't have? They're a little like human beings, who may not be aware of the fact that they miss a car or a

TV set until the Joneses next door get one. The Greeks had a word for "the," the Romans did not, but as Latin developed into the Romance languages, all these, without exception, worked out a word for "the"; and it is possible that the movement began when the Romans compared their language with that of the Greeks.

The division of words into parts of speech suits very well those languages which use many endings and internal changes. Then, according to the endings and changes that a word takes on or undergoes, you can easily classify it. In languages like Latin, Greek, Russian, or our ancestral Anglo-Saxon, nouns, adjectives, pronouns, articles where they existed, verbs, and, to a limited degree, adverbs, take on different endings, each set of which is specific for that particular part of speech, while prepositions, conjunctions and interjections don't change. This means that in those languages classification of words into parts of speech is not only easy but natural. But what if a language uses no endings, like Chinese, or has lost a great many of its ancient endings, like English today? In that case, we can either forget about classification, as the Chinese do, or fall back on a mixture of the few endings we have left plus the way the word is used, as we do in English, where we have a few endings and changes left in nouns and verbs, a few separate forms for pronouns, and nothing whatsoever for adjectives, articles, and the rest.

It is important for us to know the classification of words in our own and other languages, because that classification is a guide to the way the words are used. But we must not lose sight of the fact that the classification shifts from language to language; it may be far more complicated in one language than in another, and in some languages may be completely nonexistent.

This principle did not come to light until recently, because in former times the only languages widely known in the western world were those of the western world, all of which belong to the same family (the Indo-European)—or to another family (the Semitic) that shows strong similarities of structure to the Indo-European. It was only the study of Far Eastern, American Indian, African Negro and other remote languages that brought to light the infinite diversity of structure and classification that language can take.

accent, intonation, and the syllable

There is something more to spoken language than mere sounds, or even words and sentences. Each language has its own spoken rhythm, its rise and fall, and if this is not observed it will inevitably sound foreign.

The word "accent" comes from the Latin, and if we break it up into its component parts, we find that it originally meant a "singing upon" the word or sequence of words. We know what happens in English if you stress the wrong part of a word. A Frenchwoman once told me that when she first came to America, though she thought she knew English fairly well, she had trouble in restaurants, because she would ask for "POT-a-toes" instead of "po-TA-toes."

ENGLISH: He ANswered VEry poLITEly all the QUEStions that were ASKed.

(Initial stress in all native [ANswered] and fully naturalized [VEry, QUEStions] words. In words not fully naturalized [poLITEly], stress may be on other syllable than the initial.)

GERMAN: GNÄdiges FRÀUlein, darf ich MEInen Freund beKANNT MAchen?

(As in English. In native words, a few verb prefixes do not take stress: beKANNT, like English beCOME.)

MODERN GREEK: Ti KAnete? PoLY kaLItera. EvkharisTO paRA poLY.

(In the ancient language, accent could fall only on one of the last three syllables, but if the last syllable contained a long vowel or a diphthong, the accent could fall only on one of the last two. The rule is automatically continued in modern Greek, though vowel quantity is now lost.)

LATIN: GALlia est OMnis diVIsa in PARtes tres, QUArum Unam INcolunt AquiTÄnI.

(The accent could fall only on the second or third syllable from the end, but if the penult syllable was long [i.e., contained a long vowel, or any vowel followed by a consonant] the accent could fall only on the penult.)

SPANISH: ¿Ha leído usTED ESto? Es un arTIculo en el peRIOdico de hoy.

(Like Italian and Portuguese, generally keeps the stress on the same syllable where Latin had it.)

FRENCH: Les HOMmes aVAIent parLÉ aVEC tous leurs aMIS.

(Light stress falls on last pronounced syllable of the word [syllables containing e-mute don't count]. This is really the same rule as that of Spanish or Italian, but French has dropped many Latin unstressed vowels.)

CZECH: ROzumíte? NErozumím. MLuvíte ANglicky? MLuvte POmaleji.

(Initial stress always. Accent marks indicate length of vowel, not place of stress.)

POLISH: PrzePRAszam, KTOra goDZIna TEraz? Nie roZUmiem.

(Accent always on next to last syllable. Accent mark irrelevant for stress.)

RUSSIAN: ZDRAVstvuyte! Kak dyeLA? SpaSIbo, khoroSHO.

(Stress unpredictable, often shifts in different forms of same word: khOROshiy, khoroSHO; DYElo, dyeLA.)

JAPANESE: DŌzo YUKkuri HAnashite KUdasai; EIgo ga DEkimasu ka?

(Fairly even stress throughout, with slight tendency to initial accentuation. Long vowels and vowels followed by double consonant tend to receive slightly heavier stress.)

In words of more than one syllable, the voice bears with more vigor upon one syllable than upon others. This involves greater vocal energy expended on the stressed syllable. It also involves, normally, a somewhat higher pitch of the voice, a higher note of the musical scale. The element of energy, or vigor of utterance, properly called stress, and the element of musical pitch usually go together but can be separated if you really want to use one to the exclusion of the other. This principle is unimportant for English but comes into play in the case of certain languages whose accent involves only pitch, like ancient Sanskrit, Greek, and Latin at their purest. Today, the element of pitch is extremely important in languages like Chinese, where it distinguishes words that are otherwise alike in pronunciation. In English, pitch distinguishes such things as questions, exclamations, and emotional states of the speaker, as well as emphasis upon one part or another of the utterance ("*You* went there yesterday?"; "You *went* there yesterday?"; "You went *there* yesterday?"; "You went there *yesterday*?").

In the case of English accent, the word stress is regularly fixed on one syllable. Words of Anglo-Saxon origin are almost invariably stressed on the first syllable; in words that come to us from Latin, Greek, or French the stress may fall anywhere, but in a scheme often determined by the original language, not in accordance with the speaker's whim. French has a lighter stress than English, but regularly places it on the last spoken syllable of the word. Some languages have distinctive stress patterns which act almost as marks of identification, others have no regularity whatsoever. Within the Slavic group of languages, Czech distinguishes itself by stress on the initial syllable, Polish by stress on the syllable next to the last, while in Russian the place of the stress is unpredictable.

In addition to word stress, there is the matter of sentence stress or intonation. This is generally more difficult to acquire because it is more elusive, and there are no precise rules governing it. Also, it almost always involves pitch. A British speaker of English can usually be distinguished from an American speaker by the modulation of his voice, the rise and fall of his tone, which normally has a far greater range. Stage imitations of British or foreign accents involve a great deal of study of pitch and modulation. In acquiring a foreign language, one can master sounds, words, and grammar and still not sound like a native, and in these cases the fault usually lies with disregard of pitch and intonation.

Chinese tones distinguish meanings of words otherwise pronounced alike.

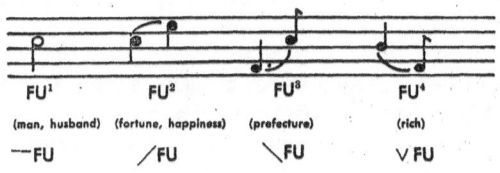

| FU¹ | FU² | FU³ | FU⁴ |

| (man, husband) | (fortune, happiness) | (prefecture) | (rich) |

—FU /FU \FU ∨FU

This disregard used to be general in the past, but recently language teachers have come to realize the importance of intonation and to make provision for it. In some language classes, the teacher demonstrates the proper modulation with a four-note xylophone, and the students are asked to imitate the "music" of the foreign sentence even before they undertake to imitate the sounds.

A further element in language that has not yet received proper attention is syllabification, or the breaking up of a word into its component syllables, and the reassembling of those syllables into a pattern of speech at the normal speed of utterance.

The reason for this neglect is that the division of words into syllables has normally been viewed as purely a written-language exercise connected with the way to break up a word at the end of a line of writing. Actually, it is far more than that.

The syllable is a spoken as well as a written unit. It consists of a group of sounds, usually a vowel preceded or followed (or both) by one or more consonants. It actually issues from the vocal organs as a unit, and is separated, however imperceptibly, from the sounds of the syllable that precedes or follows. It is, of course, true that often the syllable coincides with the word, in which case we label the word as monosyllabic, or consisting of only one syllable. But in the overwhelming majority of languages (Chinese and the languages of its family are a notable exception) many of the words are polysyllabic, consisting of two or more syllables.

The way in which these polysyllabic words are divided up, and even the way in which words of a single syllable are run into one another, differs from language to language. In English and many other tongues, there is a preference for syllables that end in consonant sounds; in fact, it has been claimed that the normal pattern for English syllables is consonant-vowel-consonant. But there are numerous languages that have a preference for syllables ending in vowel sounds, and in these languages the normal pattern, wherever possible, is consonant-vowel.

This difference of syllabic pattern makes a big difference in the way words that look similar are pronounced. The consonant endings of most English syllables tend to shorten and weaken the preceding vowel, unless it happens to be stressed. In a word like "general," where all three syllables end in consonants, the only clear-cut vowel is the stressed *e* of *gen*. The *e* of· *er* and the *a* of *al* are reduced in length and indistinct in quality, to the point where the sounds could be represented in writing by any vowel letter (if the spelling were "genirul" or "genarol," you would pronounce the word in exactly the same way).

In languages where the syllables ordinarily end in vowels, on the other hand, the vowel sound, because of its position, tends to remain clear and distinct, whether it is stressed or unstressed. Hence, in the Spanish *general*, the French *général*, or the Italian *generale,* which are divided *ge-ne-ral* or *ge-ne-ra-le*, all three or four vowels are clear and easily identifiable.

An English speaker learning a Romance language will have a tendency to divide up his words as he would in English, end his syllables in consonants, and make his unstressed vowels indistinct. But if he approaches the foreign word by breaking it up into syllables, pronouncing each syllable carefully and separately, then repeating it at a growing rate of speed, lessening the pauses between syllables, until he finally achieves normal speech rate, he will find himself pronouncing the French or Spanish or Italian word as a native would pronounce it, and will lose much of his foreign accent.

The three elements of accent (including both stress, or vigor of utterance, and pitch, or musical variation), intonation or sentence stress, and syllabification have important applications in connection with our own as well as foreign languages. Often what distinguishes a rough from a cultured form of speech is merely too much stress. Ridiculous effects of supercultivation can be attained by using too great variations in pitch. The rhythm or intonation of a sentence can make our voice dull and monotonous, or give it the animation and life that will lead people to say we are born orators. Incorrect syllabification in English leads to slipshod pronunciation, incorrect spelling, the obliteration from our speech of essential sounds and syllables, and this in turn can lead either to misunderstanding on the part of our hearers or to their setting us down as people of little education and no refinement.

Stress, pitch, intonation, and syllabification can also lead to far-reaching changes in languages. There is, for instance, a well-grounded theory to the effect that one of the major causes for the turning of Latin into the Romance languages was the addiction which the Latin speakers developed at one point in their history to a heavy, forceful form of accentuation. This heavy stress accent, by concentrating too much vocal energy on one syllable of the word, robbed the unstressed syllables of the vigor and clarity of utterance they should have had. This, in turn, obscured the all-important word endings, which bore the distinctions of gender, number, and case, and caused them in part to merge. But since these distinctions were essential for proper understanding, they now had to be made by different devices—the use of fixed word order and of many more prepositions than Latin had originally used. Ultimately, the entire grammatical structure of the language changed, and when this happened, it was no longer Latin, but Italian, French, Spanish, and Portuguese.

SAMPLES OF SYLLABIFICATION IN VARIOUS LANGUAGES

ENGLISH: gen/er/al   be/wil/der/ing   reg/i/ment
(No definite rules. That it does not go by roots is shown by "bewildering," where division by root, prefix, and ending would require be/wild/er/ing. That it does not go by the division of the language of origin is proved by gen/er/al and reg/i/ment. The tendency to end syllables with consonant sounds is quite evident.)

GERMAN: hin/aus   ver/lass/en   lang/sam/er
(Division by roots, prefixes, and endings, but with some tendency to divide as in Romance, putting single consonant sound with following vowel, as shown by Bü/cher as opposed to Buch. Nevertheless, most syllables end in consonants.)

FRENCH: i/nu/ti/le   im/pos/si/ble   fré/que/mment
(Single consonant sound between two vowels goes with following vowel, even at the sacrifice of individuality of prefixes, roots, and endings, as shown by *inutile* and *fréquemment*. Consonant groups ending in *l* or *r* (*bl, pl, tr, cr*, etc.) are treated as a single consonant, and go with the vowel following. Syllables most often end in vowels.)

ITALIAN: a/me/ri/ca/no   for/tu/na/tis/si/mo
im/por/tan/te
(Same rules as in French. The fact that Italian retains Latin final vowels, which French usually drops, gives an even higher proportion of syllables ending in vowels.)

RUSSIAN: go/vo/rit   na/zy/va/et/sya
pod/ra/zu/me/va/e/te
  (Same rules as in the Romance languages. Most syllables end
  in vowels.)
JAPANESE: ka/mai/ma/sen   o/ha/yŏ   sa/yŏ/na/ra
  (Normal syllable structure is consonant—vowel. Only consonant sound permitted at end of syllable is -n, though eli-
  sion of short *i* and *u* often gives other consonants: ka/mai/-
  ma/s[u]ka.)

SAMPLES OF LINKING (*LIAISON*)

LATIN: quae / cui/que‿est / for/tu/na‿ho/di/e, / quam /
quis/que / se/cat / spem.
FRENCH: le/s‿homme/s‿a/vaient / pris / cet/te‿é/nor/me
/ tab/le.
ITALIAN: tut/to‿il / gior/no, / no/n‿è / ve/ro?

  Not permissible in English: "Lon/g‿Is/land" for "Long
  /Is/land."
  Not permissible in German: "die‿Ei/er" for "die / Ei/er."

some laws of language

We are now in a position to set down some of the "laws" of language—statements which are valid not merely for one language, as are grammatical rules, but applicable to all languages.

1. *Language is primarily a social phenomenon.* Despite the physical-science and humanities aspects of language, its functions and uses point to an interpretation of language that stresses its importance to society and to the individual human being in his contacts with other human beings.

2. *Language is all-pervasive.* It accompanies every human activity and is the indispensable means by which that activity is coordinated and made successful. It is influenced by and in turn influences everything that the speaking community does.

3. *Language is primarily an oral means of communication.* Despite the importance of the written language, particularly in modern civilization, and of symbolical and gestural systems of meaning transfer, the primary form of language is speech.

4. *Language is normally a reflex and instinctive action.* Once it is painfully acquired by processes which can be imitative, intellective, or a combination of both, spoken language becomes as much of a reflex action as driving a car. But just as in driving we may occasionally revert to action deliberately thought out by the higher nerve centers, so in language it is perfectly possible to "think out" your speech.

5. *Language is geographically localized.* However

great or small the differences may be, language varies from area to area. The geographical differences can be recorded, and when enough of them accumulate, we are justified in speaking of separate dialects or separate languages.

6. *Language is socially stratified.* Class differences are bound to arise in language. They may be based on educational, economic, social, or occupational factors and may have considerable range. The divergences appear most in vocabulary, to a far lesser degree in grammar, least of all in sounds.

7. *Language is subject to change.* This principle applies at all times and in all places, though to varying degrees. The only language that remains completely inert is a wholly dead and forgotten language. Change appears in all segments of a language—its sounds, its words, its grammatical forms, its scheme of meanings. For what concerns sounds, there is a tendency for the changes to occur with a measure of regularity and to become universal under given conditions. The speed of change may vary.

8. *Language is subject to standardizing influences.* While the natural tendency of language is toward change and diversification, both in time and in space, man-made factors tend to pull it in the opposite direction, toward uniformity and standardization. The play of the two forces, the natural tendency to change and the man-made tendency to become conservative and uniform, may be compared to the centrifugal (fleeing the center) and centripetal (seeking the center) forces operating upon a weight which is swung in a circle, from a central point, by a cord. The "natural" tendency is for the weight to fly away from center in as many directions as there are points in the circle it describes, but the cord keeps it on its circular course and pulls it back toward center. Among the main centripetal

factors in language are a traditional and literary form, a strong central government, encouraging uniformity by such devices as schools in which the standard language is taught, routes of communication and trade by which the speakers of the language are brought together from various areas, military service, and a highly developed officialdom. Psychological factors such as a unified religion and a consciousness of unity among the speakers also encourage standardization. If the centripetal factors are nonexistent or relaxed, the natural centrifugal force of language will take the upper hand, and the language will begin to change swiftly, both in time and in space.

9. *Written-language change normally follows spoken-language change.* Since speech precedes writing, it is normal that a change will occur first in the spoken tongue and then be recorded at some distance of time in the written form of the language. This accounts for most of the discrepancies between speech and spelling in languages using alphabets and syllabaries, where the written form attempts to symbolize sounds rather than ideas. The written language, being more subject to conservative and puristic influences than the spoken tongue, normally lags behind spoken-language changes. This situation is occasionally reversed for what concerns individual words and grammatical forms, which may be introduced in writing and then spread to speech. In sounds, there is occasional reversal of the law in the attempt to pronounce words as they are spelled (for instance, "often" pronounced with a sounded *t* or "Arctic" with a sounded first *c*).

10. *Each language has its own pattern, which is independent of the patterns of other languages.* Each language is a closed corporation, with its own laws, even though it may be receptive to outside influences. This law

is particularly applicable to sound schemes and sound combinations. English permits certain consonant clusters (like the final -sts of pests, or -sks of desks), which other languages would find "impossible" and definitely reject. An initial consonant cluster like the zdr- of Russian zdravstvuytye ("hello") or Italian sdraiarsi ("to lie down") would be inconceivable in English. Certain languages, such as Hawaiian, will not permit a word or syllable to end in anything but a vowel sound.

This principle of the sound-combination pattern has already been seen in connection with syllabification. Another curious application is double-talk, in which words are created out of thin air and interspersed with legitimate words, producing a natural though incomprehensible effect, provided they fit into the permissible sound-and-combination pattern of the language. This form of linguistic creation, though generally employed for purposes of humor, may also be deliberately used to cause confusion, as in written, oral, or radio communications in warfare that may fall into the hands of the enemy.

The principle of language pattern is regularly, though unconsciously, followed in all forms of linguistic creation and innovation. The person wishing to create a new word and give it currency will ordinarily fit his word into the language's pattern, avoiding any combination that would sound unnatural to the speakers (exception is made for created forms deliberately designed to imitate the pattern of another language, like schmo, which fits not the English but the Yiddish language pattern).

The principle is also regularly applied when words are borrowed from another language. Here, however, there is a resistance arising from the fact that people of culture are aware of the correct foreign pronunciation (note the

Each of the following sentences is constructed in accordance with the pattern of sounds and grammatical endings of the language it is supposed to illustrate, with a sprinkling of authentic short words. Each can be read with perfect accent by a native, but will make no sense whatsoever. In English and Hungarian, such forms are actually used for humorous purposes, under the names of "double-talk" and *halandzsa*.

ENGLISH: Foring mests larry no granning sunners in the rones.

GERMAN: Der Schirrenhorst zerwaldet am Drosten zur Schwurrigkeit.

LATIN: Inquabatur corrivios lapulos per exteritum fularium in pirtis curibusque.

FRENCH: Le siron fordissait au prélau du magondeau répiré.

SPANISH: Cuadroscamente se enterelló al fuedrecillo para sorgarle el hacho.

ITALIAN: Corando intriscare lo stiepolo ferava cosamente al pretiro e relovò inderno.

RUSSIAN: Dorayu dostravlyat' na svuke porom ulizhenie i shchovalenie.

GREEK: Ho aphrotes ethneke gynarkois kai semandriois epi ta psanata.

HUNGARIAN: Paló rezőhöz hégy megyeleket koporáltam felszalandzsáva.

FINNISH: Vaarukka eisollu viitotta päärdeksän päikensi ullo.

CZECH: Jak čelsku bohámi istinájam su spřiležitost ido mludováti se.

JAPANESE: Taraku no iyoji sumishite do kashimasu ka.

two possible pronunciations of "foyer"; one reflects adaptation of the French word to the English sound pattern and stress, the other attempts to conserve the French pronunciation, quite foreign to English speech habits). Partial adaptations occur in words like "spaghetti" and "macaroni," where most of the Italian sounds, particularly the vowels, are changed to conform to the English sound scheme, but the foreign structure is kept in the ending and the stress.

PERMISSIBLE AND NONPERMISSIBLE GROUPS OF CONSONANTS AT BEGINNING AND END OF WORDS IN VARIOUS LANGUAGES

ENGLISH INITIAL CONSONANT GROUPS: *shr-* (shriek), *str-* (strive), *spr-* (spry), *spl-* (spleen), *skr-* (scribe). None of these initial groups would be permissible in Spanish, which requires *e-* before all initial groups of *s* + consonant (*escribir,* "to write," *estrella,* "star," etc.). All would be permissible in French or Italian except *shr-*. In German, initial *s-* before consonant would be pronounced *sh.*

GERMAN INITIAL GROUPS: *shm-* (*schmieren,* "to spread"), *shl-* (*schlagen,* "to strike"), *shpr-* (*sprechen,* "to speak"), *shtr-* (*Strasse,* "street"), *kn-* (*Knecht,* "servant"). The initial sibilant sound before a consonant in German is *sh,* whether spelled *s* (before *t, p*) or *sch* (before liquids and nasals). *Kn-,* which English once had, and still preserves in spelling (knee, know), is fully pronounced in German. None of these groups would be permissible in native French, Spanish, or Italian words, though the Neapolitan and other dialects of Italian would use the *sh* instead of the *s* sound before consonants.

RUSSIAN INITIAL GROUPS: *pt-* (*ptitsa,* "bird"), *sr-* (*sreda,* "Wednesday"), *tv-* (*Tver,* name of a Russian city), *zn-* (*znat',* "to know"), *gd-* (*gdye,* "where"). None of these groups would be permissible in English, German, or Romance, save for Italian *zn-* (*snidare,* "to uproot").

CZECH INITIAL GROUPS: *skř-* (*skřin,* "locker"), *hr-* (*hrdti,* "to play"), *stl-* (*stláti,* "to strew"), *hl-* (*hlína,* "clay"), *ml-* (*mladý,* "young"). None of these groups would be permissible in Germanic or Romance.

ITALIAN INITIAL GROUPS: *zdr-* (*sdraiarsi,* "to lie down"), *zb-* (*sbafare,* "to free-load"), *ny-* (*gnorri,* "ignorant person"), *zbr-* (*sbrigarsi,* "to hurry"), *ly-* (*gli,* "the"). These groups would not be permissible in Germanic languages. French would permit *ny-* (*gnome*), Spanish would permit *ny-* and *ly-* (*ñape, llover*). The Slavic languages would admit most of them.

GREEK INITIAL GROUPS: *ps-* (*psyche,* "breath"), *tm-* (*tmesis,* "cutting"), *pn-* (*pneuma,* "blowing"), *mn-* (*mnemonikos,* "pertaining to memory"), *bd-* (*bdella,* "leech"). These groups appear in writing in learned words of all civilized modern languages, but few pronounce the first consonant of the group (cf. English "psychology," "pneumonia," "mnemonic," etc.).

ENGLISH FINAL CONSONANT GROUPS: *-sts* (pests), *-sks* (desks), *-ndz* (ends), *-lmz* (elms), *-bz* (ribs). None of these would be permissible in any of the other languages mentioned.

FRENCH FINAL CONSONANT GROUPS: *-bl* (*possible*), *-pl* (*exemple*), *-br* (*libre*), *-vr* (*livre*), *-tr* (*notre*). It may be argued that in these groups a faint vowel sound is audible after the *l* or *r* (English would put the same faint vowel sound between the *l* or *r* and the preceding consonant).

RUSSIAN FINAL CONSONANT GROUPS: -bl' (rubl', "ruble"), -pr (Dnyepr, name of a river), -rshch (borshch, "beet soup"), -zhd' (dozhd', "rain"). None of these would be permissible in English, German, or Romance.

---

scientific aids to language learning

Instruction in language, both native and foreign, has always existed. Egyptians, Babylonians, Greeks, and Romans taught and learned languages, both their own and those of neighboring groups. This was done largely by ear.

The human ear is still probably the best all-around instrument for language learning, and certainly the one most extensively used. The contribution of modern science to the language picture lies largely in the invention of tools and instruments that help and supplement the human ear.

Three modern devices that have wide application in present-day language learning are the phonograph and the tape or wire recorder. The primary purpose of all three is to record the human voice so that it can be played back in the absence of the original speaker. The recording made on a phonograph record is permanent, that made on a tape or wire recorder can be erased when it is no longer needed and be replaced with another recording.

The value of these devices is obvious. A student may not always have access to his teacher or native speaker, but so long as he possesses one of these instruments he can hear "his master's voice" over and over again, as long and as often as he pleases. Accordingly, language records have become the vogue, especially in localities where speakers of the language desired are not available and in cases where the student cannot attend a regular language course.

An additional service performed by these devices, particularly the wire and tape recorders, is that the student may record his own pronunciation and compare it over and over again with that of the speaker. He may also compare various stages of his own pronunciation and so be able to determine how much progress he is making.

An important innovation made in language recordings is the pause of silence between words and phrases pronounced by the native speaker; this permits the student to repeat what he has just heard. Another important gadget is a throw-back device attached to a phonograph by means of which the student is enabled to play the same section of the recording over and over again.

It may be stressed that these devices are helpful not merely in learning foreign languages but in improving your command of your own language. If you have doubts concerning the "correctness" of your pronunciation, or the degree to which it coincides with the accepted general standard, you may use recordings of cultured native speakers of the standard language to improve yourself.

For what concerns professional linguists, recordings are of infinite value for determining precisely what a spoken language sounds like; in this connection, they are far more useful than any written description, however phonetically accurate. The difference is that which passes between getting someone else's account of what happened and seeing (or, in the present instance, hearing) the occurrence for yourself. The great complaint of people who study languages historically is that they do not have recordings of the language at the time it was spoken. All the written documents that come down to us from the days of the Romans, all the accurate descriptions of sounds and pronunciations left us by Latin grammarians are not as valuable as would be one single phonograph recording made in the Roman Forum in the days of Cicero.

In addition to these scientific devices which are in fairly common use, modern science has supplied us with other machines which serve to give a precise analysis of the sounds of language—the way they are produced, transmitted, and received. Certain instruments used in medicine and surgery, like the bronchoscope and laryngoscope, may also be used to determine precisely how the sounds of language are produced by the human speech apparatus. Machines exist that will determine the precise frequency, pitch, and loudness of sound waves. Other machines explore the human ear.

One recent invention that has startling features is the sound spectrograph, an instrument that translates sound frequencies into visible waves appearing on a screen, so that you may actually "see" your own voice in action. Another attachment permits a "pattern playback," whereby these visible symbols are translated back into sound. Among other things, the sound spectrograph permits us to observe variations in the sound qualities of different dialects of the same language, so that we may determine precisely what is the vowel quality in the Southern "aigg" that differentiates it from Northern "egg." It is also claimed that the sound spectrograph will permit us to gauge accurately the phonetic range of phonemes, that is to say, the variations in a given sound which are acceptable to the speaking community, and the border lines of tolerance beyond which one may not go in the production of a given sound without laying oneself open to the charge of speaking like a foreigner.

Another device which promises to have broad applications, both for the scientists of language and for the lay learner, is the so-called "speech stretcher," which slows up the recording of speech while retaining the normal pitch. With this type of "speech in slow motion" the scientist will be able to make a far better analysis of speech sounds, while the student will be able to catch little overtones and other features of speech which he could never hope to detect at normal speed.

Many other mechanical aids to the study of language are in preparation, but one in particular still in its initial stages, promises to have a definite practical application. It is a translating machine, electronically operated, which sets forth, into another language, units of one language that are fed into it. It makes allowances for the possible variations of meaning and the variations of endings and other grammatical devices. In its present state, the device still needs the aid of a human being competent in both languages to take care of these variations, but it is possible that as the machine is improved, human participation in the translating process may be cut down to a minimum. It is generally acknowledged, however, that with all possible improvements the machine will still have to limit its function to the translation of simple sentences simply arranged, and will never be able to convey literary overtones from one language into another.

Science, as we can see, is supplying language with important mechanical tools which prove of vast practical use, particularly for what concerns the study and acquisition of language sounds. There is little so far that mechanical science has been able to contribute to the other divisions of language—the study of grammatical forms and the uses and meanings of words. Despite its physical and physiological features, language remains overwhelmingly a mental or psychological activity.

3

HISTORY OF LANGUAGE

language and the world's past

Concerning the origin of language, the way in which men started to speak, there are only unprovable hypotheses and theories.

Were man's first words imitations of sounds heard in nature? Were they grunts accompanying physical exertion? Were they vocalizations of primitive chants? Were they unconscious shapings of the mouth organs designed to accompany and imitate gestures made by other parts of the body? These and similar ideas have been advanced by those who believe in a materialistic or purely evolutionary origin of man.

Studies of animal "languages," the dancing of bees in their hives, the chattering of apes, the barking of dogs, have not cast too much light on the subject. Neither have studies of how babies first learn to form speech sounds. The most these studies have shown is something that was already known—that the human being learns to speak by listening, imitating, and repeating. But there must be something for him to listen to, imitate, and repeat.

Practically all primitive accounts of language claim for it a divine origin, a gift of God to man, and man alone. While this would account for the fact that only human beings really speak, divine-origin theories have to be supplemented by additional explanations (like the Biblical episode of the Tower of Babel) to cover the variety of human speech and its obvious imperfections.

Our accounts of language do not extend any farther back than our written records, and these are quite recent in comparison with speech. While it seems likely that speech has been in existence for many tens of thousands of years, written records, however much they are stretched, do not appear to go back beyond the traditional Biblical date of creation—about 4000 B.C. In addition, they are fragmentary and unsatisfactory. Even after an ancient system of writing has been deciphered, there is no assurance that it is a perfect representation of the way people spoke—in fact, we are usually safe in making the opposite assumption.

Early historical records are scanty, and so are early records of language. One of the earliest to come to our notice is Sumerian, a tongue spoken in the Mesopotamian area, approximately where Iraq is located today. This form of speech was at least in part supplanted by Akkadian, the Semitic tongue spoken by the Assyrians and Babylonians. Almost at the same time, another great language flourished

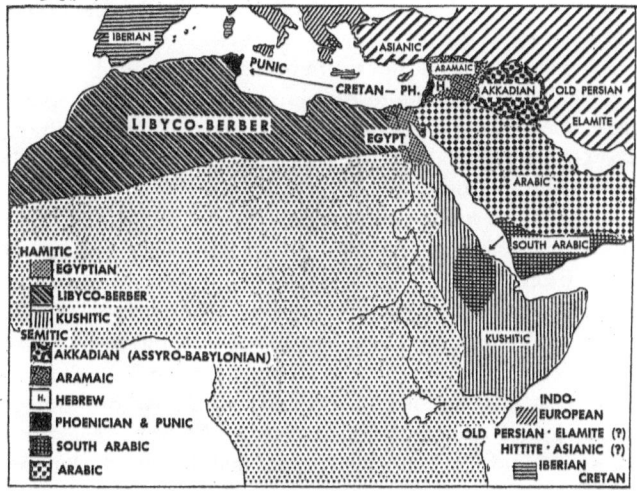

on the banks of the Nile—the ancient Egyptian of the hieroglyphic inscriptions. This tongue was of the Hamitic family, and there is a definite link between Semitic and Hamitic, so that we may safely assert that the earliest languages on record (outside of Sumerian) belonged to the same broad group.

Two other great centers of civilization and language begin to appear around 2000 B.C., one in northern India, represented by Sanskrit, the other in the eastern part of Asia, represented by Chinese. Chinese belongs to a family of languages that are spread throughout eastern and southeastern Asia and have no apparent link with any of the others mentioned so far. Sanskrit, on the other hand, belongs to a great family of languages called Indo-European, whose main representatives are in Europe and include such other groups as the Germanic (to which English and German belong), the Latin-Romance, the Slavic, the Celtic, and the Greek.

After the second millennium before Christ, our linguistic records become far more numerous and satisfactory and a great many languages begin to appear. Some of them, like Greek and Latin, still live on today, at least in their descendants. Others have utterly vanished.

Excavations and explorations have brought to light numerous languages that flourished between the dawn of civilization and the Roman era. Many of these were spoken in Asia Minor and nearby regions, where Turkish and Arabic predominate today. But in the first and second millennia before Christ the ancestors of Arabic and Turkish were spoken in regions far away from Asia Minor, and the relics found there indicate vastly different tongues—Phrygian and Lydian and Lycian and Hittite and many others. Some of these languages, like Hittite, have been

---

THE LANGUAGES OF ANCIENT ITALY (1000-500 B.C.)
(opposite)

All seem to have been Indo-European with the exception of Etruscan, the Punic of the Carthaginian colonies in western Sicily (Semitic), and the very doubtful "Iberian" of Sardinia and Corsica; some doubt attaches also to Ligurian. The closest relative of Latin was Faliscan. Next came Sicel, then Oscan and Umbrian, all of Italic stock. The Greek of the coastal cities of Sicily and southern Italy and the Gaulish of the north were Indo-European, but of different branches (Greek and Celtic, respectively). Messapian, Illyrian, Venetic, and Rhetic seem to have formed part of other Indo-European branches which later became extinct.

124

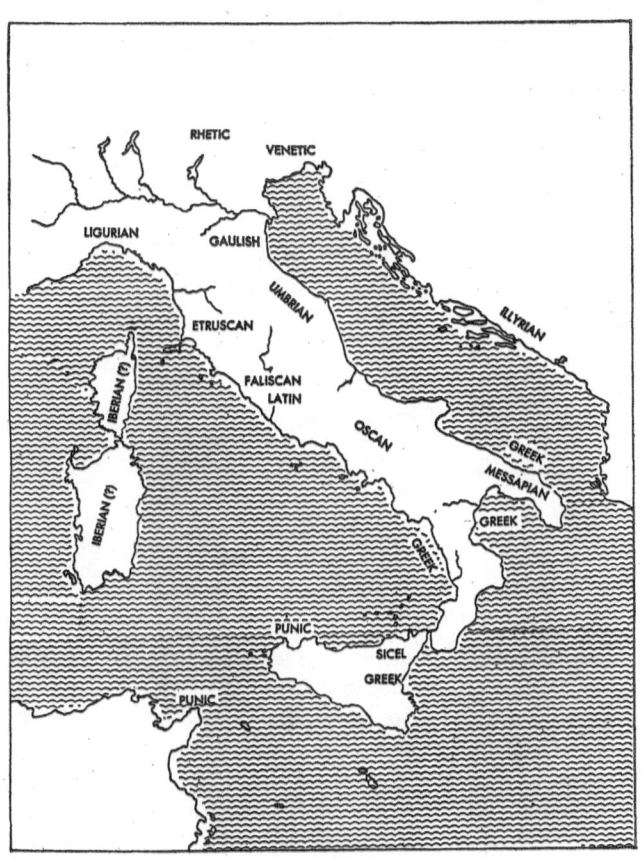

studied and deciphered with some measure of accuracy, thanks to the abundance of written records. For others, all we have is a few inscriptions, from which not too much can be told beyond the fact that the language existed.

A similar situation is met in other regions famous in antiquity. In Greece and the Aegean and Ionian islands there appears a multitude of tongues and dialects, mainly of the Greek family but quite distinct nevertheless—Doric, Aeolic, Attic, Ionian, even Minoan, whose status as a Greek dialect was settled only a year or two ago. In India, other languages besides Sanskrit appear, while on the Iranian plateau we have the rise of Persian, the imperial tongue of

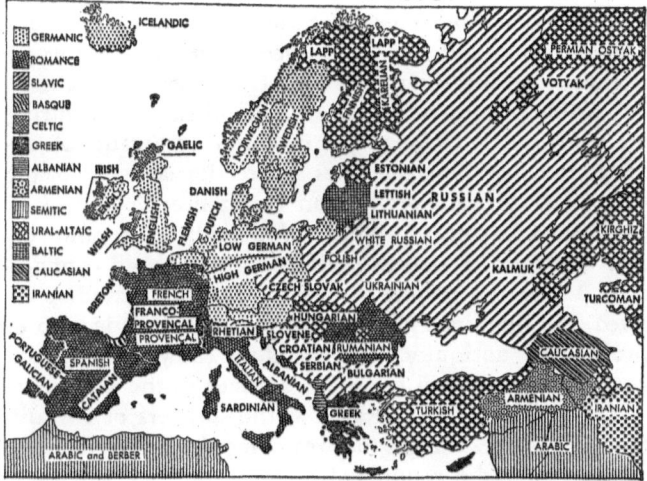

Darius and Xerxes. Besides Akkadian, many other Semitic civilizations and languages go on record, chief among them the Hebrew, Aramaic, Phoenician, and Punic, or Carthaginian. On the European mainland are found languages like the Iberian of what is today Spain, the Gaulish of what is now France, while in Italy, where the Romans kept some memory of the languages they had displaced, we find records and inscriptions of Rhetic, Liguric, Venetic, Gaulish in the north, Etruscan and Umbrian in the center, Oscan, Messapian, and Sicel in the south and on the islands.

It may be emphasized that these languages were not all

spoken at one time. They were the fruit of vast migrations and invasions, and the appearance of one was frequently attended by the disappearance of another. It is almost impossible to construct a series of linguistic maps showing the distribution of languages in antiquity because of uncertainty concerning the dates and territorial range of the languages. As each pre-Roman civilization flourished, it established its empire, which undoubtedly was to some extent linguistic as well as political, military, and commercial. But as the empire crumbled, and new invaders arrived, the linguistic picture changed. A linguistic map of pre-Roman antiquity will therefore show various languages superimposed upon one another in the same area.

This is important, because as the speakers of two different languages mingle they react linguistically upon each other. Either the conquered or the conqueror gives way and adopts the other's language, but with abundant contributions from his own. Some go so far as to say that this is not merely a matter of words but of pronunciations as well, which would mean that as the Gauls were conquered by the Romans, for instance, they discarded Gaulish in favor of Latin, but pronounced Latin with a Gaulish accent similar to the foreign accent which an immigrant to the United States displays when speaking English. The question would then be whether this accent disappeared in the course of subsequent generations of speakers, or whether it persisted across the centuries. If the latter is true, then there would be a reflection of the speech habits of the ancient Gauls in the Romance tongue of the modern Frenchmen.

A fairly satisfactory language map of at least the Mediterranean area can begin to be drawn with the establishment of Roman power throughout that area, but the subsidiary languages still spoken there, and their influence upon the predominant language are largely a matter of conjecture.

evolution of language

Like individuals, languages have personal histories. They are born of previous languages, they grow, acquiring new elements and new speakers as their life span advances, they reach their full maturity, then they decline and die, more often than not leaving descendants behind them.

There are two things to be considered in the growth and decline of a language. One is the speakers, who constitute the soul and spirit of the language. The other is the linguistic element—sounds, grammatical forms, and words, which are a tongue's physical structure and living blood stream.

A language cannot live without speakers. When the last speaker of a tongue is gone, that tongue may live on in written documents, but it is only an embalmed mummy. We occasionally see languages die under our eyes. A recent example is the Dalmatian dialect of the island of Veglia in the Adriatic, which seems to have been the last survivor of a once fairly extensive system, derived from Latin, that was spoken in the Middle Ages all along the eastern Adriatic coast. By the time the language came to the notice of the linguists, around the 1890s, only a few old people on the island still spoke it. The remainder of the population had gone over to one or the other of the two big languages of the Adriatic, Italian and Serbo-Croatian. A linguist, Bartoli by name, went to Veglia and recorded the speech of the last surviving speakers of Vegliote. A few years later these old people died, and no one was left to speak the language, which went to join the roster of dead tongues in the linguistic mausoleum.

Increase in the number of speakers is a sign of a language's healthy vitality. Decrease is a sign of decay, old age, and approaching death, which comes sooner or later to all languages, as to all men.

Figures for a language's speaking population are even today uncertain and difficult to ascertain. This is because, in spite of the institution of the census, the population figures of countries are based on political sovereignty, not on language affiliation. When we are told that the total population of the United States now stands at 165,000,000, that does not mean that we have the same number of speakers of American English. Leaving out of account very young children who have not yet learned to speak, there are in our midst foreign groups whose mother tongue is something other than English. But we are not safe in excluding these groups from our count, because most of their members have learned to speak English after a fashion. About all we can do is to subtract the foreign-born population from the total number of inhabitants, then make a rough estimate as to what proportion of the foreign-born may be expected to have learned the language, and add that tentative figure to the native-born population. The difficulty of estimating a language's speaking population is multiplied when we go back in history beyond the point where general census figures are reliable. Still, on the basis of complicated yet somewhat haphazard estimates, we may reach some conclusion as to the number of speakers of a given language at various points in its history. A comparison of the speaking-population figures for the six major languages of Europe from the year 1100 to our own times indicates that not all these languages have grown at the same rate. English and Russian, seemingly the least likely contenders at the outset of an 850-year period, are today in the lead. French and Italian, today the lowest in speaking population, were once in a far better relative position. All six of the languages, however, show remarkable growth. Another interesting chart is that of the speaking population of Chinese, which shows an increase from about 140 million in 1741 A.D., when Chinese historians first began to make tentative estimates, to the 585 million claimed by the Red Chinese government today.

The other angle of linguistic evolution, that of the language itself as apart from its speakers, shows features of growth accompanied by features of decay. The growth consists in accretions to the vocabulary both from within and from without. The decay consists in the loss of words and terms which grow obsolete and archaic. In the case of a living, vital language, accretions far surpass losses. Changes in sounds and grammatical structure, while they are of vast linguistic importance, cannot properly be classified as either growth or decay. Any language, as soon as it emerges as a language and as long as it endures as a language, possesses a full complement of both sounds and grammatical forms, which are merely subject to change. But an increase or decrease in the number of sounds or significant grammatical forms does not in itself lead to enhancement or degradation of the language as a system of communication. Hawaiian has only a fraction of the sounds that appear in English, and Chinese has no morphological endings or changes of any description, yet both are just as efficient in fulfilling their purpose as are languages far richer in sounds and morphological equipment.

It is otherwise with words. Poverty of vocabulary usually accompanies backwardness of culture. The measure of material civilization of a speaking community normally finds its reflection in the number of words at that community's disposal, because the words, in turn, represent objects and concepts. This is not to say that languages such as those of the American Indians, Eskimos, or Australian natives are not sufficient to express the notions which their speakers wish to express, and which are often far more complex than one would suspect. But if speakers of those languages wish to enter a higher civilization and still retain their languages, then they must endow those languages with new words and expressions to convey the new concepts they are acquiring—something which can ordinarily be done by borrowing words from the more civilized tongues and adapting them to their own sound-and-grammar structure.

This is a process which all existing languages have gone through. If we take two typical languages of western civilization, Latin and English, and examine their historical course, we shall observe that they both resemble tiny rivulets, issuing from the subsoil and gaining strength from tributaries as they move along until they become wide, majestic rivers. As they approach the end of their course (this is clearly perceptible in the case of the Latin

HISTORICAL GROWTH OF SIX WORLD LANGUAGES

ENGLISH	1½	5	8	123	250
RUSSIAN	1½	12	30	85	150
SPANISH	5	8½	22	58	120
GERMAN	7	10	40	80	100
FRENCH	10	12	35	52	80
ITALIAN	5	9½	25	46	60
DATE	1100	1500	1700	1900	1955

TABLE OF CHINESE SPEAKERS

1741	143½ million	1902	440 million
1800	295 "	1923	450 "
1835	400 "	1933	470 "
1849	413 "	1955	550 " (Western estimate)

COURSE OF LATIN-ROMANCE LANGUAGE STREAM

INDO-EUROPEAN	ARCHAIC	PRE-CLASSICAL		CLASSICAL		VULGAR
800 B.C.	600 B.C.	400 B.C.	200 B.C.	1 A.D.	200 A.D.	400 A.D.

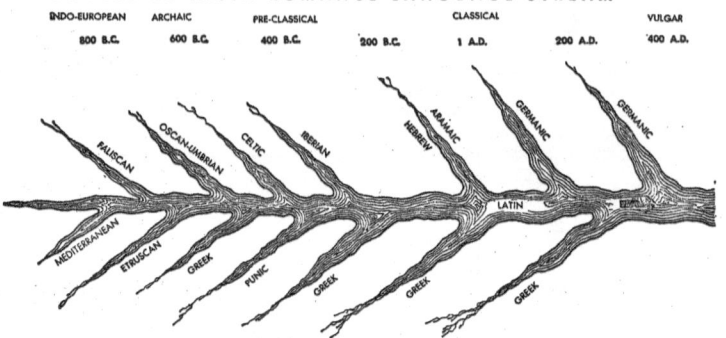

COURSE OF ENGLISH-LANGUAGE STREAM

450 A.D.	900 A.D.	1066 A.D.	1300 A.D.	1400 A.D.	1500 A.D.

WEST GERMANIC   ANGLO-SAXON   MIDDLE ENGLISH

ENGLISH

LATIN-GREEK   LATIN-GREEK   SCANDINAVIAN   NORMAN FRENCH   FRENCH   LATIN   GREEK

ITALIAN-FRENCH-SPANISH

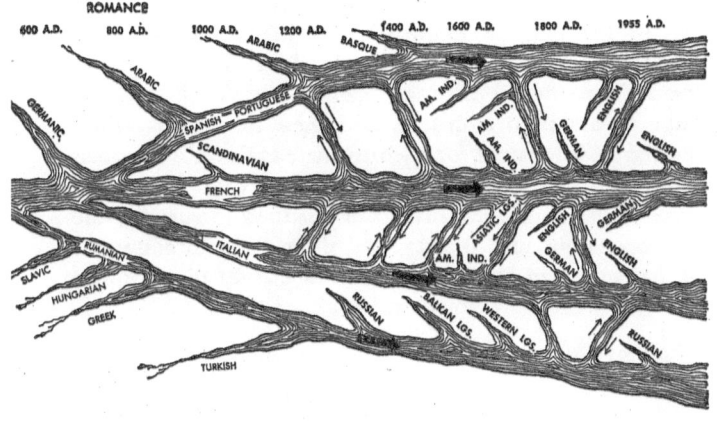

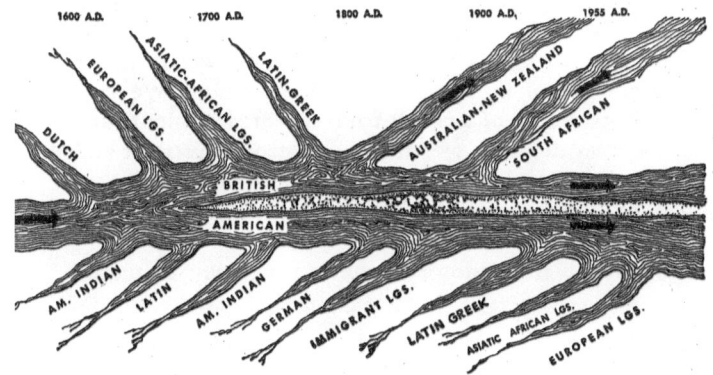

stream, while only the beginning of the process is notice-able in the case of English), they break into separate streams, much as a river does at its delta. These separate streams are the beginnings of new rivers, if the language stream is to continue, and these new rivers, often running underground for a while, issue again into the open to repeat the experience of the parent stream. If the language under consideration is not destined to survive, the delta opens out into the sea, and the river is forgotten, as has happened to so many of the languages of antiquity described in the previous chapter.

arteries of language

Languages are spread by the movements of their speakers. Within historical times, we have seen the spreading of Latin from a tiny locality near the mouth of the Tiber to the entire Mediterranean basin, northward to the Rhine and Danube, eastward to the Persian Gulf. We have seen the spreading of English from the British Isles to the vast overseas domains of America, Canada, Australia and New Zealand, and the spreading of Spanish and Portuguese to Mexico, the Antilles, and Central and South America.

But even before recorded history, vast language migrations are indicated. The American Indians seem to have brought the ancestors of their thousand tongues with them from the Asiatic continent, across Bering Strait. There is reason to believe that the numerous languages spoken by the natives of Australia and New Guinea moved originally, by an overseas route, from the Andaman Islands in the Bay of Bengal. Polynesian tongues appear to have spread in all directions from a center of diffusion in Tahiti to Samoa, Hawaii, New Zealand, westward to Madagascar, and eastward to Easter Island off the coast of South America. In Africa there are indications, supplied largely by anthropology, that the Bantu family of languages, which today occupies the entire continent south of the Gulf of Guinea with the exception of a relatively small area in southwest Africa, had its origin in the restricted region of the great African lakes and spread southward and westward in successive mi-

---

HYPOTHETICAL MIGRATIONS OF ANCIENT LANGUAGES
(next two pages)

Indo-European to all parts of Europe, Asia Minor, Persia, northern India;

Uralic and *Altaic* to Finland, Hungary, Turkey, northern and western Asia;

Chinese from bend of Yellow River to all parts of China;

American Indian from western Siberia to all parts of Western Hemisphere;

Bantu from East African lake region to west-central and south Africa;

Australian-Papuan from Andaman Islands to Australia, New Guinea, and Melanesia;

Malayo-Polynesian from Tahiti-Samoa region to Indonesia, Hawaii, New Zealand, Madagascar, Micronesia, Formosa, etc.

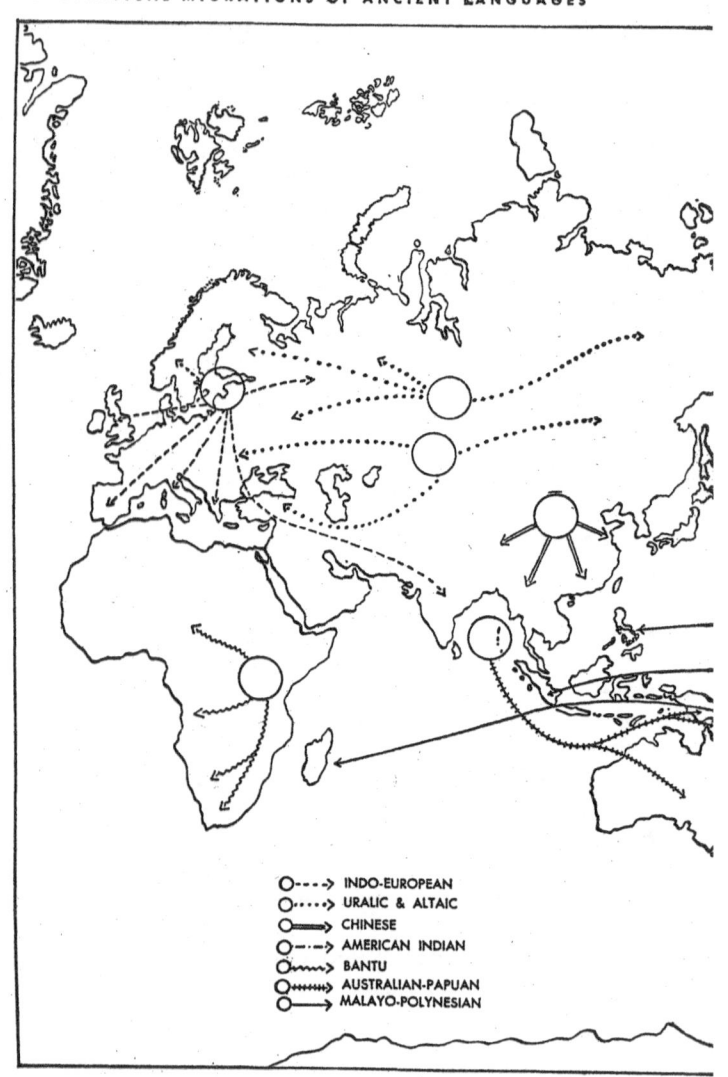

O---->	INDO-EUROPEAN
O·····>	URALIC & ALTAIC
O====>	CHINESE
O—·—>	AMERICAN INDIAN
O~~~>	BANTU
O++++>	AUSTRALIAN-PAPUAN
O——>	MALAYO-POLYNESIAN

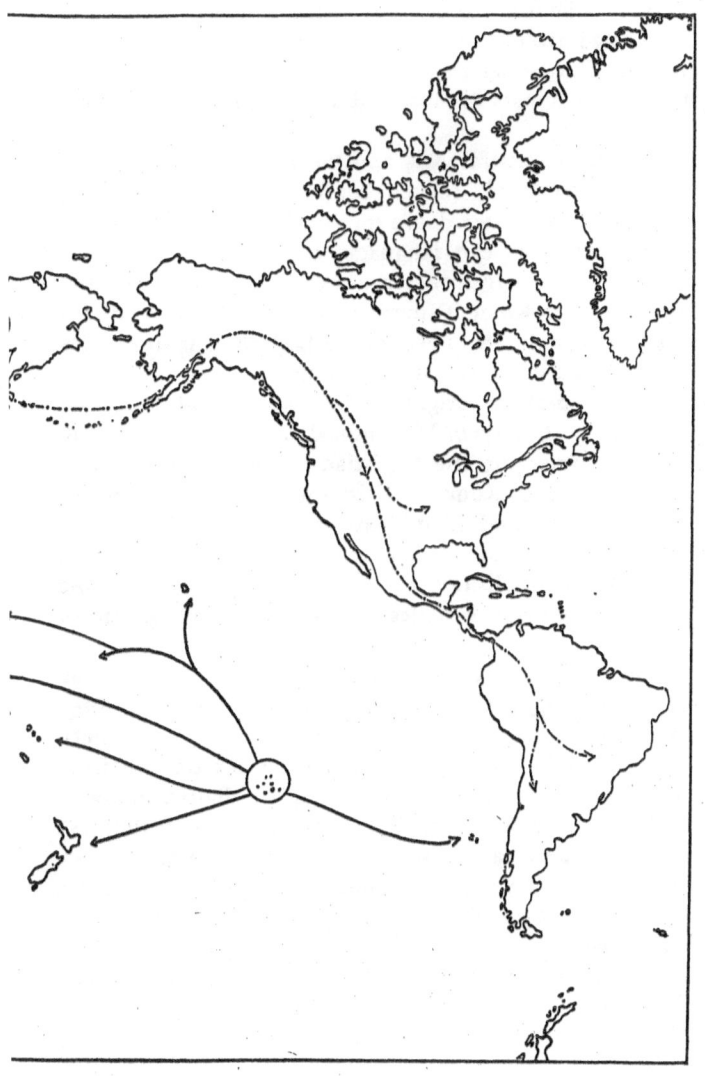

grations. The original Chinese area of diffusion was probably located around the central bend of the Yellow River, and the Chinese language moved from there in all directions to encompass the vast regions it holds and influences today.

From north-central Asia and the western regions of Siberia two seemingly related families, the Uralic and the Altaic, moved westward and southward to give rise to such present-day European languages as Finnish, Hungarian, and Turkish; their speakers were followers of Attila the Hun, Genghis Khan, Tamerlane, and the Turkish sultans who finally broke the power of the Eastern Roman Empire and turned Byzantium into Istanbul.

Semitic speakers, originally located in Arabia, moved westward in the days of Mohammed and his immediate followers, submerging the Christian lands of North Africa and their Graeco-Roman civilization, which they replaced with an Arabic and Islamic culture. But long before Mohammed, other Arabian invaders had crossed the Red Sea into Africa, establishing a ruling class in Ethiopia whose Amharic language is a descendant of the Himyaritic of southern Arabia.

The wanderings of speakers of the Indo-European family of languages, to which our western tongues belong, have long formed a fascinating though somewhat mysterious chapter in the history of language. Starting off from an original homeland located around the Baltic, in northern Europe, they moved in successive waves to the east, south, and west, each migration giving rise to a new branch of languages—Celtic, Germanic, Italic, Greek, Albanian, Balto-Slavic, Armenian, and Indo-Iranian, to mention only those that survive; but among the dead branches of the Indo-European tree are Hittite, Tokharian, Illyrian, and numerous extinct languages of the Balkans and Asia Minor—Dacian, Thracian, and Phrygian among them.

In the course of these wanderings, the Indo-European languages displaced many pre-existing tongues, some of which utterly disappeared, while others resisted and survived. A mysterious group of Iberian languages, spoken throughout Spain and probably in the western Mediterranean islands, gave way to the Latin of the Romans but left a small group of survivors in the persons of the Basque speakers of the Pyrenees. The Etruscan spoken in west-central Italy vanished before the onset of Latin, and its many inscriptions can no longer be interpreted. In India, the speakers of Indo-European languages drove before them speakers of two language groups apparently indigenous to the Indian subcontinent, the Dravidian and the Munda, ultimately relegating them to the south of the peninsula and a few isolated spots elsewhere.

Successive waves of Indo-European speakers occupied in turn the same territories, each leaving a trace of its presence. The Germanic-speaking Goths, who later lost their identity in Italy and Spain, were at one time located in southern Russia, a land that today is Slavic-speaking. What is today Germany was overrun in turn by Celts, Teutons, and Slavs, not to mention the attempted Roman invasions.

OVERSEAS MIGRATIONS OF MODERN LANGUAGES
(next two pages)

English to North America, Australia, New Zealand, South
Africa;
Spanish to Central and South America, Mexico, Antilles;
Portuguese to Brazil;
French to eastern Canada, Haiti, North Africa, Madagascar.

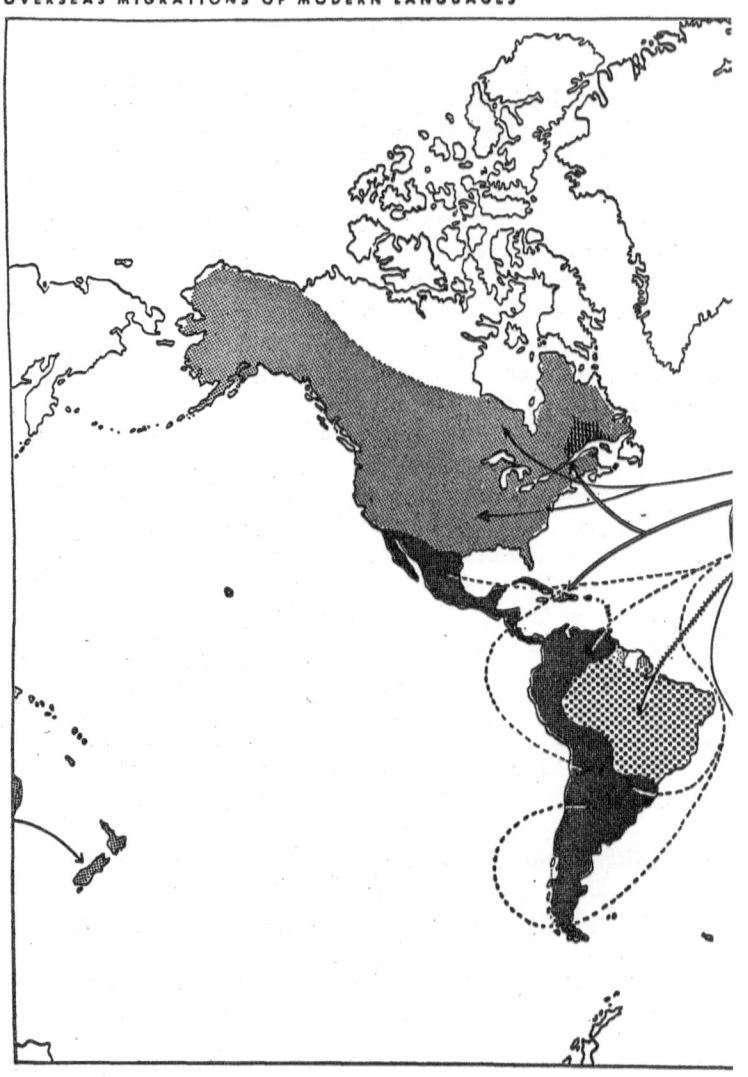

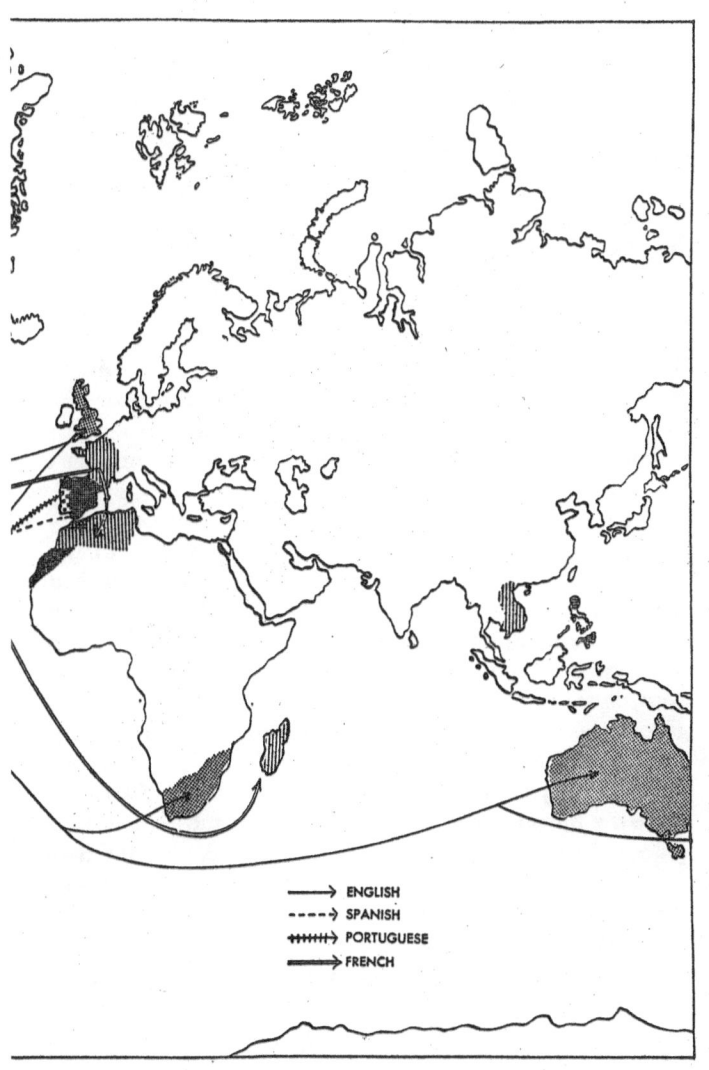

ENGLISH
SPANISH
PORTUGUESE
FRENCH

Celtic place names appear not only in the British Isles, France, Spain, and northern Italy, but also in Russia, Asia Minor and the Danubian basin. At one time practically all Germany east of the Elbe was Slavic-speaking, and this is indicated by the fact that the names of many eastern German cities, including Berlin itself, are of Slavic origin.

The sea proved no obstacle to hardy navigators in the days of sails and oars, and seaborne language migrations vie with overland routes. All the Pacific islands seem to have been stocked with peoples and languages in this fashion, but to refer to recorded history we need only recall the Anglo-Saxon and Danish invasions of the island of Britain and the later progress of speakers of European languages to the lands of America and other continents. Today a third artery, the air, is added to the two ancient courses, land and sea, that carry languages from one part of the earth to another.

Geographic factors are paramount in the spread of languages. High and difficult mountain ranges have in the past constituted an obstacle to language movement, but not an altogether impassable one. The Himalayas block off the speakers of the Chinese-Tibetan family of languages from those of Indo-Aryan speech, but Urals, Carpathians, Alps, Pyrenees, have proved no deterrent to language migrations. Great watercourses occasionally serve as barriers, but more often as vehicles of language. Flat, level ground, like the steppes of eastern Europe and western Asia, best serve the purposes of land-borne language movement. Language spreads better along the valleys and plateaus than along mountain crests, with the result that often an invading language will encircle and by-pass a group of foreign speakers, leaving them completely isolated, like a linguistic island. This has happened, for instance, along the crest of

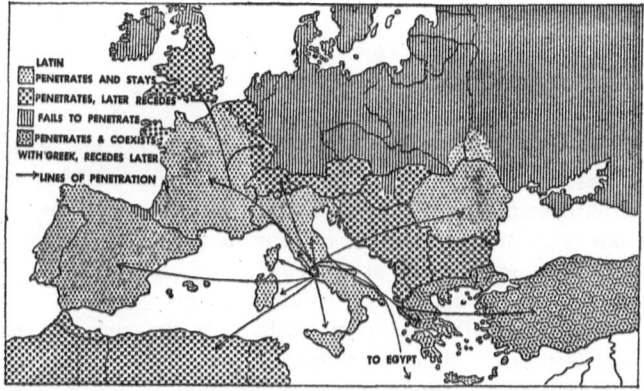

the Alps, where in the vicinity of the Austrian-Swiss-Italian border you find small groups of Romance speakers completely surrounded by speakers of German.

Today, as often in the past, the lines of linguistic penetration are not altogether physical, but cultural as well. A culture that enjoys high prestige can make itself felt as desirable without recourse to force of arms. While the material arteries of language—land and sea—take on a new element, the air, the language ways of the spirit and the mind acquire new force, derived from a variety of sources —trade, religion, diplomacy, art and literature, and, last but not least, the ever-growing consciousness of the basic unity of mankind, and the spirit of mutual tolerance and understanding which that consciousness engenders.

When two languages come in contact, they may, at least in theory, live on side by side, having nothing to do with each other. The likelihood of this, however, is on a par with the chances that two families, living next door to each other with no other neighbor within miles, will completely and utterly ignore each other.

Another possible solution is that the speakers of one language will wipe out the people who speak the other, without any further contact. This has undoubtedly come close to happening in many instances. We are told, for example, that there was little save warfare and mutual destruction between the Anglo-Saxons who invaded Britain in the fifth century A.D. and the Britons who sullenly retreated before them until they reached the mountain fastnesses of Wales and Cornwall. But even if this is largely true, it does not altogether do away with the likelihood of less lethal contacts, particularly of a linguistic nature. Prisoners questioned before they are killed, captives enslaved by their captors, occasional parleys between the two sides, would account for such slender borrowings of words as the Anglo-Saxons made from the Celts, and vice-versa, in the centuries of their unpeaceful coexistence on the British Isles.

One curious variant of this phenomenon appears in the Antilles. Before the coming of the white man, these islands had been occupied by natives speaking languages of the Arawak family; fiercer Carib speakers from the mainland, however, had invaded the islands. Since they were cannibals (the word "cannibal" seems to be derived from

"Carib"), they ate up their male Arawak captives but spared the women for other purposes. The result was that when the earliest explorers came, they found a population speaking what was to all intents and purposes two different languages; the men used Carib, while the women used Arawak. But this is an exceptional case.

When two languages come in contact, it is normal for one or the other to give way, but not without leaving its mark upon the other. There is a merger and a compromise, in which one of the two regularly comes out on top. While negotiations are in progress, so to speak, the two languages may coexist side by side for years and even centuries. In fact, under conditions of peace and civilization, the coexistence may continue indefinitely, with each of the two making contributions to the other.

When the Romans took control of Spain and France (or Iberia and Gaul, as they were designated then), they had no idea of wiping out the existing populations. They merely wanted to control, exploit, civilize, and Romanize them to the point where they, too, would become Romans like themselves. This they proceeded to accomplish by settling Roman legionaries in the conquered provinces, encouraging them to take native wives and bring up families of mixed blood that would, however, be steeped in the higher Roman tradition and culture. This far-sighted and seemingly tolerant imperial policy did not mean that the Romans could not be quite ruthless when that policy was opposed, as witnessed by Vercingetorix and Boadicea.

In the main, however, the policy worked. After a lapse of many centuries, during which each succeeding generation of Gallo-Romans and Ibero-Romans became more and more Romanized, it could be said that the Roman citizen from Iberia or Gaul was the full counterpart of his fellow citizen born on Italian soil. During this same period, the Latin of the Romans gradually took the upper hand over the Iberian and Gaulish of the original inhabitants, so that by the time the western Roman Empire came to an end in the fifth century A.D. the presence of the Roman legions was no longer needed to keep the inhabitants of Iberia and Gaul speaking Latin. It is interesting to note that in Britain, where the period of Roman occupation was shorter, the inhabitants reverted to their Celtic tongue when the Romans left. Big sociological changes require the passing of much time, whatever some of our modern sociologists may say to the contrary.

The Latin of the Romans, however, did not go entirely unscathed in the mouths of Gauls and Iberians. Barring the possibility that some of the Gaulish and Iberian traits of pronunciation may be reflected in the development of the French and Spanish of today, there is no doubt that we find in French certain words of Celtic, or Gaulish, origin that appear nowhere else in the Romance world (like *maint* or *arpente*), and in Spanish there is a corresponding body of words of Iberian origin (like *vega* and *páramo*).

When Germanic invaders later forced their way into the lands of the Roman Empire, the imperial and religious prestige of the Latin language was such that they quickly discarded their Germanic tongues and took on the language of the conquered populations. But here, too, there was a two-way exchange. Numerous Germanic words found their way into the Latin of the Romance lands and appear in the French, Spanish, and Italian of today (*guerre, choisir, honte; yelmo, brindar, blanco; albergo, drudo, scherzo*).

The Anglo-Saxons coming into Britain took little of the language of the British Celts but accepted much of the language of the Danish invaders who followed them. Most striking of all, however, by reason of the fact that the entire process can be traced, is what happened to the English of the Anglo-Saxons when they were conquered by William's French-speaking Normans in 1066. For well over two centuries the two languages coexisted, one as the tongue of the lower classes, the other as the court language of the aristocracy. Eventually it was the French of the Norman nobility that gave way, but the victory of English was attended by such an influx of French words, reinforced by the cultural Latin of the clergy and the scribes, that today it is an open question whether Germanic or Latin-Romance elements predominate in our English vocabulary.

Two other historical experiences may be mentioned. One is the story of Spanish at the time when Spain was almost completely submerged by the Arabic-speaking Moors. It took the Spaniards somewhat more than seven centuries to eject the Moors from their land, and during this period there was much contact between Spanish and Arabic. The ultimate result was that Spanish emerged with thousands of Arabic words in its vocabulary, but little else to mark the conflict.

The Spanish and Portuguese of the explorers and *conquistadores*, moving to Latin America, largely repeated the experience of Latin with the tongues of the Gauls and Iberians. In all the countries where the white men came, they were a minority, imposing their language by a combination of force of arms, conversion, cultural prestige, and intermarriage with the conquered natives. Today, in various areas of Central and South America and Mexico, the native languages still coexist with Spanish and Portuguese. They may be said to be gradually dying out, but the process is extremely slow and, in some areas, imperceptible.

Portuguese predominates in Brazil, and Spanish elsewhere. There is plenty of interaction on the part of the European languages with the native ones, and a considerable influx of native words into the Portuguese and Spanish, which are everywhere official. Beyond vocabulary, however, the influence of the native languages is hardly felt. Certain features of intonation, the special pronunciation of certain sounds in various Latin-American countries are at times attributed to the influence of the native Indian languages, but this is strongly disputed. Many traits which were at one time hastily attributed to such influence have since been discovered to come from European sources.

One interesting experiment made some years ago dealt with the dialect of a Sicilian town whose inhabitants are descendants of people who emigrated to Sicily from northern Italy during the Middle Ages in order to escape religious persecution. The dialect they had brought with them was a north Italian dialect, radically different from the Sicilian spoken all around the town. It was ascertained that while there had been plenty of borrowing of Sicilian words, there had been practically no borrowing of Sicilian sound patterns or grammatical structure.

These identical results appearing in such widely diversified languages as English, where far more than half the words are borrowed, but the sounds and structure remain essentially Anglo-Saxon; Spanish, as it appears in the lands of Latin America; and dialects whose historical migrations can be traced, lead to the conclusion that when two languages come in contact they may coexist for indefinite periods, but usually one or the other gives way; the surviving language accepts contributions from its rival which are often vast so far as vocabulary is concerned, but scanty in the matter of sounds and grammar. The borrowed words are generally fitted into the sound-and-grammar pattern of the borrowing language to the point where they become completely naturalized and cannot be distinguished from native words.

FROM OSCO-UMBRIAN: *bufalus* (ultimately becomes English "buffalo"); *lingua* ("language"); probably *caseus* (gives rise to our "cheese").

FROM VENETIC: *gandeia* (later becomes *gondola*).

FROM CELTIC: *lancea* ("lance"); *carrus* ("car"); *veredus* ("horse"; later becomes German *Pferd*); *ambactus* ("serf"; later gives rise to French *ambassade,* and English "embassy and "ambassador").

FROM SICEL: *campus* ("camp").

FROM ETRUSCAN: *Ruma* (later *Roma,* Rome); *satelles* ("body-guard," later our "satellite"); *caerimonia* (from the name of the town of Caere; later "ceremony"); *fenestra* (later Italian *finestra,* German *Fenster,* "window"; English "fenestration"); *autumnus* ("autumn").

FROM MEDITERRANEAN LANGUAGES: *viola* ("violet"); *lilium* ("lily"); *laurus* ("laurel"); *ficus* ("fig"); *citrus* ("citrus").

FROM GREEK: *kamara* (gives rise to both "camera" and "chamber"); *talanton* ("talent"); *macina* (Latin form of Greek *mechane,* gives rise to "machine"); *kerasos* (Latin *cerasus,* gives rise to "cherry"); *platea* ("place"); *kolaphos* (Latin *colapus, colpus,* gives rise to "coup" and perhaps to "golf"); *kybernan* (Latin *gubernare;* "govern" and "cybernetics"); *thriambos* ("triumph" and "trump").

FROM ARAMAIC: *abba* ("abbot").

FROM EARLY CELTIC: crag, bug (originally meant "ghost").

FROM LATER CELTIC: glen, bard, wraith, heather, clan.

FROM LATIN DURING ANGLO-SAXON PERIOD: mint (L. *moneta*), cheese (L. *caseus*), street (L. *strata*), kitchen (L. *coquina*), cheap (L. *caupo*), cup (L. *cuppa*), cross (L. *crux;* "cross" ultimately replaced native English "rood").

FROM GREEK, THROUGH LATIN, DURING THE ANGLO-SAXON PERIOD: bishop (G. *episkopos*); church (G. *kyriake*), priest (G. *presbyter*), school (G. *schole*).

FROM THE SCANDINAVIAN OF THE DANES: they, knife, dirt, guess, leg, want, window, ill, low, weak, both, skin, hit, take, cut, sky, are.

FROM FRENCH, AFTER NORMAN CONQUEST: dainty, roast, beef, peach, crown, state, court, sir, pray, fine, robe, dress, chair, park, pain, city, rage, river, air, piece, seem, large, nice, real, cry, move, please, wait, people.

FROM MODERN FRENCH: foyer, ballet, champagne, rouge, garage.

FROM LATIN, AFTER NORMAN CONQUEST: bonus, bus, exit, extra, item, muscle.

FROM GREEK ROOTS, OF RECENT COINAGE: allergy, protein, electric, atmosphere, cosmetic.

FROM ITALIAN: piano, tempo, campaign, vista, gala, wig, cash, pilot, flu, laundry, pants.

FROM SPANISH AND PORTUGUESE: cargo, mosquito, cork, alligator, guerrilla, ranch, burro, cocoa, Negro.

FROM DUTCH: drawl, deck, gin, nap, tub, stripe, leak, snap, switch.

FROM GERMAN: halt, poker, stroll.

FROM SLAVIC: bolshevik, robot, polka.

FROM ARABIC AND PERSIAN: alcohol, syrup, mattress, magazine, jungle, shawl, van, check, lemon, sugar, spinach, rice, rose, tiger, tape.

FROM THE LANGUAGES OF INDIA: loot, punch, bungalow, cot.

FROM CHINESE: tea, yen.

FROM JAPANESE: kimono.

FROM AFRICAN LANGUAGES: hoodoo, jazz, coffee.

FROM AMERICAN INDIAN LANGUAGES: hurricane, potato, tobacco, lagniappe.

---

language and colonialism

Colonialism is based not on temporary military occupation but on permanent conquest. The course of language under these circumstances is partly dictated by the behavior and attitude of the two groups concerned.

When speakers of one language colonize lands originally held by speakers of another, we may expect one of three things to happen. If the newcomers are more numerous and enjoy a higher standard of civilization than the original inhabitants, they may, to all intents, render the latter's languages extinct. This has either happened or is in the process of happening in North America and Australia, where successive waves of English-speaking settlers have driven the scanty aboriginal populations farther and farther back, relegating them to the least desirable sections of the country, where their numbers dwindle, and imposing their own language everywhere. The fact that the colonists may later break political ties with their homeland is linguistically inconsequential. Their language remains substantially a dialect of the tongue of their country of origin, and a widely transplanted, widely diffused language results.

Where the two populations are approximately equal in numbers, or, failing that, where conditions favor a merger, the result is such as has been outlined in the preceding chapter. One or the other of the two languages wins out, but with extensive accretions from the other, which disappears as a separate language in that area.

There is a third possibility, appearing particularly in regions that are already densely populated when the colonizers arrive, or where the colonists are in such scanty numbers that they do not succeed in imposing themselves culturally, or are so set upon maintaining their separate individuality that they have little or nothing to do with the conquered population. Here the effects of colonialism upon language may be varied, but there is a striking similarity in the ultimate outcome.

During the last two or three centuries, in countries like India, Pakistan, Burma, Ceylon, and various regions of Africa, the British occupied the country with a small force of soldiers and administrators but made no attempt either to send out a large body of settlers or to have their military forces and officials intermingle and intermarry with the native population. The linguistic set-up of the country was left undisturbed, but English was superimposed as a language of civil and military administration, and as such was

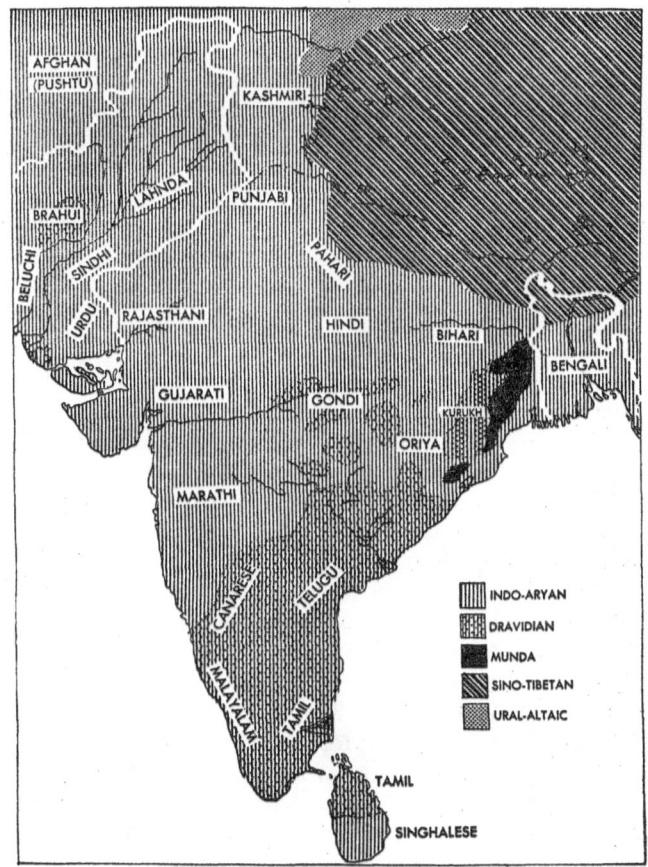

Legend:
- INDO-ARYAN
- DRAVIDIAN
- MUNDA
- SINO-TIBETAN
- URAL-ALTAIC

learned by a considerable number of the natives. By reason of political circumstances, this colonial form of occupation ceases after a period of many years, often centuries. At this point, the native population, left politically to its own devices, has the choice of obliterating all trace of the former occupation, which will include going back to the exclusive use of its own language or languages, or of retaining whatever features of the former administration it deems desirable, including the official language. The experience of the British in this connection is paralleled by that of the Dutch in Indonesia, of the French in Indochina, of the Americans in the Philippines. It may soon have to be repeated by the French in North Africa.

In all these cases, the liberated colonial population has chosen to go back to its own language or languages. Where there was too great a confusion of native tongues, one has been selected to serve as the national, official language. In the Philippines, out of some sixteen more important native tongues, Tagalog was chosen, though it is the language of only a fraction of the population. In India, Hindi, one of the Indo-Aryan tongues of the northern part of the peninsula, serves the purpose, but numerous other languages, both of Indo-Aryan and of Dravidian stock, are granted recognition. In Pakistan, the Urdu of West Pakistan is grudgingly accepted by the Bengali speakers of East Pakistan. In Indonesia, a pidgin form of Malay that was already current as a trade language throughout the islands was refined and given official standing with the new name of Bahasa Indonesia, or Indonesian Language. Vietnamese serves the purpose in most of Indochina, and there is little doubt that if Morocco, Tunisia, and Algeria ever declare their full independence from France, the popular Arabic will be reestablished as an official tongue.

All this would seem to indicate a desire on the part of former colonial populations to reject the official tongues imposed by their former masters and to declare their linguistic independence. But a curious situation arises, fostered largely by the multiplicity of native tongues. During the period of colonialism, the official language of the colonizers invariably served as a tongue of common intercourse among native populations speaking mutually incomprehensible languages. The eradication of this long-standing habit is a difficult task, with the result that even today the use of English, French, and Dutch is widespread in the former colonies.

To this must be added the factor of the world-wide prestige and usefulness of such languages as English and French, which act as keys to unlock the doors of western culture and science. The native of India, Indochina or Pakistan who steps beyond his national borders will find little use for his native Hindi, Vietnamese, or Urdu, but with English or French he is in possession of an international passport. It is therefore not too surprising that when the free Asian and African nations held their widely heralded conference at Bandung in Indonesia, the official language of the conference was English, which most of them held in common, with French holding the post of secondary language.

One may deplore the methods by which colonial languages were spread to undeveloped lands, but the results of that diffusion are in existence and must be reckoned with as objective realities. They may not be everlasting, and it is possible that in half a century all traces of the European languages of colonization will have disappeared from the lands where they once held sway, but this is far from a certainty.

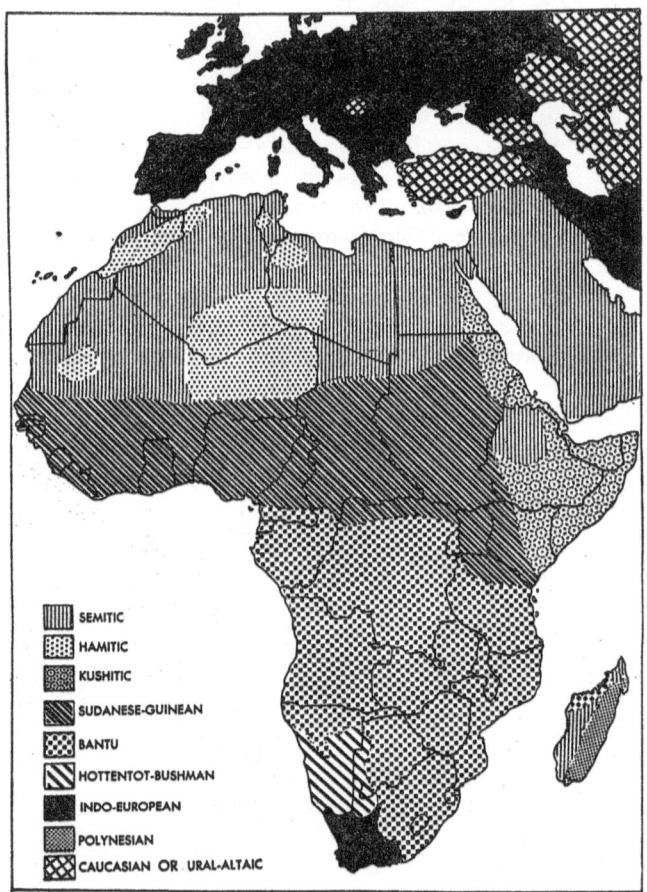

SEMITIC

HAMITIC

KUSHITIC

SUDANESE-GUINEAN

BANTU

HOTTENTOT-BUSHMAN

INDO-EUROPEAN

POLYNESIAN

CAUCASIAN OR URAL-ALTAIC

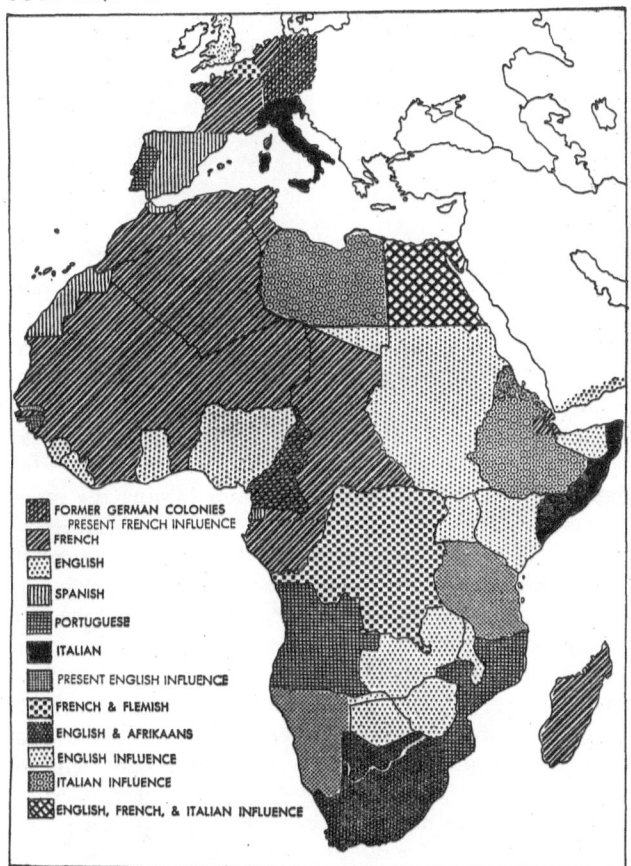

FORMER GERMAN COLONIES
PRESENT FRENCH INFLUENCE
FRENCH
ENGLISH
SPANISH
PORTUGUESE
ITALIAN
PRESENT ENGLISH INFLUENCE
FRENCH & FLEMISH
ENGLISH & AFRIKAANS
ENGLISH INFLUENCE
ITALIAN INFLUENCE
ENGLISH, FRENCH, & ITALIAN INFLUENCE

There are numerous regions where colonialism still endures, and here, of course, the European languages are still officially in the saddle. English, French, Portuguese, Italian, and Spanish still appear as official languages in vast areas of Africa and Oceania. Traces of German, Italian, and Japanese influence endure to this day in former colonies of those countries. Linguistic colonialism is very much in a state of flux.

The field of colonies and former colonies lends itself admirably to the study of the two great tendencies of languages, centrifugal and centripetal (see page 108). The establishment of the languages of colonization, their gradual spreading to larger and larger numbers of the colonial populations, their tendency to press the native languages into the background and render them less important may be described as highly centripetal. But the return of the native languages to an official status, and their joining the ranks of the great world languages in demanding universal recognition and consideration is, of course, part of the centrifugal movement. The clash of these two historical movements is significant in the extreme, but we are not yet in a position to determine the outcome. We may, however, point out that the arising of the clash is itself an indication that historical movements seldom proceed in a single direction but rather resemble the swing of a pendulum. At the turn of the century, it was so universally believed that the world's future belonged to a few great western languages that the many constructed languages purposely devised for international use at that period all went on the assumption that nonwestern languages need not be in the least taken into account. This point of view seems quite outmoded today. Yet some still try to justify it on the ground that technological science, being western in its inception, must move all nonwestern peoples to accept the combination of languages which were its original vehicles.

The practical significance of the superimposition of colonizing languages upon native languages of Africa, Asia, and Oceania is that in many cases these European tongues will serve as substitutes for the native languages of vast areas in which a westerner may wish to carry on his activities. If you expect to do business in Algeria, it will be best to know both Arabic and French; but if you know only the latter, the chances are that it will enable you to carry on. The same may be said of English in India, Pakistan, Ceylon, or Burma, of Dutch in Indonesia, of English and Spanish in the Philippines, of Portuguese in Angola and Mozambique, of Italian in Somaliland, Eritrea, and Libya. For an undetermined period of time, the language of colonization still carries a cash value.

trade and military influences on language

As against the permanent contact between two languages established by colonialism or migration, there are the occasional contacts which are the result of trade, travel, and temporary military occupation.

Languages give and receive trade terms. usually the

names of products. "Kapok," "copra," "mango," "chutney" are characteristic, as are also names of fabrics based on the locality from which they come, like "calico," "shantung," "worsted," and "denim." Trade influences lead to an enrichment of the vocabulary to the same extent that trade gives rise to a more abundant and varied standard of living. Among names of everyday articles of consumption which first came to English as the result of trade are such commonplace terms as "chocolate," "coffee," "tea," "tomato," and "maize"; more recent borrowings are "broccoli," "zucchini" and "avocado."

The linguistic influence exerted by a temporary military occupation has lately come in for a good deal of scrutiny, by reason of American military commitments to far-flung lands. A thorough study of this influence casts light upon what must have happened in the past under similar circumstances. It also tends to confirm what was established in the previous chapter, namely, that not too much language mingling is to be expected from a purely temporary contact, and that the element of time is extremely important for the achievement of linguistic results.

American military occupation of countries like Germany, Italy, Japan, and Korea; American military installations on British and French soil, and similar recent occurrences have had as their principal permanent result the extension of the American "O.K." to practically all areas of the earth. For this, the friendly meaning of the expression and also the fact that it seems to fit in with the sound habits of practically all languages seem to be responsible. Beyond that, we find the most startling variation in the adoption of what might be termed "G.I. vocabulary" by the populations with which the soldiers came in contact.

Extensive penetration of two expressions, "G.I." and

"jeep," was noted, but with the cessation of hostilities both faded into the background. From all countries where American soldiers were stationed, come reports of the adoption of words like "Coca-Cola," "Pepsi-Cola," "ice cream," "chewing gum." They sometimes take strange forms, like the *pepusikora* (Pepsi-Cola) of Japanese or the *ciuinga* (chewing gum) of Italian. But it will be noted that even though these words may have been carried by soldiers, they do not differ in kind from the trade words described above.

From Britain comes a report of greater interchangeability of English words originally restricted to Britain or America, like "lorry" and "truck," or "petrol" and "gas." This, however, may well be due to trade and travel interchange rather than to straight military influence. The same may be said of the universal use of "nylon" in all countries reporting.

From Germany come stories of American English verbs, adjectives, and nouns to which German endings are affixed, like *fixen* used in the place of the customary *reparieren,* itself a borrowing. There are also wholesale loan translations of English sentences, like *eine harte Zeit zu geben* in the sense of "to give someone a hard time." The similarity between the two languages, of course, lends itself to this process. From the Russian side of the occupation line, come words like the German *Ami-töter* ("American-killer") or the Russian *drug* ("friend"), applied to a Russian-made cigarette designed to break the American strangle hold on the German black market.

Italy reports a wholesale invasion of terms and words from American English, but most of them are of the trade-and-travel variety. Individual terms that seem due to G.I. influence are *sciuscia'* ("shoe-shine," "bootblack"), *okeyna* and *segnorina,* two terms used to describe Italian girls who fraternized too freely with the Americans (*okeyna* is built on the stem of O.K., "one who freely says O.K.," while *segnorina* is a peculiar crossing of Italian *signorina* with Spanish *señorita*), and *vacca,* a term which in Italian means "cow," but which coincided phonetically with "WAC." Other random creations, which by now have disappeared, were *brekkare* and *spiccare* ("break" and "speak" with Italian verb endings), *teghedizi* ("take it easy") and *tumorro* ("tomorrow"; both were used to refer to someone who was lazy). One change affecting the grammatical structure of the language, though not permanently, was the use of the Italian verbs exclusively in the infinitive form (*Voi dove andare?*, "You where go?"). This was designed to supply an escape hatch from the complicated endings of the Italian verb, but it gave Italian a quaint pidgin flavor, and many Italians jokingly fell into the habit among themselves. One German word that had fully as much currency in Italy as "O.K." was *kaputt,* "dead," "finished," "done for"; it was even used as the title of a literary work.

Japanese and Korean adopted many loan words from the English of the American soldiers, but for Japanese, at least, this was merely the continuation of an ancient process, whereby the Japanese language has supplied itself with abundant western terminology. Three interesting "military" expressions which apparently had not found their way into Japanese previously were *herro* ("hello"), *goombai* ("good-bye"), and *sutinka* ("stinker"). The Americans in turn adopted and brought back to the States expressions like *ano ne* (a general exclamation of surprise or inquiry), *taksan* ("much," "lots of"), *skoshi* ("little," "few"), and *ichi ni san* "one, two, three"), but these were quickly lost and are seldom heard today.

French, which readily adopts American cultural and

trade expressions, particularly of a sensational nature (witness *le jitter-bug, les shorts, la starlette, le boyfriend, le nioulouque,* which is the French phonetic rendering of "new look"), and even gives new uses to them (*il a les yeux swing,* "he has swing eyes"; *elle est très pin-up,* "she is very pin-up"), seems to have taken little or nothing from the American military as such.

The conclusion to be drawn from these modern observations is that it takes far more than a mere temporary military occupation to produce a lasting and considerable linguistic effect. There has to be an element of time, coupled with a desire to blend.

The time element accounts largely for the different results achieved by Latin upon conquered populations. The lands where the Romans held sway for many centuries eventually turned into Romance-speaking countries. Where the time of occupation was shorter, as in Britain, the inhabitants reverted to their original tongue, though with numerous borrowings from the language they had learned. Where there was neither time nor a desire to blend, as in the Roman occupations of parts of what is today Germany, the results were limited to an exchange of loan words, the sort of thing that might as easily result from a trade-and-travel process, from which it is often indistinguishable.

WORDS OF MILITARY ORIGIN

GERMANIC INTO VULGAR LATIN AND ROMANCE

Brand ("sword") becomes Italian *brando,* Old French *brant.*

Helm ("helmet"), appearing in three Germanic versions, Gothic *hilms,* Frankish *helm* and Old Norse *hjalm,* replaces

Latin *galea* and gives rise to Italian *elmo*, Spanish *yelmo*, French *heaume*, etc.

Werra (Frankish, "war") replaces Latin *bellum* and becomes Spanish and Italian *guerra*, French *guerre*. In a Spanish diminutive form, "little war," it turns into *guerrilla*.

Germanic *triuwa* or Gothic *triggwo*, from the same root as English "true," becomes *truce, tregua.*

Warnjan, akin to English "warn," becomes *guarnire, garnir.* Coming from French into English, it gives rise to "garnish," "garrison," etc.

Marahskalk, "horseshoer," becomes *maréchal* and "marshal." The horseshoer was an important official at the Frankish court. Note the root of English "mare."

Frankish *kotta* and *fano* (the first akin to English "coat," the latter to German *Fahne*) give rise, respectively, to *cotte* (coat of mail) and *gonfanon, gonfalone*, "battle standard."

Frankish *hapja, halsberg, herialt* give rise to French *hache* ("ax"), *haubert* ("hauberk"), *heralt* ("herald").

Frankish *skara* gives rise to Italian *schiera* ("rank"), while Gothic *skarja* turns into Italian *sgherro, scherano* ("henchman").

More recently, Middle High German *helmbart, landsknecht, faldastol, bolwerk* give rise to French *hallebarde, lansquenet, fauteuil, boulevard*, while Dutch *haakbuse* become *harquebuse*, from which English forms "blunderbuss."

FRENCH AND OTHER LANGUAGES INTO ENGLISH

"Army," "navy," "enemy," "arms," "battle," "siege," "sortie," "sally," "soldier," "guard," "sergeant," "archer," "rank," "round robin" (*rond ruban*). *Poilu* and *maquis* come from the two World Wars. From Italian, generally through French, English borrows "attack," "reprisal," "cannon," "regiment," "infantry," "artillery," "colonel," "enfilade." From German come "blitz," "panzer," "Luftwaffe," "Wehrmacht," "schnorkel," "flak" (*Flugzeugabwehrkannonen* is the full form). "Forlorn hope" is Dutch *verloren hoop,* "lost troop." "Uhlan" and "janissary" are Turkish; "admiral," "assassin" and "jihad" are Arabic; "Molotoff" ("cocktail") and "chetnik" are Slavic. "Tommy" is British. "Jeep," "gremlin," "snafu," "expendable" are our own creations.

MONEY TERMS

ETRUSCAN, SICEL, GREEK INTO LATIN

As (unit of system of weight or coinage divisible into 12 parts), possibly from Etruscan. Was at first a rectangular, later a round, bronze coin. Later becomes English "ace."

Nummus, from Sicel or Sicilian Greek. Gives rise to "numismatic."

Libra, probably from Sicel *lithra,* unit of weight or money. Gives rise to Italian *lira,* English abbreviation £ for "pound" (in money) and *lb.* for unit of weight.

Talentum, from Greek *talanton.* Gives rise to "talent."

Native Latin money terms are *denarius* (from *decem,* "ten"), *sestertius* (from *senis-tertius,* "2½"), *pecunia* (from *pecus,* "sheep"; so called because Servius Tullius stamped coins with images of animals).

LATIN-ROMANCE INTO ENGLISH

Money, from French *monnaie,* Latin *moneta;* the latter word comes from the root of *moneo,* "to warn," and was at first applied to Juno, whose sacred geese by their cackling had

saved the city from a Gaulish surprise attack. The temple of
Juno Moneta was later a mint. The word "mint" is the
Anglo-Saxon development of *moneta,* while "money" is the
same word imported later by the Normans.

Salary, from Latin *sal,* "salt." Part of the pay of Roman soldiers was in salt, important for preserving meats.

Dime, from Old French *disme,* Latin *decima,* "tenth."

Quarter, from Latin *quartus,* "fourth."

Crown, from Latin *corona* (coin stamped with crown). This
word is used in Czech (*koruna*), Swedish (*krona*), Danish
and Norwegian (*krone*).

Pound, from Latin *pondus,* "weight."

GERMAN INTO ENGLISH

Dollar, from *Thaler* (from *Joachimsthaler*), first coined in the
valley of St. Joachim in Bohemia in the 16th century.

Nickel, from *Kupfernickel,* "Old Nick's copper," so nick-
named because difficult to mine.

Native English money terms are *farthing* (¼), *penny* (Anglo-
Saxon *pening*), *shilling* (Anglo-Saxon *scilling*); other Anglo-
Saxon money terms were *sceatta* (modern German *Schatz,*
"treasure") and *styca* (English "stick," modern German *Stuck,*
"piece").

SERBO-CROATIAN, IRAQI FROM LATIN

Dinar (from *denarius*).

HUNGARIAN FROM ITALIAN

Florint, from *fiorino,* "florin," originally a coin of Florence.

when language migrates

In ancient times, migrations were mass movements that very often involved entire populations. The Gauls, Romans, and Dorians who moved westward and southward from what seems to have been the original homeland of the Indo-Europeans on the shores of the Baltic moved as a unit.

Yet, even in those days, there is evidence that mass migrations involved a separation, possibly of individuals, more probably of clans and tribes; that some went and some stayed behind, perhaps to move at a later date and in another direction. If we accept the view that the ancestors of the speakers of today's Indo-European languages originally spoke the same tongue, there is no tenable theory save that the language was diversified by migration, by the loss of contact among the speakers, by innovations that crept in among one group and never reached the other. It may seem strange that by this process we have ultimately reached the vast differences that appear between Hindustani and Welsh, or between Russian and English, but when there are no centralizing forces at play the centrifugal tendencies of language work overtime.

In more recent times, we have such phenomena as Elizabethan English that comes to America, seventeenth-century French that moves to Canada, post-Columbian Spanish and Portuguese that move to Mexico, Argentina, and Brazil. Here the situation is different, because the links are not broken and the speakers keep in touch with the homeland, though by devices that are often primitive, like sailing ships that crossed the Atlantic twice a year.

Under these semimodern circumstances, the centrifugal tendencies of language are, of course, sharply braked. Changes and innovations that are made in the mother country eventually reach the colonies, where they may or may not meet with favor. Colonial innovations, on the other hand, have an excellent chance of reaching the home country, along with the products or descriptions of customs to which they refer. The interchange is such that while most technological and literary words that were evolved in London and Manchester eventually spread to Boston and New York, the "tomahawk" and "wigwam" and "wampum" of the colonists soon appeared in literary works published in Britain. The pronunciation of new waves of colonists serves to check the tendency of the colonial language to go off at a complete tangent. The fact that common institutions have already emerged and lie within the tradition of both groups, that there is a consciousness of unity on the part of both, that they have both achieved a permanent civilization, is bound to keep the language one.

At the same time, divergences inevitably appear, so that after a period of noncommittal silence on the subject one begins to hear of "the barbarous language spoken in the American colonies," "the strange pronunciation affected by French Canadians," "the deviations of the Castilian language in the overseas colonies."

These divergences generally fall under two large headings: vocabulary and pronunciation. Grammar is little, if at all, involved. It would be, of course, if there were no correctives and things were allowed to go on unchecked, but in recent centuries that has no longer been possible.

In vocabulary, the innovations are made on both sides of the ocean, but they are perhaps more numerous in the new land, where new objects and activities have to be named. These novelties, which represent very imminent realities to the colonists, are often nothing but a literary device to the dwellers in the homeland. A certain tree indigenous to Venezuela may mean a great deal to the Venezuelans, yet be nothing but a vague word to the Spaniards of Spain and, we might add, to colonists in Argentina, where the flora and fauna are much different from those of Venezuela. The result is that while the general Spanish vocabulary is enriched by a new name, the word will truly live only for a fraction of the total body of Spanish speakers.

In the matter of pronunciation, an interesting phenomenon has been noted. The pronunciation of a language which keeps on evolving at a normal rate in the mother country often crystallizes, or at least becomes quite conservative, in the colony. Because of its isolation, the colony tends to keep the speech of the period of its founding. This is true of American English, which is in many ways more conservative of Elizabethan habits of pronunciation than is the English of Britain; and American conservatism both of speech sounds and of speech forms is most noticeable in those regions, like the Appalachians and the Ozarks, where the colonists have become isolated and segregated from the bulk of the population, so that overseas and even local innovations have failed to reach them. The same is true of French-speaking Canada, which in many respects keeps the speech of seventeenth- and eighteenth-century France; it is true of Brazil, whose Portuguese has a slightly archaic flavor; it is true of many, though by no means all, the regions of Spanish America.

If we needed any confirmation of this general principle that the more remote, outlying, and isolated colonies tend to be more conservative in their speech forms, we could obtain it from the Romance languages. The more outlying of these, like Portuguese and Rumanian, show archaic and conservative features which reflect an earlier stage of the Latin language, whereas French and Italian, located in a more central position with respect to the pulsating heart of the Empire, the city of Rome, where most slangy innovations occurred, display a later stage of Latin.

A still more modern language process is displayed by the languages of immigrant groups coming not as colonists to an undeveloped land but as minorities to a land previously settled. Such groups normally give up their foreign tongue within a few generations and become completely absorbed by the linguistic majority; but there are numerous exceptions in cases where the immigrant group constitutes a local majority. This may happen in the farmlands of Pennsylvania, the forests of Minnesota, the sheep ranges of Idaho, or even in the heart of a great city like New York.

The so-called Pennsylvania Dutch (a much better name would be Pennsylvania Germans) came to America from the Palatinate section of western Germany, bringing their German customs and their Franconian dialect with them. They were so numerous that at one time Benjamin Franklin expressed the fear that they might make German the official language of the Commonwealth of Pennsylvania. This did not happen, but they have continued to dominate the life of York and Lancaster counties and have clung to their tongue of origin. But this has become so interlarded with English words and expressions from their American environment that it has developed into what might be described as a brand-new Germanic language, rooted in German, but with many accretions from English and a few special features of its own. Books and newspapers are published in Pennsylvania German, and it is seriously studied as a separate language in at least one great American university.

Something similar, though on a more diffused scale, has happened to the Scandinavian communities of Minnesota and Michigan, German groups in Wisconsin and Ohio, Italian groups in New York and other eastern states, Slavic groups in Pittsburgh, Ohio, and Chicago. There is even a community of Basque speakers in Idaho, to which many Basques have migrated from northeastern Spain to carry on their traditional calling of sheepherding. Yiddish communities appear in most of our large cities.

Nowhere, however, has there been quite the same development that is in evidence in the Pennsylvania German community. What normally occurs in a foreign-language group transplanted to an English-speaking environment is that English, the language of the broader community, is gradually assimilated and the point of complete saturation is achieved in the course of three generations.

Meanwhile, the foreign tongue brought by the immigrants tends to crystallize and become conservative. In an Italian community in Brooklyn will be found the speech forms current in the Italian dialects of origin forty or fifty years ago, rather than those employed in Italy today. Customs and ways of life usually parallel the language. Eventually, the old dialects die and English becomes the universal tongue of the new generations.

The crystallization is not complete, but this is due to infiltrations from English rather than to any influence from foreign-language developments overseas. Picturesque but transitory jargons spring up, in which English words are appropriated and fitted into the foreign-dialect pattern, with little regard for the fact that there are perfectly good equivalent words in the official foreign tongue. The results are often ludicrous, particularly when the borrowed English word happens to coincide phonetically with a foreign word of totally different meaning (consider, for instance, the New York Italian *sciabola* and *sciabolatore*, borrowed and adapted from English "shovel" and "shoveler," which in the Italian of Italy would have the legitimate meaning of "saber" and "swordsman").

Similar developments occur in other tongues, wherever large bodies of foreign speakers enter as immigrants. In Argentina, where nearly half the population is of Italian origin, there exists an Italian-Spanish blend called Cocoliche, which is aided and abetted by the fact that Italian and Spanish are so similar in sounds, structure and vocabulary. Another similar pidgin brand of Italian and French appears in southern France, to which many Italians have migrated.

Under modern conditions, these language blends are bound to be temporary and transitory, since the centripetal power of national tongues is too great to be resisted. While they endure, however, they serve to illustrate in graphic fashion the way in which many of our modern standard languages were formed.

SAMPLES OF MIXED (PIDGIN) LANGUAGES

The following excerpts are from the Bible translations of John 3:16 which appear in the American Bible Society's *Book of a Thousand Tongues.*

ENGLISH: For God so loved the world that He gave His only-begotten Son, that whosoever believeth in Him may not perish, but may have everlasting life.

AFRIKAANS (DUTCH WITH SOME ENGLISH AND BANTU ADMIXTURE), SOUTH AFRICA: Want so lief het God die wêreld gehad, dat Hy sy eniggebore Seun gegee het, sodat elkeen wat in Hom glo, nie verlore mag gaan nie, maar die ewige lewe kan hê.

HAITIAN CREOLE (FRENCH WITH SOME AFRICAN ADMIXTURE), HAITI: Car Bon Dieu té r'aimé créatures-li si tant, que li baille seul Pitite-li, pour que ça qui croit-n'en li pas perdu, mais pour li gagné la vie éternelle.

INDO-PORTUGUESE (PORTUGUESE WITH DUTCH AND INDIAN ADMIXTURE), CEYLON: Parque de tal maneira Deos ja ama per o mundo, que elle ja da seu Filho unigenito, que quemseja te cré n'elle nadia perece, mas acha vida eterna.

PAPIAMENTO (SPANISH OR PORTUGUESE WITH DUTCH AND AFRICAN ADMIXTURE), CURAÇAO: Pasoba Dios a stima mundu asina tantu qu El duna su unicu Yin, pa tur qu quere den djé, no bai perdí, ma haya bida eternu.

MALTESE (ARABIC WITH ITALIAN ADMIXTURE), MALTA: Ghaliex Alla hecca hab id dinia illi tâ l'Iben tighu unigenitu, sabiex collmìn jemmen bih ma jintilifx, izda icollu il haja ta dejem.

MALAY (LITERARY COMPROMISE OF INDONESIAN LANGUAGES), INDONESIA, MALAYA: Karna dĕmikian-lah Allah mĕngasehi isi dunia ini, sa-hingga di-bĕri-nya Anak-nya yang tunggal itu, supaya barang siapa yang pĕrchaya akan dia jangan ia binasa, mĕlainkan bĕroleh hidup yang kĕkal.

Newspaper account of royal wedding.

PIDGIN ENGLISH (ENGLISH WITH MELANESIAN ADMIXTURE), NEW GUINEA: Good news e come up long England. Long Friday twentieth November, number one piccininni belong king belong you and me King George VI long England e marry. All e save e long this feller king all time e come up long house picture now you and me stand up. Now number one piccininni belong e marry. Im e got two piccininni. Now Princess Elizabeth in e got marry long one feller man name belong Duke of Edinburgh. All e hurrah much long this feller princess.

Some other examples of Pidgin English.
Wata he kai-kai 'im. (The water ate him—He drowned.)
Have got wata top-side. (He's crazy.)
Belly belong me plenty walk about (I have a stomach-ache.)

PENNSYLVANIA GERMAN (in its purest form, this is merely a German Franconian dialect; in popular speech, it may become mixed with terms borrowed from English):
The Lord's Prayer: Unser Vadder im Himmel, maag Dei Naame heilich sei. Dei Reich soll kumme. Dei Wille soll gschehne uff der Aerd, graad wie im Himmel. Unser notwennich Brot gebb uns heit. Un vergebb uns unser Schulde, so wie mir annere vergewwe, wu uns schuldich sin. Un fiehr uns net in Versuchung, awwer mach uns vum Iwwel frei.

Popular poem.
> Heut is 's xäctly zwanzig Johr
> Dass ich bin owwe naus;
> Nau bin ich widder lewig z'rück
> Un steh am Schulhaus an d'r Krick
> Juscht nächst an's Daddy's Haus.

liturgical languages

A liturgical language is one which is used exclusively, or primarily, in the religious service of a given community. It may or may not have wide currency outside of that function, but it normally serves to color the community's thinking, gives the members of that community a sense of unity, and inevitably spills over into its literature and rhetoric. Religion is of vast importance to most human beings, and it is not surprising that it greatly affects language.

As a spoken tongue, the liturgical language is often extinct, but it almost invariably was a spoken tongue in the earlier life of the community. We are hardly in a position to judge definitely whether the language of the Egyptian hieroglyphic inscriptions and the Sumerian and Akkadian cuneiform tablets, which is largely bound up with religious worship, was precisely the same as the spoken tongue of the multitudes living at the time when those carvings and tablets were produced. The chances are that it represented a somewhat antiquated and archaic form of that spoken tongue even then. This conclusion is based partly upon its serious religious content, but even more upon the general fact that the written language always tends to be slightly archaic and conservative.

The Vedic form of Sanskrit employed in the Rig-Vedas of ancient India led to the classical Sanskrit of the epics, which in turn became the Prakrits of medieval India and ultimately the Indo-Aryan vernaculars of today. But Vedic, whatever may have been its status as a spoken language, continued to serve for a time as the sacred tongue of

Hinduism, while classical Sanskrit, long after its "death" as a spoken tongue, continues to be the official language of Buddhism. Avestan, the language of Zoroaster, is still liturgically used today by the fire-worshiping Parsees.

In the western world, we find Hebrew and Aramaic serving both Judaism and Christianity, though the latter chose as its later vehicles Greek and Latin. Hebrew, discarded by the Jews themselves in favor of Aramaic as a spoken language, came back into favor and was assiduously cultivated by the Jewish communities throughout the classical and medieval periods and on into modern times, when we have its restoration as a fully popular spoken language in the new state of Israel. Its experience may be unique, but it proves that a tongue can pass from the liturgical to the popular status, thus reversing the traditional process.

When the Christian religion began to expand, its original vehicle was Aramaic, the language spoken by Christ and His followers. But Aramaic was a language of little international diffusion, though it had been and was current in the lands of the Near East. The truly international tongues of the period were Greek, the language of culture of the classical world, and Latin, the language of political and military administration throughout the Roman Empire. It was therefore natural for the new mass religion to turn to these two languages and use them as media for its expansion.

The fact that Latin and Greek were so used in the early days of Christianity gives us considerable reassurance concerning their spoken use and particularly concerning the connection between their spoken and their written form. Languages used as the instruments of mass propaganda must be popular spoken tongues; they cannot under any circumstances be artificial literary tools, or they will fail in their purpose. The early Greek and Latin translations of the Bible, including even St. Jerome's Vulgate, composed about 400 A.D., are, by reason of their use, fair indications of the state of the spoken Greek and Latin tongues.

In return for their services as instruments for the spreading of the Gospel, these languages were reinforced and perpetuated by their use in that capacity. The invaders that poured into the Roman Empire from the fifth century on could do little to offset the mighty religious prestige of Greek and Latin. Latin in particular could have succumbed to the many waves of Germanic speakers that swamped the lands of the west, but since the newcomers were invariably converted to Christianity, and the official language of western Christianity was Latin, the barbarians regularly accepted the language along with the religion.

Today, after an interval of a millennium and a half, Latin and Greek still continue to serve the western and eastern Christian churches. In between, they served the world of medieval and Renaissance scholarship, and Latin came close to occupying the post of international language in the Middle Ages. Priests of the Roman Catholic Church are able today to communicate with one another in Latin, whatever the country from which they come.

In Christianizing peoples who were not in direct contact with the Graeco-Roman tradition, the early missionaries found it expedient to depend upon the popular languages of the groups they were trying to convert. The result is that the earliest written document of numerous languages is a translation of all or part of the Bible. This is true of Gothic, first of the Germanic languages of which we have satisfactory records. It appears in a Bible translation composed by Bishop Wulfilas, himself a Goth, who around 400 A.D. translated the Bible into Gothic for his people, at that time located on the northern shores of the Black Sea. Five centuries later, the first written document of a Slavic tongue appears in the form of a Bible translation composed by Cyril and Methodius, two Greek bishops from Constantinople, for the Slavs who had followed the Germanic invaders into central Europe. The language of this translation is sometimes referred to as Old Bulgarian but more often goes by the name of Old Church Slavonic. Numerous other languages, including Armenian, Albanian, and Finnish, have a Bible translation as their earliest written record.

Arabic, originally restricted to the Arabian peninsula, became a world language by reason of the fact that it was the spoken tongue of Mohammed and his followers, who spread the Islamic religion to vast regions of the earth. As a result of religious expansion, Arabic became the popular language of North Africa, Egypt, and the states of the Near East (Syria, Jordan, Lebanon, Iraq); but the influence of Arabic is felt wherever there are Moslems, in precisely the same way that the influence of Latin follows the Roman Catholic faith. In the same fashion that Latin broke up into separate Romance languages, spoken Arabic diverged into a series of spoken dialects; but the classical Arabic of the Koran is still in written use everywhere in the Arabic-speaking world, regardless of the local spoken form.

The linguistic influence of Arabic, a Semitic language, upon languages of non-Semitic stock has been enormous. The Persian of Iran, the Urdu of Pakistan, the Pushtu of Afghanistan are all basically Indo-European languages; all three, however, are written with modified forms of the Arabic alphabet and are replete with Arabic words and forms. The western languages have borrowed heavily from

Arabic, which in the Middle Ages was the tongue of an imposing culture. English words like "magazine," "alcohol," "sofa," "syrup" are Arabic in origin.

Numerous other liturgical languages are in use today, in addition to the half dozen giants we have mentioned. In Egypt, Nubia, the Sudan, and Ethiopia there is in liturgical use a language called Coptic, which is a direct descendant of ancient Egyptian and is used by African Christians who refused to go over to Islam. Liturgical forms of Old Slavonic appear in Serbia, Bulgaria, Macedonia, Rumania, and even Soviet Russia. A liturgical form of old Armenian is in use in Armenian churches. Even Aramaic, in a modified and modernized form called Syriac, is used in the church services of Near Eastern Christians.

The influence exerted by liturgical languages upon their users is profound. There is normally a carry-over from the language of the religious services to the common tongue, which is felt in pronunciation, grammar, and particularly in vocabulary. In countries where the liturgical language is not altogether foreign, broad areas of it lie in the common domain. There is no need to translate to Italian or Spanish speakers such Latin phrases as *Pax vobiscum* or *Requiescat in pace*. The restraining influence of liturgical Latin and Greek has been responsible for conserving many language forms that would otherwise have disappeared from modern Romance and modern Greek. In English, we may note that the influence of the language of the King James Bible, which contains, from twentieth-century standpoints, numerous archaisms, is still very much felt. Forms like "behold," "unto," "ye," "thou," "spake" would probably have utterly disappeared from the language had it not been for their constant recurrence in Biblical contexts.

Nor should we forget the purely alphabetic influence

TABLE OF ALPHABETIC DEVELOPMENT

Semitic name of letters	North Semitic	square Hebrew	Greek name of letters	Greek	Cyrillic	Roman
ALEF	𐤀	א	ALPHA	A	A, Я,Ѧ	A
BETH	𐤁	ב	BETA	B	В, Б	B
GIMEL	𐤂	ג	GAMMA	Γ	Г,Ґ	C, G
DALETH	𐤃	ד	DELTA	Δ	Д	D
HE	𐤄	ה	EPSILON	E	Е,Є,Э	E
VAV	𐤅	ו	DIGAMMA	F		F
			UPSILON	У	У,Ү	V, U, Y, W
ZAYIN	𐤆	ז	ZETA	Z	З	Z
CHETH	𐤇	ח	ETA	H	И,Й	H
TETH	𐤈	ט	THETA	Θ	Θ	
YOD	𐤉	י	IOTA	I	І,Ј	I, J
KAF	𐤊	כ	KAPPA	K	К	K
LAMED	𐤋	ל	LAMBDA	Λ	Л,Љ	L
MEM	𐤌	מ	MU	Μ	М	M
NUN	𐤍	נ	NU	N	Н,Њ	N
SAMEKH	𐤎	ס	XI	Ξ		
AYIN	𐤏	ע	OMICRON	O	О,Ю	O
PE	𐤐	פ	PI	Π	П	P
TSADE	𐤑	צ			Ч,Ц,Џ	
QUF	𐤒	ק	KOPPA	Ϙ		Q
RESH	𐤓	ר	RHO	P	Р	R
SHIN	𐤔	ש	SIGMA	Σ	С,Ш,Щ	S
TAU	𐤕	ת	TAU	T	Т	T
			PHI	Φ	Ф	
			CHI	X	Х	X
			PSI	Ψ	Ж,Ѧ	
			OMEGA	Ω		

Additional Cyrillic characters: Ъ, Ь, Ы, Ѣ, Ћ, Ђ

exerted by liturgical languages. Those countries to which Christianity came from Rome have almost universally adopted the Roman alphabet, while the Greek alphabet of the Eastern Church has formed the basis of the Cyrillic used by many Slavic nations. In Yugoslavia, the Catholic Croats and the Orthodox Serbs both use the same spoken language, but while the Croats write it in Roman, the Serbs use Cyrillic. In India, the Moslem speakers of Urdu use Arabic characters, but the Hindu speakers of Hindi, a language extremely close to Urdu, use the Devanagari characters of ancient Sanskrit. It may almost be said that liturgical language and alphabetic notation go hand in hand.

(*opposite*)

NOTE: North Semitic alphabet gives rise on the one hand to Hebrew, on the other to Greek. Cyrillic alphabet devised in 9th century A.D. on the basis of Greek, with an assist from Hebrew. Roman alphabet comes from Greek through Etruscan. Semitic and Hebrew alphabets consist exclusively of consonants; some of these are adapted to serve as vowel symbols in Greek, Cyrillic, and Roman. Some of the Cyrillic characters appear only in Russian; others only in Ukrainian, or Serbian, or Bulgarian, or Old Church Slavonic. The Arabic alphabet, which, with modifications, serves also Persian, Urdu, etc., and the Devanagari of ancient India, from which most of the modern alphabetic forms of India, East Pakistan, Burma, Ceylon, and Thailand are derived, also stem, more remotely, from the North Semitic alphabet.

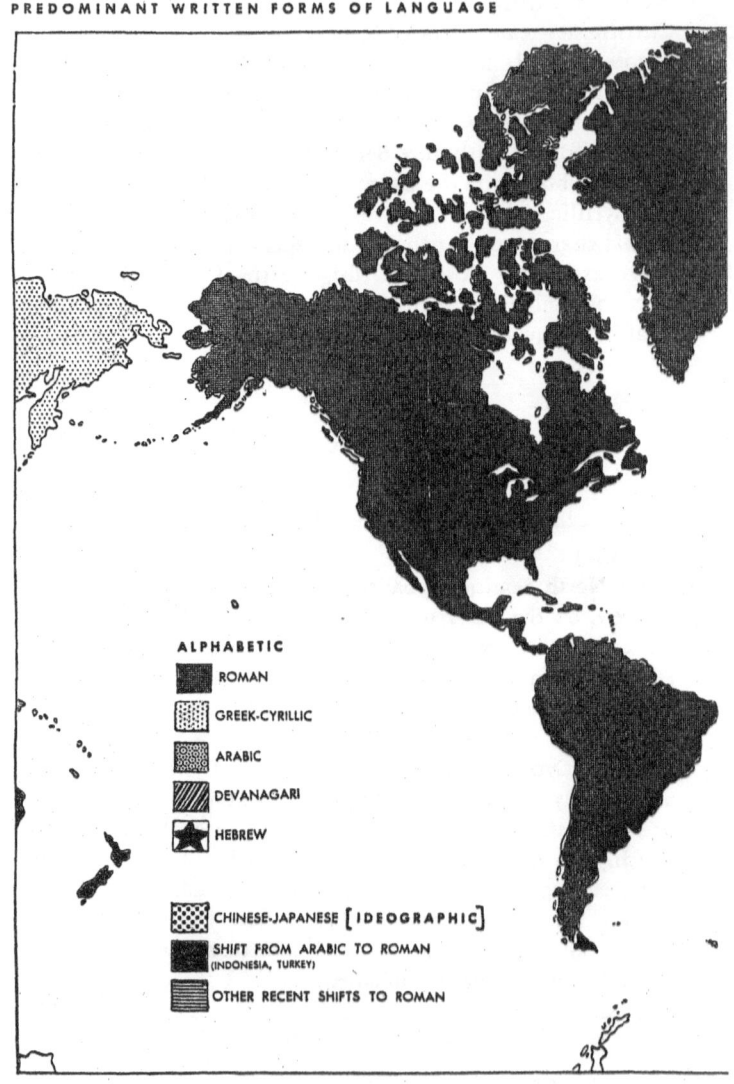

ALPHABETIC

ROMAN

GREEK-CYRILLIC

ARABIC

DEVANAGARI

HEBREW

CHINESE-JAPANESE [IDEOGRAPHIC]

SHIFT FROM ARABIC TO ROMAN
(INDONESIA, TURKEY)

OTHER RECENT SHIFTS TO ROMAN

4

SOCIOLOGICAL IMPLICATIONS OF LANGUAGE

language cycles and zones

The life cycle of the individual language is its total history, from birth to death, or at least from its first historically recorded emergence to the point where it ceases to have a living body of speakers who employ it as a mother tongue.

By this criterion, we may say that languages like Sumerian, Akkadian, ancient Egyptian, Gaulish, Etruscan have fully run their life course. Other languages, like Hebrew, Greek, English, French, are still in the process of completing their life cycle.

The life span of a language is fully as unpredictable

as that of a man. Some tongues have a short history, at least so far as the records indicate, others are very long-lived. Some "die" by our definition, then come back to life (this is the case with Hebrew). Others "live on" in their descendants, like Latin. The exact time when a language becomes extinct is hard to determine. The Vegliote mentioned on page 129 is one of the few cases on record for which even an approximate death date is possible. Surprising discrepancies appear in estimates made for some of our best-known languages. The date for the extinction of Latin as a universal popular tongue has been placed as far back as the third or fourth century A.D. and as far forward as the eighth or ninth.

The life cycle of a language is marked by a period of emergence, in which the written documents are few and unsatisfactory, as is the case with Latin between 500 and 300 B.C. Then comes a period of full development, attended by literary growth and a marked vocabulary increase. The decline of the language does not always or necessarily coincide with its vulgarization in the puristic sense, but rather with a loss of speakers, and is frequently accompanied by the emergence of new languages.

Often a language becomes predominant in a certain part of the world, setting up what amounts to a partial and temporary universality. Appearances in this respect are somewhat deceptive, however. The fact that at one historical period we find records only of Sumerian, or of Egyptian, or of Akkadian does not at all mean that no other languages were spoken. The impression is fostered that when Greek and Latin ruled the classical world practically nothing else was spoken. But even in the Mediterranean basin there is abundant trace of other contemporary tongues, even if these were not fully recorded. And it must also be remembered that while the beginnings of the great western civilization were occurring in that area, there were other areas of the earth in which other civilizations and other languages flourished. The rise of the Chinese culture and language coincided roughly in time with the emergence and spreading of the Hellenic civilization and its immediate predecessors. The art of writing appeared simultaneously in the East and in the West, and without any known link.

Predominance of one language does not imply lack of coexistence, peaceful or otherwise, with others. There is little in our historical records to indicate that the Romans made any conscious effort to do away with other languages, while geographical remoteness meant that cultures and languages could flourish in different areas of the earth completely unknown to one another, and without the possibility of clashing.

With the improvement of travel and communications, the spirit of peaceful linguistic coexistence not merely was fostered but became a conscious phenomenon. The Renaissance in particular, with its growing use of national languages, brought about a realization of the multiplicity of tongues and the need for mutual tolerance. The Greeks had referred to all non-Greek speakers as *barbaroi*, or "babblers"; he who did not speak Greek did not speak at all; he merely made sounds. Of this spirit of linguistic intolerance there are numerous examples in later centuries (the Slavs, for instance, call the speakers of German by a name that means "mute"); but proximity coupled with a measure of equality brought about the admission, at least on the part of the more enlightened, that there could be other languages, even of a civilized variety, in addition to one's own tongue.

B.C.

Area	2000	1500	1000	500
FAR EAST	Chinese	Chinese	Chinese	Chinese
SOUTHERN ASIA	?	Vedic	Sanskrit	Sanskrit
NEAR EAST	Sumerian Hittite Akkadian Elamite	Sumerian Hittite Assyro-Babylonian Elamite	Sumerian Hebrew Aramaic Phoenician Assyro-Babylonian Persian	Hebrew Aramaic Chaldean Babylonian Persian
MEDITER-RANEAN BASIN	Egyptian Cretan	Egyptian Mycenean	Egyptian Greek Etruscan Italic Celtic Iberian	Egyptian Greek Punic Etruscan Gaulish Iberian Latin Osco-Umbrian
NORTHERN EUROPE	Indo-European ?	Indo-European ?	Germanic? Slavic?	Germanic Slavic
WESTERN HEMISPHERE	?	?	?	Mayan ?

I	500	1000	1500	1955
Chinese	Chinese	Chinese	Chinese	Chinese Japanese
Sanskrit	Prakrits (Pali, *etc.*)	Prakrits	Hindi Urdu, *etc.*	Hindustani Indonesian Bengali
Hebrew Aramaic Persian	Aramaic Arabic Persian	Arabic Turkish Persian	Arabic Turkish Persian	Arabic Turkish Hebrew Persian
Latin Greek	Latin Greek	Greek French Spanish Italian Arabic	Greek French Spanish Portuguese Italian Arabic	Greek French Spanish Portuguese Italian Arabic
Germanic Slavic	Anglo-Saxon Scandinavian Old High German Gothic Slavic	English German Dutch Scandinavian Slavic	English German Dutch Scandinavian Russian Polish, *etc.*	English German Dutch Scandinavian Russian Polish Czech Ukrainian Serbo-Croat
Aztec Inca ?	Amer. Indian	Amer. Indian	Amer. Indian	English Spanish Portuguese French

Recent extensions of this spirit of peaceful coexistence are profound. Fifty or even thirty years ago, the admission of an Oriental language like Chinese, or even of a Slavic tongue like Russian, to the parity that they encounter today in UN circles with western tongues like English, French, and Spanish would have been unthinkable. The present period may well be defined as one of conscious peaceful linguistic coexistence, though it is a question whether this situation will continue or will lead to new hegemonies in the field of language.

In its period of predominance or fullest development, a language will commonly tend to extend its sphere of operations and influence and create for itself a wider zone or *Lebensraum*. This phenomenon, as we have seen, is often accompanied by diversification. The ancient Phoenicians sent out colonists from their cities of Tyre and Sidon, and Phoenician colonies sprang up all over the Mediterranean and the Black Sea. Among these colonies was the city of Carthage. We may presume that at the outset the language of Carthage coincided precisely with that of Phoenicia, but in the course of time it became differentiated, and the ancient historians speak of the Phoenician of the homeland and the Punic of Carthage as two different tongues. Perhaps the differences were no greater than those separating the King's English from the American language, but they were noticeable nevertheless.

It sometimes happens that a language, in sending out its offshoots to form separate language communities, loses its own homeland. This is in part illustrated by the Hebrew of the Jews, which practically disappeared from Judaea while spreading to numerous Jewish communities in North Africa, only to return to Palestine after the lapse of many centuries.

The operating area of a language includes all territories in which that language is spoken as a mother tongue, but it also extends to other regions where the language is described as official. Colonies, of course, fall under this heading, but there are many instances where bilingual or trilingual situations exist, particularly along the international borders of countries where a single language is both official and national. In a country like France, whose language extends far beyond the French borders into neighboring Belgium and Switzerland, there are extensive areas where the mother tongue of the inhabitants is something other than French, though French is spoken and understood by practically everybody and is the tongue of all official business. Breton appears in Brittany, Basque and Catalan at the two ends of the Pyrenees, German in Alsace and parts of Lorraine, Flemish on the North Sea coast, Italian in the vicinity of Nice. In all these areas it may be said that the language zones overlap and that there is, to use the language of diplomacy, a conflict of interests. There usually is also, however, peaceful coexistence. The situation is not too different from that prevailing in the religious field in areas where followers of two different faiths live side by side.

The language community is composed of all speakers of the language. It may or may not coincide with the political grouping of those living under one government. It need not at all coincide with the geographical boundaries of a given religious faith, and it is altogether unconnected with factors of race and color.

It has been customary in the past for centralized governments to endeavor to enforce some measure of conformity and standardization in language among those who were subject to them, though the measure of this has varied. Both linguistic and religious unity help to fasten the hold of a government upon its subjects, but it has been abundantly proved that political unity can be achieved despite differences in practically all the factors of linguistic or religious uniformity.

The ideal of one race, one color, one language, one religious faith for one nation is not merely outmoded. It has never really existed and is in large measure the product of diseased imaginations.

The great empires that preceded the Graeco-Roman world were composed of many races, languages, and religions, though one of each of these usually predominated. In the Roman Empire were peoples of many races, tongues, and religious faiths, and it was one of the boasts of the Empire that it ultimately extended Roman citizenship to all freemen living within its boundaries. Loyalty was to a cultural ideal and a set of political institutions rather than to any racial, religious, or even linguistic theory.

The Middle Ages advanced the cause of religious unity

to the evident disadvantage of racial, national, and linguistic ideals. All who believed in Christ formed part of
the Christian community, regardless of their other affiliations; all who believed in the teachings of Mohammed
were members of the Islamic community, in which the
Arabic language played a necessary but secondary role. In
the medieval world, language, race, and color mattered
little; what mattered was a man's faith in Christ, Jehovah,
Allah.

The Renaissance, with the rise of national states, brought
forth on the one hand the ideal of a national grouping;
on the other, it gave reinforcement to the medieval fealty
to an individual or a crown. But personal loyalty gradually
lost force as national loyalty became more firmly established. By the end of the eighteenth century, the national
ideal, partly based on language as a unifying force, took
the upper hand.

At this point, however, we have strange divergences.
Some political units were formed and maintained largely
on a national-linguistic basis, with a conscious attempt to
bring about linguistic conformity among their members.
Revolutionary and Napoleonic France, in which the
French language was extolled as the nation's symbol, is
fairly characteristic. At the outset of the revolutionary
movement, outlying provinces of France, in which the
popular language was German, Italian, Catalan, Basque, or
Breton, were encouraged to cultivate their own languages,
on the theory that this would contribute to the spreading
of the revolutionary movement and give it an international
character. But this policy was soon reversed, and French
was exalted as the tongue of freedom *par excellence*. This
spirit prevails in France to the present day, and linguistic
nonconformity is frowned upon, to the point where letters

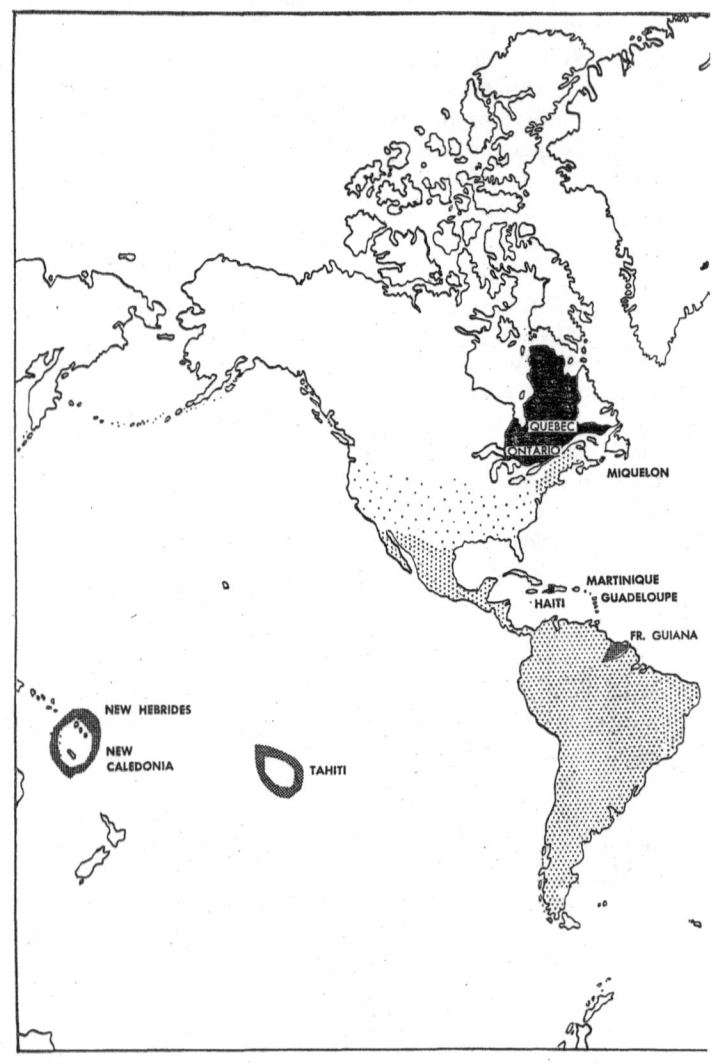

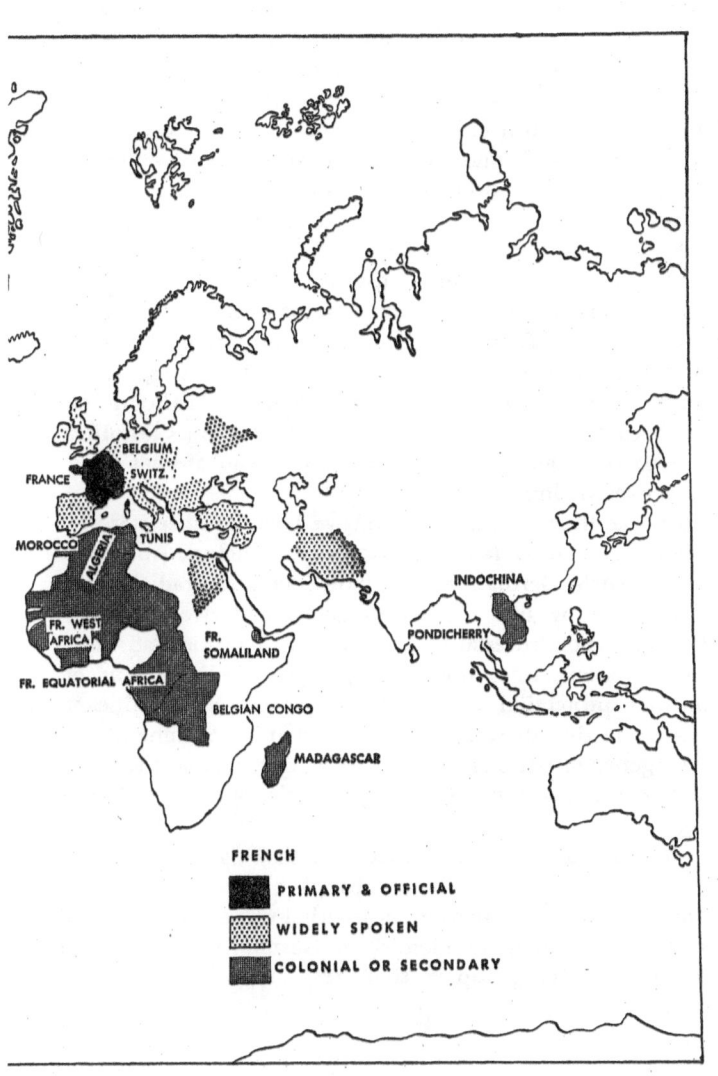

FRENCH

PRIMARY & OFFICIAL

WIDELY SPOKEN

COLONIAL OR SECONDARY

addressed in Breton or other minority tongues are returned to their senders. Something similar appeared in the new American nation, where the use of languages like the French of the Huguenots, the German of the Pennsylvania Dutch, the Swedish of Delaware, the Dutch of New York were discouraged, and newcomers were given to understand that English alone would lead to citizenship and its fruits.

A contrasting situation appears in countries like Holland and Belgium, where a division took place that was based not on linguistic but on religious lines. The Flemish of the northern Belgian provinces is to all intents the same language as the Dutch of Holland, yet the Flemish speakers preferred to go with the French-speaking Walloons of southern Belgium, who were, like themselves, Catholics, and parted company with the Dutch, who at that time were overwhelmingly Protestant.

In a country like Switzerland we have another state of affairs. Here, three languages (four, if we include Romansh with French, German, and Italian) had been traditionally living side by side for centuries; so had two religions, Catholic and Protestant. The Swiss Federation had been formed along lines not of language or religion but of mutual protection and mutual respect. No significant change in this attitude appeared, either at the time of the emergence of nationalisms or at a later date, and the Swiss state continues to be essentially what it was in the Middle Ages.

It is of interest to note that in both Belgium and Switzerland there appear large groups of French speakers, whose linguistic affiliation lies with France, not with the Germanic speakers of Flemish or German who constitute the other large group in their respective countries. Linguistically and culturally, French-speaking Belgians and Swiss are French, yet this in no way interferes with their Belgian and Swiss political allegiance, and movements to detach them from their national states and link them to the political body of France are wont to die a-borning. Precisely the same may be said of the Italian and German speakers of Switzerland.

But this fealty to an existing set of political institutions to the detriment of linguistic affiliations is far from universal. The old Austro-Hungarian Empire, originally constructed on the medieval basis of personal fealty to an emperor-king, was rent asunder by nationalistic dissensions based largely on linguistic factors. The Italians of Trieste and the Trentino looked to Italy, the Croats and Serbs of Croatia, Dalmatia, and Bosnia looked to Serbia, the Rumanians of Transylvania wanted to be joined to Rumania, the Poles of Galicia dreamed of a reunited Poland, while Czechs, Slovaks, and Hungarians, who had no foreign state beyond the border to which to turn, sought national independence. It was the Austro-Hungarian situation, more than anything else, that inspired Wilson to seek his far-famed "self-determination for small nations," so completely at variance with the economic realities which demanded the continuation of a large, self-contained Danubian state. Without going into the political or economic merits of the solution adopted at the close of World War I, it may be remarked that the solution itself was based almost exclusively on linguistic factors.

In view of all these contrasting pictures, a redefinition of the linguistic community may perhaps be in order. The language community, while it may be at times identified with factors of race, nationality, or religion, can be fully independent of all of them. There is a link among the

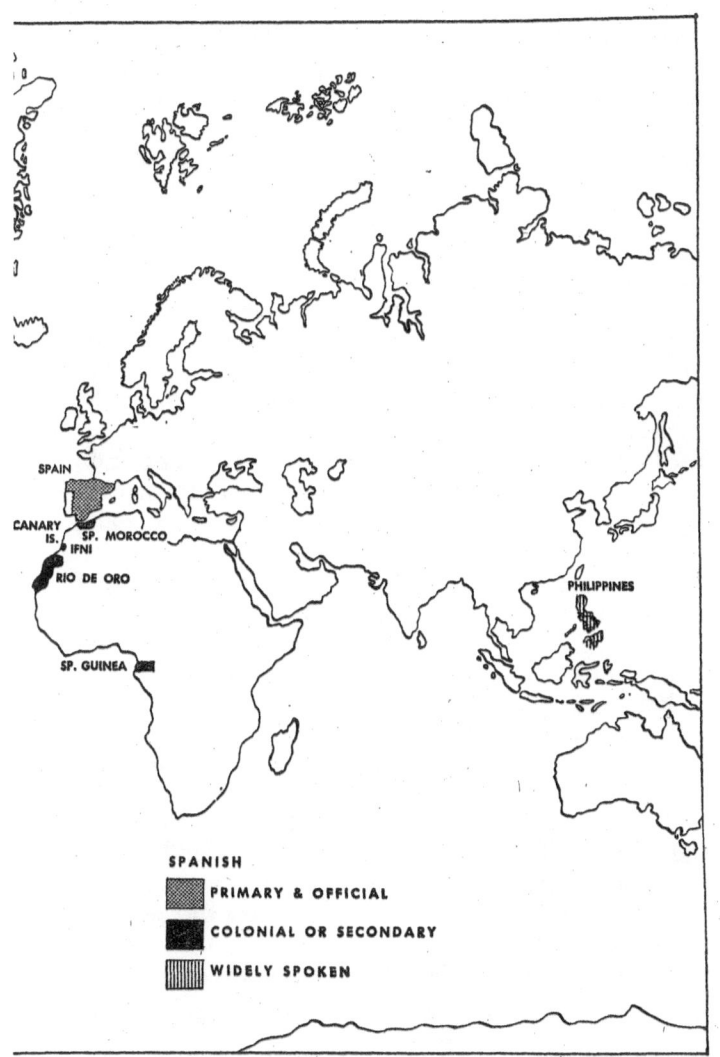

SPAIN

CANARY
IS.   SP. MOROCCO
      IFNI

RIO DE ORO

SP. GUINEA

PHILIPPINES

SPANISH

PRIMARY & OFFICIAL

COLONIAL OR SECONDARY

WIDELY SPOKEN

speakers of one language, but this link does not depend upon any of the other factors described. The community of English speakers may live under the British Crown or the American Constitution, it may be composed of people of white, black, brown, red or yellow skin, it may contain the world's major religious faiths. Almost the same may be said of the community of Spanish speakers, which includes Spaniards, American Indians, Sephardic Jews, African Negroes, and brown Filipinos. Too much cannot be predicated on language, which is only one of the various methods by which people group themselves.

Yet it is undeniable that language is one of mankind's great unifying forces, possibly the greatest, because it is the most unconscious and the one calling for the least active participation on the part of the individual. The American, placed among a group of assorted foreigners, will naturally gravitate toward the Englishman, who speaks his language. It is not by accident that we have such groups as the English-Speaking Union, or that the Spanish speakers have coined for themselves the term *hispano,* which is not at all the same as *español,* and gather together in such festivals as *el Día de la Raza* ("the day of the race"), a complete misnomer, since it is based not at all on race but exclusively on language.

Religion and nationality call for a conscious act of the intellect and the will, though they are as much a part of our heritage as is language. But language is spontaneous. An Italian who has been struggling with the German of Zürich and Luzern will thrill when he gets to Lugano, though he is as much in Switzerland, a foreign land, as he was before. The language community must be reckoned with as one of the major sociological forces at work in the world. Its links with other sociological factors are obvious, yet it is equally obvious that the language community can operate independently of them all. What historical study fails to establish is which of the four factors—race, nationality, religion, language—is the most powerful and evokes the deepest loyalties. Historical episodes show the triumph of one or another at various times and in accordance with no predictable pattern.

language minorities

A minority group implies the existence of a majority. The term "minority" has of late become of vogue among sociologists and psychologists who wish to find an explanation for juvenile delinquency and slums, and they customarily apply it to what former generations used to call "immigrant groups." This usage is quite legitimate, but it is somewhat at variance with the way the term is used in Europe, and particularly the way it was used at the time of Wilson's self-determination.

The linguistic minorities of Europe are usually found along the borderlines of countries, and they often, but not always, have affiliations, linguistic and otherwise, with the countries across those boundaries. In France, one could reasonably speak of linguistic minorities which are Breton in the northwest, Basque and Catalan in the southwest,

Italian in the southeast and in Corsica, German along the eastern border. Italian and German speakers have affiliations with the large nations that speak their language; Basques and Catalans extend on both sides of the Franco-Spanish border, so that if one wanted to carve out a Basque or Catalan nation one would have to take contributions from both countries; the Bretons are unaffiliated, unless one chooses to link them to the Welsh of Britain, from whom they stemmed many centuries ago. A special situation exists for the Provençal speakers of the south of France. Once upon a time they enjoyed full cultural autonomy and had a very highly developed literature; today Provençal has sunk to the level of local *patois,* and attempts to revive it as a literary language have not had signal success. It is doubtful if any Provençal speaker entertains any separatist thought, since he knows French, uses it well, though with a slight accent, and feels himself part of the great French nation. This, however, cannot be said of all the members of the other groups. Some Basques and Bretons dream of self-determination in the Wilson style, some Niçois, Corsicans, and Alsatians would prefer union with Italy or Germany, while other Corsicans would not mind a small but separate, or at least autonomous, Corsican nation.

Similar outlines could be drawn for the Basques, Catalans, and Galicians of Spain (the Galicians of northwestern Spain have their linguistic affiliation with Portugal); for the Irish, Scots, and Welsh of the British Isles; for the French, German, and Slovenian minority groups of northern Italy; for the Italian, German, Hungarian, Albanian, and Bulgarian groups of Yugoslavia; for the Hungarians, Germans, and Bulgarians of Rumania, and so on *ad infinitum.* It would be hard to find a single country of Europe that is not endowed with one or more linguistic minorities. The map of Europe, drawn with reference to the language groups, looks like a crazy-quilt.

The situation is greatly complicated by the fact that the minority areas are seldom, if ever, simon-pure. There are regions where the language group that constitutes the country's majority appears as a minority, with the minority constituting the local majority; a political parallel is the western counties of North Carolina, a strongly Democratic State, in which the Republicans predominate. There are regions in which not one but half a dozen minorities are hopelessly intermingled. A plebiscite carried on in some of these areas would conceivably produce a plurality vote, but by no stretch of the imagination an absolute majority, which is why Wilson's self-determination ran into inequities almost as bad as those it tried to remedy.

Exception must, of course, be made for countries like Switzerland and Belgium, where language does not constitute a major barrier to national unity, but such areas are few in comparison with those where language makes the big difference. No true understanding of the European history of the last hundred years is possible without a clear realization of the linguistic issues involved.

Linguistic minority problems of the old-world type are fortunately few in the western hemisphere, although there are a few seeming parallels to the European situation, such as the French-speaking group of eastern Canada and the Spanish speakers of our southwestern States. In both cases, the parallel is supplied by the fact that the linguistic minority was on the scene before the present-day majority arrived. This element is psychologically important, because it contributes to the minority's feeling, expressed or covert, that the majority is an intruder. This is the very same feeling that leads to irredentism and similar troubles along the European frontiers, to such an extent that some nations have undertaken to solve their problems by a wholesale transplanting of populations to the side of the border where their hearts lie.

The linguistic minorities of the United States are for the most part composed of immigrant groups that arrived here after the country had been settled, and these regularly accept cultural and linguistic integration as the price they have to pay for the hospitality and opportunities they receive. By historical standards, their absorption is quick; in a century or less, the English-speaking majority absorbed the Huguenot French, the Dutch, the Delaware Swedes, the Florida Spaniards, and vast waves of later arrivals, particularly the Irish, Germans, and Scandinavians of the mid-nineteenth century. By human standards, the process is somewhat slow, since it involves more than one generation and often extends over a period of nearly a century. The process is now largely completed for the Italian, Jewish, and Slavic groups that arrived between 1880 and 1914. It is being somewhat painfully repeated for the Puerto Ricans, who are American citizens but belong to an altogether different national and linguistic culture. Despite the wishful thinking of certain anthropologists and social scientists, there is no substitute for time.

One favorable element in the absorption of immigrant groups is that they come to a country already settled, in which a predominant pattern already exists. Another is that in a very large number of cases there is an active desire to become part of the American, English-speaking culture; even where this desire does not appear in the first generation, it comes very much to life in the second. A third advantage is the large number of different language-and-

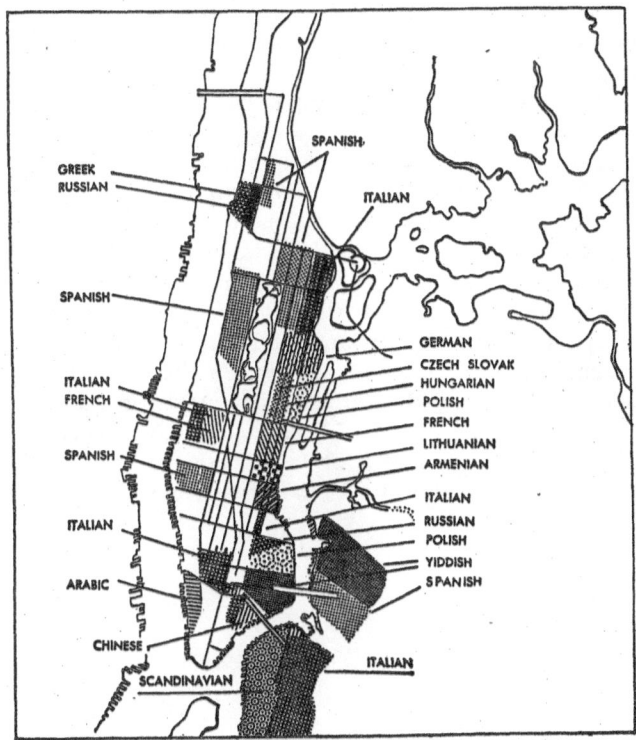

culture patterns gathered together in a single American locality, which ordinarily prevents any one of them from becoming a local majority.

New York, probably the most international city in the world, is a good example of this situation. In the early decades of this century, it was quite possible to draw a map of the city's various boroughs indicating the mother country of the bulk of the population in each district. Today, such a map would be considerably more blurred and less well defined, though one may still speak of areas that are predominantly Jewish, Italian, German, Irish or Puerto Rican.

The amalgamation of languages accompanies the disappearance of the original national consciousness, and the new English speaker tends more and more to think of himself as an American. Here perhaps we may note a basic difference between language, religion, and race in connection with national spirit. Race and color may lead to separate groupings within the national body, but do not act as a national barrier. Religion is usually retained without detriment to the national sentiment. Language, on the other hand, goes hand-in-hand with national feeling. This state of affairs is by no means universal, now or in the past; but it seems to be quite characteristic of the American culture.

language as the standard bearer
of culture

The word "culture" is used by the anthropologists in a sense quite different from the average acceptance. In their parlance, it is not a mark of superior literary or artistic achievement or even superior breeding. It is rather the sum-total of all the traditions, customs, beliefs, and ways of life of a given group of human beings. It is obvious that, in this sense, every group, however savage, undeveloped or uncivilized it may seem to us, has a culture.

To the professional anthropologist, there is no intrinsic superiority of one culture over another, just as to the professional linguist there is no intrinsic hierarchy among languages. All cultures are viewed as objective phenomena and are objectively studied. This strikes the layman as strange and, in a sense, with good reason. How is it possible to view the antics of a Papuan native as on a par with our own activities, which are the fruit of thousands of years of intellectual evolution and technological improvement?

Yet, precisely because of this known process of slow development and growth, the anthropologist is often able to prove the basic similarity of human activities. There are, in the world, groups that are quite unable to count beyond ten (which they do on their fingers), but our Roman system of numerals indicates that we originally started the same way; each figure I represents a finger, and the figure V represents the entire hand with all its fingers stretched out and the three middle ones omitted for convenience, while X is simply two outstretched hands, joined at the wrists.

People once thought of the languages of backward groups as "savage," "undeveloped" forms of speech, consisting largely of grunts and groans. While it is possible that language in general began as a series of grunts and groans, it is a fact established by the study of "backward" languages that no spoken tongue answers that description today. Most languages of uncivilized groups are, by our most severe standards, extremely complex, delicate, and ingenious pieces of machinery for the transfer of ideas. They fall behind our western languages of civilization not in their sound patterns or grammatical structures, which usually are fully adequate for all language needs, but only in their vocabularies, which reflect the objects and activities known to their speakers. Even in this department, however, two things are to be noted: 1. All languages seem to possess the machinery for vocabulary expansion, either by putting together words already in existence or by borrowing them from other languages and adapting them to their own system. 2. The objects and activities requiring names and distinctions in "backward" languages, while different from ours, are often surprisingly numerous and complicated. Where a western language will distinguish merely between two degrees of remoteness ("this" and "that"), some languages of the American Indians will distinguish between what is close to the speaker, or to the person addressed, or is removed from both, or is out of sight, or is in the past or in the future.

This study of language, in turn, casts a new light upon the claim of the anthropologists that all cultures are to be viewed independently, and without ideas of rank or hierarchy. Without delving too far into the philosophy of the matter, it may be remarked that it should be possible to segregate the objective and scientific from the aesthetic or purely practical aspects of both a culture and a language, and to view them from one standpoint or the other, according to circumstances and needs.

Language normally gives a series of near-perfect clues for the study of the culture, since it brings in all those points of view and distinctions which the speakers consider essential, along with an oral description of objects and activities known to them. Language is a complete index of racial and national characteristics. From it we can glean information concerning customs and habits, religious and superstitious beliefs, work or allied activities (hunting, fishing, agriculture, stock raising), food and drink, attitudes toward such things as sex, family life, age and etiquette, political and legal institutions, art, music and dancing, architecture or other forms of construction, attire and amusements, past history and contacts with other groups.

One curious reflection of this state of affairs appears in our own English vocabulary, which is filled with foreign words carried into English in varying adaptations. These have to be explained with reference to the customs and institutions involved, existing in the foreign culture but not in our own. A reference to a "burnoose" or a "fez," a dish of "kouss-kouss" or a cup of "arrack," a "minaret" or a "muezzin," a "jihad" or a "hadj" bring us in touch with Islamic culture and the things and doings and ideas it possesses and we don't. "Boomerangs" and "billabongs," "taboos" and "luaus," "rajahs" and "rupees," "kamikazes" and "samurais" are all words of this kind, pointing to the realities of other cultures which enter the scope of our own only by grace of the writers and the lexicographers. But, more often than we suspect, there is an interpenetration of cultures. When we speak of "tea," "coffee," "chocolate," "pajamas," words which are in our everyday vocabulary, few of us stop to think that the objects they describe were not at all times part and parcel of our culture but came to us from foreign civilizations. There are loan words and there are loan customs; both can become naturalized to the point where all realization of their alien origin is lost.

It is still an open question among linguists and anthropologists whether, once the language is established, it acts upon the speakers, constraining their behavior into certain molds and practically compelling them to think and act along certain lines. Those who sustain the affirmative of this proposition claim, for instance, that the western languages, with the careful distinctions of time expressed in their verbs ("I am coming," "I had come," "I shall come," etc.), force their speakers to have a rigid time sense, leading to a civilization in which timetables, timeclocks, classroom bells and interest on money loaned for a stated period of time play prominent roles. All this is open to question, but it furnishes an interesting topic for discussion.

On the affirmative side, there is little doubt that the language is the typical, not to say necessary, vehicle for the expression of a given culture. The English language, having lived among English speakers for centuries, has become better suited to give voice to their ideas than is Russian, or Chinese, or Hindustani. It has all the words and expressions that English speakers need, simply because it was slowly and painfully built up to express those needs. In another language, the same ideas would have to be expressed clumsily and by means of circumlocutions. Coinages like "overtime" and "overhead" are peculiar expressions of the Anglo-American capitalistic structure; it is doubtful if they can be directly rendered into Russian, which can speak of *komsomols* and *kolkhozes* where we would have to use such awkward combinations as "Communist youth organizations" or "collective farms."

Once this relationship between the language and its speakers has been established, it is difficult to deny that the established language exerts a definite influence upon the behavior of the speakers, particularly of the younger generations. But it seems equally difficult to deny that the original movement was from the speakers to the language, and that the resulting culture is primarily the product of the activities of the speakers, rather than the compulsive effect of language.

With all due respect to the anthropologists and their equalitarian philosophy, furthermore, it may be pointed out that there is another sense in which the word "culture" may legitimately be used, and that is precisely to establish a hierarchic distinction between those groups which have had a long period of material and intellectual development and those which have not. Languages that are the expression of a civilization in which there exist literacy and literature, a high standard of material production, scientific and technological progress, widespread political, social, religious, and economic organization may in this sense be said to be culturally superior, or to reflect a higher culture.

LANGUAGE VEHICLES OF THE WORLD'S MAJOR CULTURES *(next two pages)*

Western: Latin, Greek, Hebrew, English, French, Spanish, German, Italian.
Far Eastern: Chinese.
Indic: Sanskrit.
Soviet: Russian.
Islamic: Arabic.

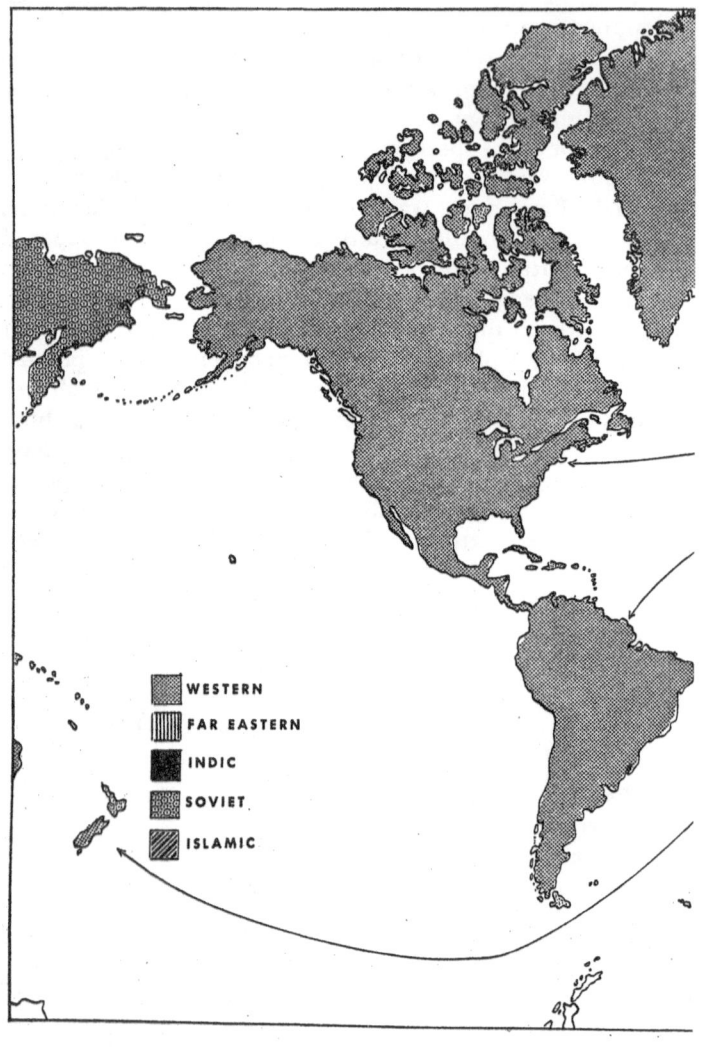

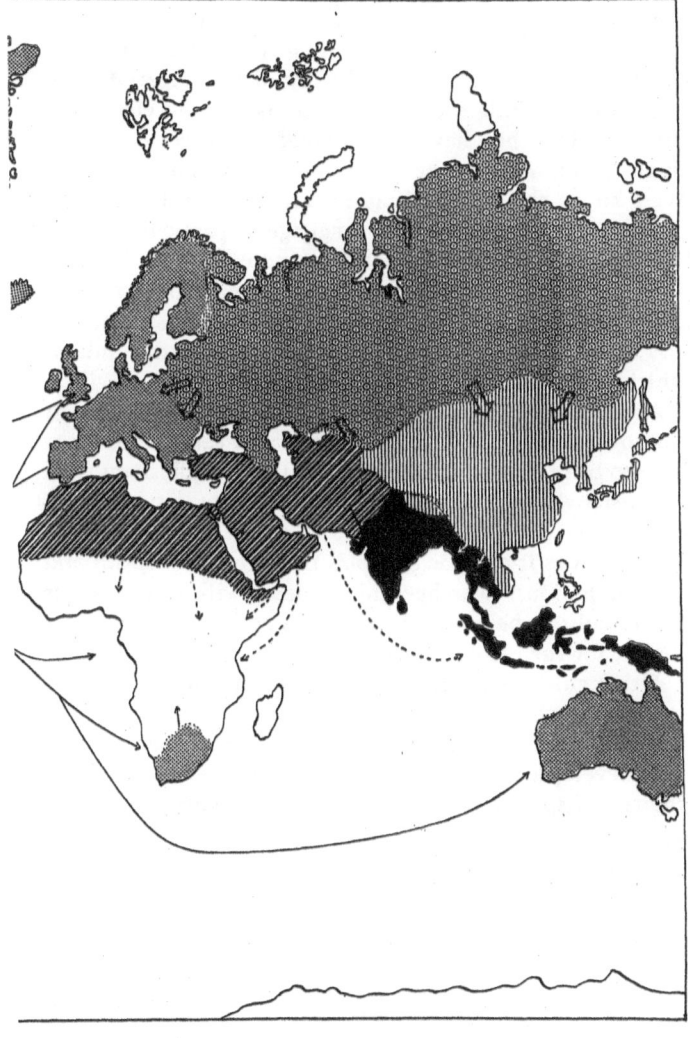

Cultural languages, in this acceptance of the word, are the tongues that have been the vehicles of western civilization—Hebrew, Latin and Greek, English, German, French, Spanish, Italian, and some of the minor languages of western Europe. While each of these bears its own characteristic imprint, they have also merged together to form a single background for the common civilization we of the West know, and this civilization cannot be said to belong to any one western nation or language in particular.

Other great cultures worthy of note are the Islamic, whose vehicle is Arabic; the Far Eastern, which was initiated by Chinese but has added to itself Japanese, Korean, and most of the cultures of southeastern Asia; the Indian, which, beginning with Sanskrit, marches on to the civilizations of modern India and Pakistan, casting its influence in part over the Far East and Indonesia. A special spot may have to be reserved for the Soviet culture, which stems from a Russian base that is largely western but tends to differentiate itself more and more from the ideology of the West even as it encroaches upon numerous European and Asiatic nations; whether this process will continue, or Soviet culture be reabsorbed into its constituent parts is a matter for the future to decide.

Other cultures are, for the time being at least, minor and secondary, whatever their anthropological interest may be. There is nothing, however, to prevent them from growing and developing, and the next few centuries may witness the rise of spectacular new cultures in various areas of the earth.

geography of language

The term "linguistic geography" has been pre-empted by the linguists for purposes of their own. They use it to indicate the study of dialects, which they carry on by sending field workers into all sections of a country with precise instructions to get from the less educated natives their way of expressing certain key words and concepts. The results are recorded in a linguistic atlas, which is a long series of maps of the country, each map devoted to a single word or expression carefully transcribed in phonetic characters as it is voiced in each of the localities polled.

The results of this method of study have been striking. They have shown that the seeming linguistic uniformity that prevails in a country like the United States or France is a figment of the imagination, and that actually there exists an almost infinite series of local dialects, as numerous as are the localities examined. If the sum-total of all local forms for each such locality transcribed on the various maps is taken as a unit, you have an accurate picture of the dialect of the locality, and no two such dialects are found to be exactly alike. The differences apply for the most part to sounds and vocabulary rather than to grammatical structure. By examining the linguistic atlas of the United States, we discover that there are at least a dozen local ways of saying "dragonfly," each totally or partly unrelated to the others. We also find that there are three or four distinct ways of pronouncing certain vowel sounds which the layman, and even Webster's dictionary, think are standardized throughout the country.

In European countries like France or Italy, where the local varieties of language are far more divergent than they are with us, the person who examines the linguistic atlas is in for some startling surprises. He discovers, for instance, that although *cheval* is the standard French word for "horse," not all Frenchmen use it by any means. Many use a similar word derived from the same popular Latin *caballus* but differently pronounced as *keval, kaval,* etc., while others use words derived from the more aristocratic Latin *equus,* which assumes such forms as *ève, ek,* etc. In the Italian atlas it will be found that instead of the standard or Florentine *ragazzo* or *fanciullo* for "boy," you may get such local popular forms as *burdel* in the North, *toso* in Venice, *pupo* in Rome, *guaglione* in Naples, and *picciotto* in Sicily. The linguistic atlas therefore turns out to be one of the very best and most useful tools for the study of language in a given area in modern times, and linguistic geography has accordingly become a highly important branch of the field of language.

But the use of the term in the sense described above leaves us without a suitable term to describe what the layman would normally understand by "linguistic geography" —the study of the distribution and arrangement of languages throughout the earth, with some consideration of the number, culture, and importance of their speakers. For this highly practical facet of language study, the terms "geolinguistics" and "geography of language" have been suggested.

The geography of language, the distribution of the world's tongues, or at least the major ones among them, together with a basic description of the people who speak them, can be studied in the present, in the past, and to some extent even in the future, by projecting present-day trends and formulating estimates. It is a subject of great practical importance under given circumstances. During World War II, the O.W.I. had a special office entitled "Media Analysis Bureau" in which many dozens of people were employed to trace the precise relationship of languages to world areas, estimate the probable number of people who could be reached with each language, and figure out the propaganda devices (printed word, radio broadcasts, direct personal approach, phonograph recordings, etc.) by which they could be made to see our side of the issues that then troubled the world. When our forces were about to seize control of French West and Equatorial Africa, it became quite important to know what native African tongues were spoken in each section of those colonies, and how the natives could be best informed of the fact that our activities were not at all directed against them, their interests, or their institutions. When the war emergency was over, there appeared, as a by-product of the Bureau's labors, several excellent works dealing with the distribution and nature of the West African languages, the newspapers and other printed media of communication existing in their area. A good deal of this material has found its way into scientific manuals and now remains at the disposal of organizations and individuals (missionary bodies, trading groups, even searchers for uranium ore) who may be interested in that region.

Of all the sociological aspects of language, the distributional one is perhaps the most important. It is basic to an understanding of the role that language plays in international affairs, the aspirations and ambitions of various cultural and national groups, whose interests very often clash, and the possible ways in which those clashing interests may be reconciled without open conflict.

To the individual, a certain amount of instruction in the geography of language is essential. It is the only way in which he can make an intelligent language choice based upon realities rather than prejudices or hearsay. It supplies him with necessary information about world issues and world movements. Coupled with information of a similar nature about religions and races, it supplies a firm basis for the understanding of the international currents that carry mankind along the course of the river of history. It also leads to a lessening of prejudice and intolerance, by presenting the facts of foreign nations and cultures in their proper perspective. If intolerance must persist after these facts are known, it at least puts the intolerance on a more rational rather than a purely emotive and ignorant plane.

The geography of language is perhaps the language angle that has most generally been neglected in all the official language study carried on in our institutions of learning. The result is that the most fanciful and incorrect answers are given to such questions as: "How many people in the world speak Russian?", "What is the language of Brazil?", "How many languages (approximately) are in spoken use throughout the world today?", "In what countries of the world may you expect to use the Spanish you are learning?", "With what language, other than Hungarian or Czech, could you expect to get along fairly well in Hungary or Czechoslovakia?"

If language is to be viewed as a sociological topic, then the geography of language is its most sociological aspect. It deals not with grammatical perfectionism, nor the laws of sound, nor literary values, but with the least common denominator of sociology—human beings.

Since population figures are in many cases uncertain and in
all cases shifting from year to year, the languages have been
arranged in groups, in order of probable numerical importance. The factor of bilingualism and plurilingualism must
be taken into account; e.g., speakers of Czech who also speak
good German are counted twice, under Czech and under
German.

OVER 50 MILLION

Chinese (all dialects)
English
Hindustani (Hindi and
    Urdu)
Spanish
Russian
German
Japanese
Indonesian (Malay)
French
Bengali
Italian
Portuguese
Arabic

40-50 MILLION

Ukrainian

30-40 MILLION

Bihari (India)
Telugu (India)

25-30 MILLION

Polish
Korean
Tamil (India)
Marathi (India)

20-25 MILLION

Turkish
Javanese
Vietnamese (Annamese)
Punjabi (India)

15-20 MILLION

Dutch (including Flemish
    and Afrikaans)
Rumanian
Gujarati (India)
Rajasthani (India)

10-15 MILLION

Kanarese (India)
Malayalam (India)

Oriya (India)
Burmese
Persian (Iranian)
Serbo-Croatian
Czech
Hungarian (Magyar)
Siamese (Thai)
Hausa (West Africa)
Lahnda (India)

5-10 MILLION

Greek
Tibetan
Swedish
Swahili (East Africa)
Bulgarian
Byelorussian (White Russian)
Yiddish
Berber
Galla (Ethiopia)
Amharic (Ethiopia)
Sundanese (Indonesia)
Catalan
Nepali (India)
Pushtu (Afghanistan)
Singhalese (Ceylon)
Bisaya (Philippines)

1-5 MILLION

Kurdish (Iran, Iraq, Turkey)
Azerbaijani (USSR, Iran)
Uzbek (USSR)

Mossi (West Africa)
Fula (Africa)
Ruanda (Africa)
Quichua (South America)
Finnish
Armenian
Luba (Africa)
Frisian (North Sea Coast)
Tagalog (Philippines)
Khmer (Cambodia)
Danish
Mandingo (Africa)
Kherwari (India)
Slovak
Norwegian
Sindhi (India)
Pahari (India)
Yoruba (Africa)
Ibo (Africa)
Zulu (South Africa)
Fanti (Africa)
Xhosa (South Africa)
Somali (East Africa)
Lithuanian
Assamese (India)
Malagasy (Madagascar)
Madurese (Indonesia)
Ilocano (Philippines)
Hebrew (Israel)
Umbundu (Africa)
Slovene (Yugoslavia)
Guaraní (South America)
Aymará (South America)

Lettish (Latvia)	Georgian (Caucasus—Soviet
Albanian	Union)
Bicol (Philippines)	Estonian
Mordvin (USSR)	Breton (northwest France)
Gondi (India)	Basque
Welsh	Balinese (Indonesia)
Romansh, including Friulian	Kashmiri (India)
(Switzerland, northeast	Sardinian
Italy)	Irish and Scots Gaelic

Note: Welsh, Romansh, Basque, Irish come so close to one million that their inclusion is justified on grounds of probable growth within the next five years.

---

what makes a language important?

Linguistically and scientifically, all languages are equally important. Practically, from the standpoint of the average individual, business organization, or government, the importance of languages shows enormous variations.

As was said on page 33, it has been estimated that there are in spoken use today throughout the world 2796 languages, exclusive of dialects. Out of this seemingly very large number, over 1000 are languages of American Indian groups, most of which do not have more than a few hundred or a few thousand speakers, and whose general cultural, commercial and political importance is low, particularly in North America. In Mexico and Central and South America the picture changes somewhat, since many of the American Indian languages are still quite alive. Quichua, the South American language once spoken by the Incas, is estimated to have some four million speakers, distributed from Ecuador to northern Argentina, with the bulk concentrated in Peru. Tupi-Guaraní is spoken in Paraguay by the majority of the population. Large groups of Aymará speakers appear in Bolivia, and in Mexico and Guatemala two or three million people still speak tongues inherited from the Aztecs, Toltecs and Mayas.

Another five hundred languages, in round numbers, are used by various African Negro tribes south of the Sahara. Among the more important are the Hausa of Nigeria and the Swahili of East Africa, which are said to number about fourteen and about eight million speakers, respectively. Many others approach or surpass a million speakers.

The islands of the Pacific, including Australia, New Zealand, and New Guinea, account for at least five hundred more languages, none of which comes near the one million mark. Five hundred more small languages appear in Asia, particularly in the southeastern portion, the Philippines, and the islands of Indonesia. Here it must be noted that the official *Bahasa Indonesia* (Indonesian Language) of the new republic is in the nature of a compromise language, devised for government purposes and incorporating most of the elements of the older Malay, which long served the area as a trade language.

Numerous other small languages appear in the Asiatic

portion of the Soviet Union, in the Near East, in North Africa, Egypt, the Sudan and Ethiopia. The truly significant languages, most of which are European or Asiatic in origin, do not exceed one hundred. Only thirteen of them, as we have seen (page 34), have fifty million or more speakers.

The question of numbers is linked with that of distribution. A language that appears in scattered areas all over the world, like English, is of greater practical value than one that is restricted to a single area, however vast that area may be. Linked in turn with distribution is the cultural prestige of the language, the way it is accepted, learned, and used by people to whom it is not native. Cultural prestige is inextricably bound up with past history, which means that certain languages live, so to speak, on accumulated capital. But history does not stand still, and new forms of cultural prestige spring up all the time. French acquired an international predominance which goes back to the days of the Crusades, when the Arabs called all Crusaders "Franks" by reason of the leading role played by the French in that world-shaking movement; later, during the Renaissance and in the Revolutionary and Napoleonic eras, France was again in the lead of Europe, both in military affairs and in literary output; this was reflected in the intellectual and diplomatic predominance of French from the seventeenth to the nineteenth century. Today, with the loss of colonial possessions and military prestige, French tends to lose some of its cultural predominance, while the slack is taken up by English on one side of the Iron Curtain, Russian on the other. German, which acquired wide distribution and international and scientific prestige in the eighteenth and nineteenth centuries, finds itself rivaled by the same contestants. Italian, a great language of both culture and trade in the Middle Ages and early Renaissance, has sunk to a secondary position by reason of its lack of military and political strength.

Some Oriental languages, once thought of little importance in a predominantly Occidental civilization, are clamoring for recognition. Two that have behind them the prestige of an ancient and widespread culture are Chinese and Arabic, but Japanese and possibly Hindustani and Indonesian may one day be in a position to advance serious claims. Spanish and Portuguese have behind them the weight of a civilization that goes back to Roman days, coupled with the factor of an ever-growing speaking population.

Industrial, commercial, and scientific factors have of late assumed great importance. They signify on the one hand the power of peaceful penetration, on the other the ability to make themselves heavily felt in modern warfare. Here English holds, at the moment, a decisive lead, but it is already being rivaled by Russian. English may at an early date have to meet competition from resurgent western and eastern tongues whose speakers are putting forth a mighty effort to forge ahead in the technological welter of twentieth-century civilization.

Widespread literacy plays an important role in the modern world, since a literate population is, on the whole, bound to be more efficient in all significant divisions than an illiterate one. The attempt to extend literacy to all of the world's peoples is proceeding at great speed and, in the main, successfully. But there is no doubt that a country like India, where between 80 and 90 percent of the population is still illiterate, is bound to find itself at a great temporary disadvantage in the face of such literacy figures

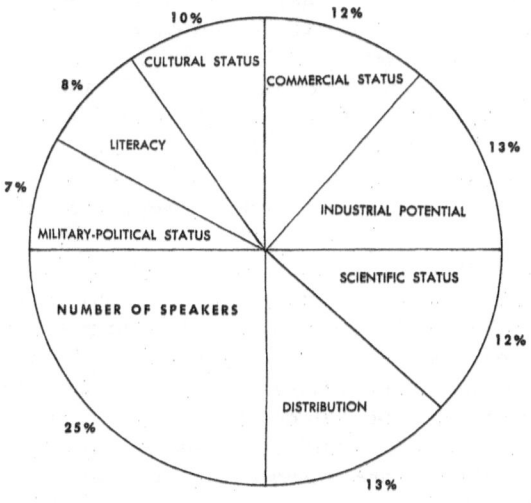

as the 95 percent of the English-speaking world or the 99 percent of Japan.

Advocates of an international language often indulge in the pastime of working out a weighted index to be applied to existing languages—so much for speaking population, so much for distribution, an allotment for cultural prestige, another for commercial importance, still another for scientific, artistic, literary, or even political maturity and advancement. Of course, a slice is reserved for military power, which has so often in the past determined the course or survival of languages.

The trouble with this game is that while some of the elements that go into the weighted index are easily evaluated on a purely objective basis (population and distribution in particular lend themselves to this treatment), the same cannot be said of the more subjective features, which often defy evaluation. A western eye and ear may prefer Italian art and music to the forms evolved in China, Japan, and India, but will the Orientals agree to such an evaluation? Political maturity is especially subject to individual judgments, while the ultimate test of military power is war, which everybody deprecates and wishes to avert, at least in words.

For what concerns the individual in his choice of a language or languages on which to concentrate, there is an easier evaluation based on the individual's own requirements and preferences. Granted that the objective factors of population and distribution are what they are, the person with scientific leanings will do well to consider primarily the languages whose scientific output most directly concerns him, while the one interested in art, music, and literature can let his tastes guide his choice. As of the present, the general scientific and technological output that appears in English, German, French, or Russian outstrips that which appears in Chinese, Arabic, or Hindustani. The sum-total of the artistic, musical and literary production of Italy, France, or Germany surpasses that of Portugal or Indonesia. For industrial and commercial production, statistics are available, and there is also the possibility of basing a choice upon the region in which one expects to carry on one's activities.

The factors that make a language important, either in the absolute or to the individual, are not altogether permanent, and it is not to be expected that they will ever become so. All that can be hoped for is that they remain stable during the lifetime of the individual.

International aspects of language

The dynamism of language is such that we may expect history to repeat itself. In the past, certain languages, having assumed preponderance for reasons of one kind or another, usually connected with physical force but occasionally of a cultural variety, have driven other tongues underground, rendered them obsolete, caused their disappearance by what might be styled inanition or starvation.

One glaring instance of such a historical process is the disappearance of Etruscan before the onset of Latin. For centuries before the appearance of Latin in historical records, Etruscan was the predominant language of central Italy, sending out colonies that extended northward to the Alps, southward to Capua and beyond, not to mention the possibility of some insular outposts in the eastern Mediterranean. When the Roman speakers of Latin appeared on the scene, they coexisted for centuries with the speakers of Etruscan, taking from them many elements of civilization, including an alphabet which the Etruscans had borrowed at an earlier period from the Greeks. Roman tradition states that at one time Rome was ruled by Tarquinian, or Etruscan, kings, whom the Romans got rid of eventually to set up a republic. Both peaceful and warlike contacts between Etruscans and Romans went on for many centuries. As the Romans and their language expanded, the civilization of Etruria seemed to wither away.

There is some likelihood that Etruscan continued in use as a spoken language during the earlier centuries of the Christian era. Eventually, the language vanished utterly and completely. The Etruscan race as such did not die out, as evidenced by the fact that its physical characteristics can still be recognized in the present-day inhabitants of Italian Umbria and Tuscany. What happened was that the original speakers of Etruscan died away and their descendants became Romanized as to customs, institutions, and, above all, language.

It is fashionable among some linguists to suppose that Etruscan traits of pronunciation may still be detected in the dialects of central Italy. Other linguists claim that the city of Rome itself fell linguistically under the spell of adjoining rural populations whose original language had been Sabine, while the purest brand of Latin spread to the regions of Etruria. This would mean that the Italian dialects of Tuscany today are the closest descendants of Latin, while the dialect of the city of Rome is a Latin diluted with Sabine and Oscan infiltrations. All this is hard to prove, but what requires no proof is that Etruscan disappeared as a living, spoken tongue, and that Latin everywhere replaced it.

In more recent times, we have seen the gradual recession and even the complete disappearance of existing languages and dialects before the drive of a more aggressive national tongue. In medieval Spain, the Leonese and Aragonese dialects, once equally important with Castilian, were crowded farther and farther back against Portuguese and Catalan until only traces of them are left today, while Castilian occupied the territory they once held. The official Francien dialect of Paris has made serious inroads into the other French dialects, both in the north and in the south of France. The Italian dialects, hardiest members of the dialect world, feel the pinch of standard literary Italian. Even in the United States, it is claimed that the southern and eastern American dialects are tending to give way be-

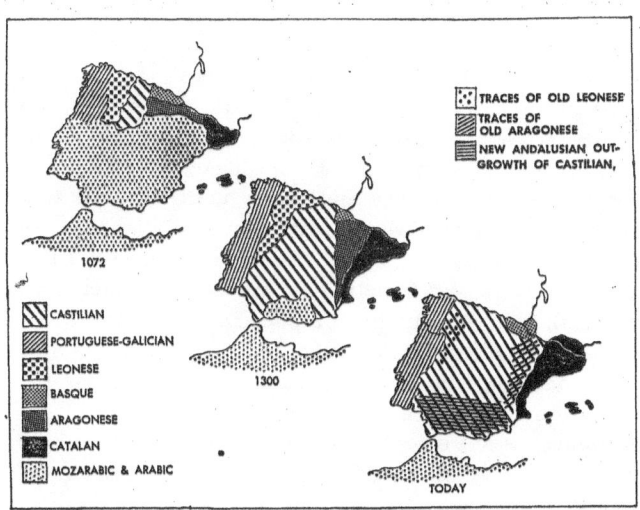

TRACES OF OLD LEONESE
TRACES OF OLD ARAGONESE
NEW ANDALUSIAN OUT- GROWTH OF CASTILIAN,

1072

CASTILIAN
PORTUGUESE-GALICIAN
LEONESE
BASQUE
ARAGONESE
CATALAN
MOZARABIC & ARABIC

1300

TODAY

EXPANSION OF CASTILIAN

As Castilian speakers take the lead in the reconquest of Spain from the Moors, their speech acquires greater prestige than that of adjoining groups (Leonese, Aragonese) and tends to squeeze them against Portuguese and Catalan. The latter, farther removed from Castilian, show greater resistance.

---

fore the expansion of Midwestern, or General American, refined and unified by movie, radio, and TV use.

All this, of course, is an example of the way in which centripetal forces take the upper hand over the natural centrifugal tendencies of language when the artificial, man-made factors of civilization gain the upper hand. In each of the cases described above, a central government, a common literary tradition, and the will to national unity have been at work. Under the circumstances, the question is whether not only the dialects, but also the smaller, less important languages will eventually be squeezed out of existence by a few large, important tongues which serve as mouthpieces for the new and larger political units that modern conditions have created. Specifically, should we expect in a more or less distant future to see such languages as Dutch and Scandinavian replaced, on their own home soil, by an international English; or Polish and Czech succumb to the Russian of the Soviet Union? Will the time come when the world's major languages will become the world's only languages?

Prophecy is not easy. Events, as they unfold, have a way of making fools of would-be prophets and speakers of oracles.

In the past, we have witnessed the disappearances described above; but history is also full of successful resistance movements. The speakers of Catalan have managed to save their language, even though the speakers of Leonese and Aragonese did not save theirs. Breton, Welsh, Scots Gaelic, Irish, Basque are all living monuments to the proposition that a language, however small and shrunken, can survive if there is a will on the part of its speakers to make it survive, even when the speakers are forced to become a part of a much larger political unit that worships at other linguistic shrines. Lithuanian, Lettish, Estonian have so far survived the pressure of Russian. Even in cases where the original language is forgotten and the language of the larger group adopted, there are striking instances of the survival of the will to rehabilitate and resuscitate the "dead" language, as proved by Hebrew and Irish.

At the same time, the power of attraction exerted by a

great national language which is the vehicle of political, military, scientific, cultural, and commercial power is undeniably similar to the force exerted by a magnet upon a piece of iron. Individuals and groups naturally gravitate toward what has prestige. The Dutch and Scandinavians may not give up their languages, but it is likely that more and more of them may get to learn English, and that more and more Czechs and Poles and Rumanians may get around to learning Russian.

Stalin once expressed the idea that the world's language picture was headed not so much toward a single international language as toward a series of regional languages that would have practically universal currency in their own areas. This idea may yet turn out to be the one closest to the truth.

Let us note, however, all the signs of linguistic nationalism that are resurgent in various areas of the world. There are also other instances where nationalism is not involved, yet a separate language, divorced from the mother speech, springs into being nevertheless. The Creole of Haiti is at present used in the Haitian literacy campaign instead of the official French, and the Melanesian pidgin English (or Neo-Melanesian, as some linguists choose to call it) is similarly used instead of official English in areas held by English-speaking powers. This is being done on the ground that it is easier for the natives to become literate in a language they habitually use than in one with which they are unfamiliar. Whether this point of view will eventually turn out to be correct remains to be seen.

Rightly or wrongly, big languages are widely viewed as carriers of imperialism, an imperialism that may be merely cultural but is nonetheless regarded with suspicion. For this point of view, history supplies abundant justification.

Languages, being standard-bearers of culture, must necessarily carry with them ideas and attitudes, points of view, and ways of life. The spreading of English to the countries of continental western Europe is accompanied by the spreading of Anglo-American customs, beliefs, and traditions. It matters little whether the language is regarded as a cause or a symptom. The link is there, as proved by the progressive Americanization of countries that until a few years ago would have regarded our mechanized living and boogie-woogie antics with amused contempt.

By the same token, it is undeniable that the spreading of the Russian tongue to the lands beyond the Iron Curtain goes side by side with the adoption of collectivistic ideas whereby men are reduced to the level of bees and ants.

Linguistic nationalism on the part of countries in danger of being swallowed up by cultural imperialisms is perhaps the best form of defense. Signs of it are on the increase everywhere, but so are signs of capitulation to the big languages. It is impossible to tell at this stage which of the two tendencies will eventually win out.

language and the world's future

It may not seem at first glance that the movement on behalf of a single international language for universal use is a compromise between the aggressive tendencies of the large languages and the resistance movements of the small ones, yet this is the way in which the international-language movement is regarded by many of its sponsors.

Speakers of small languages such as Norwegian or Finnish find themselves at a decided disadvantage. In any international gathering, public or private, their language is out of the running. They cannot seriously expect an English, or French, or Russian speaker to have learned a minor language that serves only three or four million people. They must therefore defer to the larger language, learn it, and speak it. Even if they succeed in doing so, they seldom achieve the proficiency of native speakers. This means that they find it more difficult to present their viewpoints, reply to questions, make witty repartee in case of need.

Many of them have resigned themselves to this state of affairs and have industriously proceeded to learn more English, or French, or German, or Russian, so as to be able to hold their own with the speakers of those tongues. But a good many others have said to themselves: "Why must we be in a position of perennial inferiority when we face an English or French speaker? Why must we be expected to learn their languages, when they never make an attempt to learn ours? Why can't there be a compromise language, in which we shall have equality of opportunity with them, and in which they will stumble around as much as we do, be at a loss for a word or a construction as much as we are, and be made to realize, as we constantly are, that their languages are not the only ones on earth?"

This thought, expressed or unspoken, accounts for much of the success of such constructed languages as Volapük and Esperanto in the minor countries of Europe, Asia, and Latin America. The constructed language, whatever its framework or the source of its vocabulary, has the merit of being "neutral," at least to the extent that it is not the native speech of any national group. By reason of its roots, it may be easier for some than for others, but everyone will have to make some effort to acquire it.

Against this tendency there are the objections of those who claim that constructed languages are unnatural, that they have not grown, so to speak, out of the soil, by the slow, painful process that has attended the development of the national tongues. It is a little strange that this argument should arise in this era of extensive artificiality, when the automobile replaces the horse, the movies replace the living actors on the stage, and the canned music of the radio and the juke-box replaces the living orchestra, but the argument is there. People who would like to have an international language that would do away with linguistic difficulties, interpreters, translations and all the other evils we have inherited from Babel, but at the same time dislike the idea of an "artificial" language, are then wont to advance the candidacy of living national tongues. Usually they propose the big and important ones, like English, French, or Russian. Of course, in a world of clashing imperialisms, there is not much chance that such a tongue may be adopted for international use, save by force of arms.

Other remedies that are suggested are small national tongues, like Swedish or Finnish, which cannot by any stretch of the imagination be said to be the vehicles of any imperialism; or modified national tongues, like Basic English, which would turn out to be more difficult to the natural speakers than to foreigners trying to learn them.

The idea of big zonal languages advanced by Stalin has given rise to interesting modifications. One group suggests that the world be carved indeed into four or five major linguistic zones, each of which would be dominated by one major language. Spanish, Russian, Chinese, and Hindustani are suggested for, respectively, the Atlantic community, the Soviet Empire, the Far East, and southern Asia. But it is proposed that English and French be added to each of these zones to serve the purposes of transfer from one zone to another. In actual practice, this would mean that English and French would become the true international languages, and the others, being restricted to a single zone, would eventually wither away.

It is not surprising that some people, to speed up the process, would immediately eliminate the intermediate step and would create what they call the "Bilingual World," in which English and French would serve side by side as universal media of communication, repeating to some extent the experience of Latin and Greek in antiquity.

It is to be expected that both these plans would run into opposition from the Russians and Red Chinese, who would charge western cultural imperialism, and with some reason. Without the participation of the Communist countries and the neutrals, the Anglo-French bilingual world would become simply what Stalin envisaged—a zonal language scheme for the countries of the west.

Outside of the dubious accusation that the constructed languages are artificial, there are two other drawbacks. One is that their vaunted "neutrality" is questionable, since they are almost without exception based on the classical and the western tongues, thus representing one type of culture to the exclusion of the others. The second is that there are a good many of them (certainly two hundred, and probably more), each with conflicting claims that somehow remind one of the claims of the national languages.

Without going back into the earlier languages of this type (the original ones appeared in the seventeenth century), it may be pointed out that after a period of vogue for Volapük, which was brief but intense, Esperanto came to the fore. But Esperanto was soon rivaled by all sorts of derivatives, each claiming to be an improvement on Dr. Zamenhof's original. In recent times, a good deal of noise has been made about Interlingua, a language concocted by a group of linguists who labored for long years on the usual theory—that the international language should represent a cross section of the main western tongues, with Slavic, Oriental, and other groups carefully shut out. The present duel between Esperanto and Interlingua is attended by an interesting feature: while the Esperantists envisage their language as one designed for universal spoken use, the Interlinguists prefer to regard their creation as something to serve, primarily in written form, international scientific congresses, which in their minds justifies the language's western structure and vocabulary.

The situation is further complicated by the almost total indifference to the question on the part of important international bodies, such as UN and UNESCO. In the ten or more years of its existence, UN has never deigned to cast a glance at the problem, despite the fact that its gatherings are the most glaring examples of the need for an international language.

This indifference is not shared by the world's populations, which realize to a far greater extent than their rulers that a world language would prove to be a signal boon to trade and travel, as well as to international relations and the spirit of tolerance and friendship about which so many fine words are spoken. Gallup polls conducted in various countries of the free world have indicated that at least three fourths of those consulted would favor an international tongue to be imparted to all of the world's children from the time they are in kindergarten.

This passive show of hands, however, is insufficient to solve the problem, which requires the active participation of the governments.

What we have in the meantime is the gradual extension, by natural processes, of Stalin's zonal languages, coupled with linguistic nationalism that acts as a counterpoise. Among the zonal languages, the most dynamic and expansionistic at this time are English and Russian. English extends its tentacles more and more into every corner of the free world, where it is welcomed for practical reasons rather than because of any intrinsic merit. Russian is gradually imposing itself not only over the non-Russian populations of the Soviet Union but also over the European satellites.

Chinese, traditionally an imperial language, is backed by its enormous speaking population and has resumed its historical process of penetration into eastern and southeastern Asia. Hindustani bids fair to impose itself over the hundreds of millions in India and Pakistan, but its progress is slow. Arabic retains its traditional position in the Moslem world and may acquire a new force of expansion if North Africa frees itself of French rule. Spanish and Portuguese continue to expand, not by the acquisition of new territory but because of the vast population increase in the countries of Latin America. French, German, Italian, and Japanese have all lost ground in recent years, but they are languages of hardy vitality, as they have proved in the past, and it would be an error to strike them from the books. Little can as yet be said for Indonesian, while Bengali may be swallowed up by its relative Hindustani.

*First part of the Lord's Prayer in Volapük, Spelin, Esperanto,
Ido, Latino Sine Flexione, Romanal, Nepo, Interglossa, and
Interlingua.*

VOLAPÜK: O Fat obas, kel binol in süls, paisaludomöz nem ola!
Kömomöd monargän ola! Jenomöz vil olik, äs in sül, i
su tal!

SPELIN: Pat isel, ka bi ni sieloes! Nom el zi bi santed! Klol el
zi komi! Vol el zi bi faked, kefe ni siel, efe su sium!

ESPERANTO: Patro nia, kiu estas en la ĉielo, sankta estu via
nomo; venu regeco via; estu volo via, kiel en la ĉielo, tiel
ankaŭ sur la tero.

IDO: Patro nia, qua esas en la cielo, tua nomo santigesez; tua
regno advenez; tua volo facesez quale en la cielo, tale anke
sur la tero.

LATINO SINE FLEXIONE: Patre nostro, qui es in celos, que tuo
nomine fit sanctificato; que tuo regno adveni; que tua
voluntate es facta sicut in celo et in terra.

ROMANAL: Patro nostri, qui est en cieles, sanctificat estas nomine tui, advenias regne tui, fias volite tui, sicut en ciele,
et en terre.

NEPO: Vatero nia, kotoryja estas in la njeboo; heiliga estu
nomo via; kommenu regneo via; estu volonteo via jakoe
in la njeboo ebene soe na la erdeo.

INTERGLOSSA: Na Parenta in Urani: Na dicte volo; tu Nomino
gene revero; Plus tu Crati habe accido; plus u Demo acte
harmono tu Tendo epi Geo homo in Urani.

INTERLINGUA: Nostre Patre qui es in le celos, que tu nomine
sia sanctificate; que tu regno veni; que tu voluntate sia
facite como in celo assi etiam in terra.

While all these languages attempt to be "neutral," Volapük and Spelin lean in the direction of German and Romance, with logical and synthetic word building. Nepo attempts to give representation to Slavic as well as to Germanic and Romance. Interglossa combines Latin and Greek roots with Chinese syntax. The others lean toward Latin-Romance, with Latino Sine Flexione using Latin pure and simple, but without classical endings.

5

LANGUAGES IN COMPARISON

how language affiliations
are determined

When people speak of *language families,* they do not use the term "family" in quite the same sense in which it is used genetically. The fact that people speak the same, or related, languages does not mean that there is a link of race or blood, though such may quite well be the case. Languages are acquired and cast off by their speakers, and an American or Brazilian Negro, racially related to the African Negroes of West Africa, will normally speak native-speaker English or Portuguese and have no knowledge whatsoever of the Guinean speech of his ancestors. It is therefore unscientific in the extreme to establish any link between racial origin and language, even by implication, as when people in the last century spoke of a "Mongolian" race and "Mongolian" languages.

The continuity of language is unbroken so long as there are speakers, regardless of who those speakers are. A language may be lost by the group that originally spoke it, but be acquired by a totally different group. The *language* goes on.

It was once generally believed that all languages stemmed from the original speech of Adam, differentiated in accordance with the Biblical episode of the Tower of Babel. This explanation may yet be confirmed, literally or figuratively, and all languages may someday be traced to a single common parent tongue. This, however, is not too likely.

During the Middle Ages, people who gave the matter any conscious thought (and they were not many) assumed that all the languages they knew anything about stemmed in some way or other from the Biblical Hebrew of the Old Testament. This point of view gradually changed as more languages came to light, until most linguists of the nineteenth century categorically denied that there could be any unity of origin, or monogenesis, in language. The linguists of today are not quite so sure, since they have found out more about the remarkable changes that may occur in a single language when groups of its speakers lose contact with one another.

We are today in a position to state definitely that certain languages (Latin, German, Irish, Russian, and Hindi, for example) are so linked as to betray a common origin. What we are not in a position to do is to carry the linking process still further so as to establish a connection among various larger groups, such as Indo-European, Semitic, and Ural-Altaic.

The process of establishing the link is an interesting one. At first glance, it would seem that if a considerable body of words appearing in one language is to be found in another, the connection of origin between the two languages would be established. But this fails to take into consideration two elements, one of which is perhaps trifling, but the other one of which is fundamental.

Since each language consists of hundreds of thousands of words, and since each word consists of a limited set of sounds to which a meaning has been given, it would be strange if the words did not sometimes coincide in sound and meaning by mere chance. This happens perhaps more often than we think. A glaring example of chance resemblance is English "bad" and Persian *bad*, both with the same meaning, though the words are not related in origin. With slight shifts of sound, we have Italian *donna* and Japanese *onna*, both of which mean "woman," or Russian *khoroshiy* and Japanese *yoroshii*, both of which mean "good."

But these chance similarities of sound and meaning are on a par with the chance of precisely the same bridge hand being dealt twice in an evening. Far more basic is the fact that since languages do not live in isolation but come into contact with other languages, they may borrow words and even constructions from one another. This can happen at a phenomenal rate; over half the vocabulary of many languages comes from foreign sources. English is an excellent example of this. Starting out with a basic Anglo-Saxon vocabulary that certainly did not exceed 100,000 words, English has gone on to add to itself hundreds of thousands of

Here is striking proof of the fundamental kinship of all the languages of Europe, outside of Finnish, Hungarian, Turkish, and Basque—the little numeral "three":

German—*drei*

Dutch—*drie*

Icelandic—*thrír*

French—*trois*

Spanish—*tres*

Portuguese—*três*

Italian—*tre*

Rumanian—*trei*

Swedish, Norwegian, Danish—*tre*

Russian, Serbo-Croatian, Bulgarian—*tri*

Polish—*trzy*

Czech—*tři*

Greek—*treîs*

Albanian—*tre*

Lithuanian—*trỹs*

Irish—*trí*

Welsh—*trī*

Esperanto—*tri*

BUT

Finnish—*kolme*

Hungarian—*három*

Turkish—*üç*

Basque—*hirur*

In Asia, the Indo-Iranian languages of India agree with the Indo-European tongues of Europe:

Sanskrit—*trayah*

Hindustani—*tīn*

Bengali—*tin*

But the Semitic, Dravidian, Sino-Tibetan, Khmer, Japanese-Korean, and Malayo-Polynesian do not:

(Semitic) Arabic—*thalāth*
(Dravidian) Tamil—*mŭndrŭ*   Telugu—*mŭdŭ*
(Sino-Tibetan) Chinese— *·san*   Siamese—/*săm*
  Burmese—\ *thoun*   Tibetan—sum
(Khmer or Cambodian) Khmer—*bei*
(Japanese-Korean) Japanese—*mitsu*   Korean—*seit*
(Malayo-Polynesian) Indonesian—*tiga*

---

additional words from Danish, French, Latin, Greek, and
other sources. If one were today to try to classify English on
the basis of its vocabulary alone, one would be tempted to
call it a Romance rather than a Germanic language, though
the higher frequency of occurrence of the Anglo-Saxon
words would give a clue to its true nature.

Vocabulary is therefore an uncertain criterion on which
to base language kinship, though it may be remarked that
there are certain basic words, like names of family relationship and numerals, which are rather seldom borrowed.
The best that can be said is that word similarities have to
be used with extreme caution, and the possibility that they
may have been borrowed has to be taken into account.

Present-day sound schemes normally tell nothing or next
to nothing about a language's affiliations. French and
Italian are very close in origin, yet the sound schemes of
the two languages are quite different, whereas the sound
schemes of Italian and Japanese, which are unrelated, show
striking similarities.

The only element of language that remains is the structural or grammatical, the way in which the language
changes or arranges its words to convey subsidiary meanings. Since this structural element often changes in the
course of time, it is important that we try to trace it back

to an earlier form. This is possible with some languages and not with others.

If we take modern English and compare its *grammatical* arrangement with that of Latin, we shall not be conscious of any striking similarities; but if we push English back to its original Anglo-Saxon form, it becomes evident that there is great similarity between the structure of English and Latin. The likeness, in fact, is unmistakable and can by no stretch of the imagination be attributed to mere chance. Something of the same nature occurs when we compare Hebrew and Arabic, but not when we compare Hebrew and Latin. So we are forced to the conclusion (supported also by similarity in the basic vocabulary and by a certain regular pattern appearing in the shift of sounds from one language to the other) that there is an intimate link between Latin and Anglo-Saxon, and another intimate link between Hebrew and Arabic; but no definitely provable connection between the two pairs.

Wholesale shifts of sounds in basic words are corroborating evidence. We notice, for example, that in words which neither Latin nor Anglo-Saxon is too likely to have borrowed from a foreign source, Latin shows *p* where Anglo-Saxon shows *f* (*pater*, "father"; *pedem*, "foot"; *pecus*, "fee"; *plenus*, "full"). This correspondence is proof of a genetic link even more than outright identity of sound would be, since identity could more easily be ascribed to borrowing.

Once the existence of a family relationship is established, it becomes easier to determine the precise subgroups and branches of the family. Latin and Anglo-Saxon are related, like brothers who have a common father. But Latin gave rise to direct descendants—French, Spanish, Italian, and other Romance tongues. Anglo-Saxon, on the other hand, shows even more direct links with the known ancestors of Dutch, German, and Scandinavian than it does with Latin. Therefore, within the larger group, we have two subgroups, one headed by Latin, the other by the common ancestor of Dutch, English, German, and Scandinavian. Today, French, Spanish, and Italian may be said to be brothers; the Germanic languages are likewise brothers; but since the ancestors of the Romance and of the Germanic languages were brothers, then it follows that any individual Romance language is a first cousin to any individual Germanic language; and this, quite aside from the fact that they have lived in contact with each other and have borrowed heavily from one another.

The processes described above are, of course, oversimplified; but they serve to give an idea of how languages may be grouped and affiliated and of the limits beyond which the process cannot go. In the case of languages whose past history is unknown and for which there are no historical records, like the American Indian tongues, there is little possibility of pushing them back to an earlier stage, when they may have shown similarities since lost; and the process of classification and affiliation is correspondingly more difficult. On the basis of our present knowledge, we have a dozen or more definitely established language families, clearly subdivided into subgroups, plus a very large number of languages and groups of languages for which classification is at present either impossible or only hypothetical. These families show the same discrepancies as individual languages; some are very large, others very small, some important from a practical angle, others unimportant.

From the standpoint of the individual, language classification has a corollary. Since what is known and familiar is normally easier than what is unknown and unfamiliar, there will be greater ease in acquiring a language of a group of which we already know a member. Practically, this means that if you are already acquainted with Latin or French you will have an easier time with Spanish or Italian; if you already know Hebrew, Arabic should hold no terrors for you.

language families

Among the language families of whose connections we are certain, first place in numbers and cultural importance goes to Indo-European, which includes more than half of the world's total population. The living subdivisions of the family are: 1. Indo-Iranian, covering most of the languages of northern India, as well as the main tongues of Iran, Afghanistan, and Baluchistan; about 300 million people speak languages of this branch. 2. Armenian, a language of no more than four million speakers, astride the Russian-Turkish frontier. 3. Albanian, the tongue of no more than two million people in Albania and nearby Balkan countries. 4. Balto-Slavic, subdivided into two sections, the Baltic (Lithuanian and Lettish, or Latvian; a total of no more than five million speakers), and the Slavic, which includes Russian, Ukrainian, Polish,

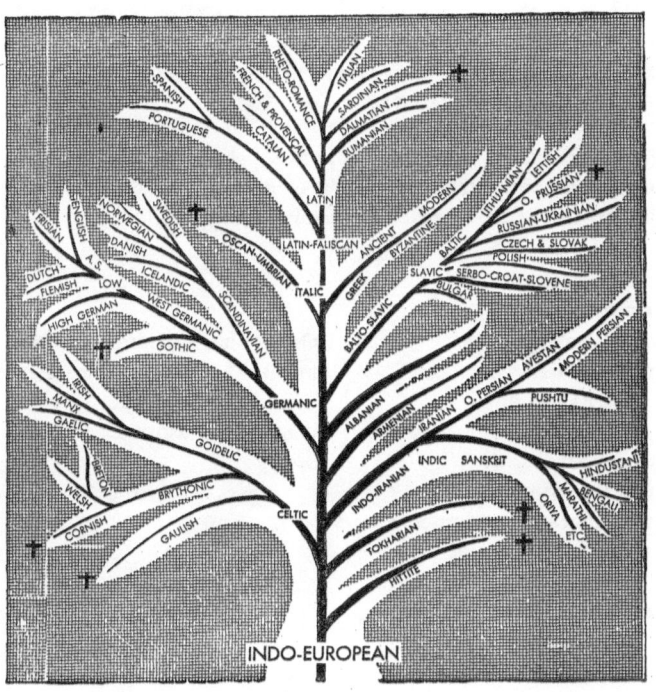

INDO-EUROPEAN

THE INDO-EUROPEAN FAMILY TREE

Crosses indicate extinct branches and languages. It is probable that numerous other languages of antiquity belonged to the Indo-European family. The eight existing branches are Indo-Iranian, Armenian, Albanian, Balto-Slavic, Greek, Italic-Romance, Germanic, Celtic.

(Asterisks placed before the Indo-European roots indicate that
the forms reconstructed from a comparison of attested languages are to be regarded as purely hypothetical.)

SANSKRIT mātár-
AVESTAN mātar-
GREEK mḗtēr, mā́tēr   On the basis of these attested
LATIN māter   forms, the "mother" root of
ARMENIAN mair   the Indo-European parent
ALBANIAN motrë   language is assumed to have
OLD IRISH māthir   been
OLD SLAVIC matere
OLD HIGH GERMAN muoter   * mā́tēr-
ANGLO-SAXON mōdor

SANSKRIT dáśa
AVESTAN dasa
GREEK déka   On the basis of these attested
LATIN decem   forms, the "ten" root of the
ARMENIAN tasn   Indo-European parent lan-
OLD IRISH deich   guage is assumed to have been
GOTHIC taíhun
ENGLISH ten   * dek̂m-
GERMAN zehn

GREEK kardía
LATIN cord-   On the basis of these attested
ARMENIAN sirt   forms, the "heart" root of the
OLD IRISH cride   Indo-European parent lan-

LITHUANIAN širdìs
OLD SLAVIC srъd'ce
GOTHIC haírto
GERMAN Herz

guage is assumed to have been

* k̂erd-

SANSKRIT kravís
GREEK kréas
LATIN cruor, crúdus
LITHUANIAN kraũjas
OLD SLAVIC krъv'
RUSSIAN krov'
OLD HIGH GERMAN hrō
ANGLO-SAXON hrā
ENGLISH raw

On the basis of these attested forms, it is assumed that there was in the Indo-European parent language a root
* kreu-
which could assume different, though related, meanings in all these languages: "blood," as in Russian; "meat," as in Greek; "raw," as in English. Note the original relationship between the native English "raw" and the "crude" borrowed by English from Latin.

Czech, Slovak, Serbo-Croatian, Slovenian and Bulgarian, with between 200 and 250 million speakers. 5. Greek, the present-day language of Greece and adjacent areas, with no more than ten million speakers. 6. Italic or Romance, including French, Spanish, Portuguese, Italian, and Rumanian, with well over 300 million speakers. 7. Germanic, including English, German, Dutch, and the Scandinavian tongues (Swedish, Norwegian, Danish, Icelandic), with a total of nearly 400 million speakers. 8. Celtic, including Irish, Scots Gaelic, Welsh, and Breton, with a total of perhaps five million speakers.

The Indo-European languages seem to have originated around the shores of the Baltic and to have spread out fanwise to the south, southeast, and southwest. Their parental name, Indo-European, indicates the major localities where they are spoken. They cover not only most of Europe and vast expanses of southern Asia, but also, as languages of migration, most of the western hemisphere, Australia, New Zealand, South Africa, and, as colonizing languages, other regions of the earth.

They have been and are the vehicles of western culture, though with a considerable admixture from another language family, the Semitic. In their Indo-Iranian branch, they are also the vehicle of the culture of India, and in their Slavic branch, of the Soviet culture (if we wish to view this as separate from the culture of the West). Indo-European is also the family of languages concerning which the greatest amount of information is at our disposal, though in this respect the Semitic family rivals it.

The links among the Indo-European languages are indisputable. Some possibility of connection appears for them as a group, on the one hand with the Semitic-Hamitic family, on the other with Ural-Altaic.

First to appear chronologically, and vying with Indo-European for what concerns the amount of historical information available, is the Semitic-Hamitic family, whose members cover North Africa, the East African coast down to the southern borders of Somaliland, the Near East, and the Arabian Peninsula. The present-day total number of speakers is in the vicinity of 100 million. The main branches are: 1. Semitic, subdivided into Northern, represented by Hebrew, and Southern, represented by Arabic and several tongues of Ethiopia (including Amharic, the country's official language). 2. Hamitic, subdivided into:

a. Lybico-Berber (Kabile, Shilh, Tuareg, and other languages of North Africa and the Sahara). *b.* Kushitic (Somali, Galla, and other East African and Ethiopian tongues). *c.* Coptic, today merely a liturgical language, derived from ancient Egyptian.

Fewer than 100 million people speak Ural-Altaic tongues, which extend across northern Asia from the Pacific to the Urals and have extensive spearheads in Europe, of which the best-known are Finnish, Hungarian, and Turkish. But the Ural-Altaic family is one concerning whose unity there is doubt. If this unity is rejected, we must postulate two separate families, Uralic (or Finno-Ugric) and Altaic. The Uralic, or Finno-Ugric, languages include Finnish, Estonian, Lapp, several tongues of northeastern European Russia, Hungarian, and some groups of Siberian tongues. The Altaic tongues include Tungus or Manchu; Mongol; and Turkish and allied languages, spoken by the Tatars, Turkomans, and Kirghiz.

The fourth language family is again subject to doubt. It is the Japanese-Korean, which some linguists prefer to view as two separate families. Japanese has nearly 100 million speakers, while Korean has over 30 million.

The Sino-Tibetan languages of southeastern Asia are second only to the Indo-European in number of speakers, of which they have probably over 600 million. The subdivision most commonly made for these languages is 1, Chinese-Thai and 2, Tibetan-Burmese. Doubt attaches to the classification of the languages of Indochina, some of which, like Vietnamese (or Annamese) seem to show links with Sino-Tibetan.

In southern India is a language family with about 100 million speakers, called Dravidian. The languages of this family were probably native to all or most of India before

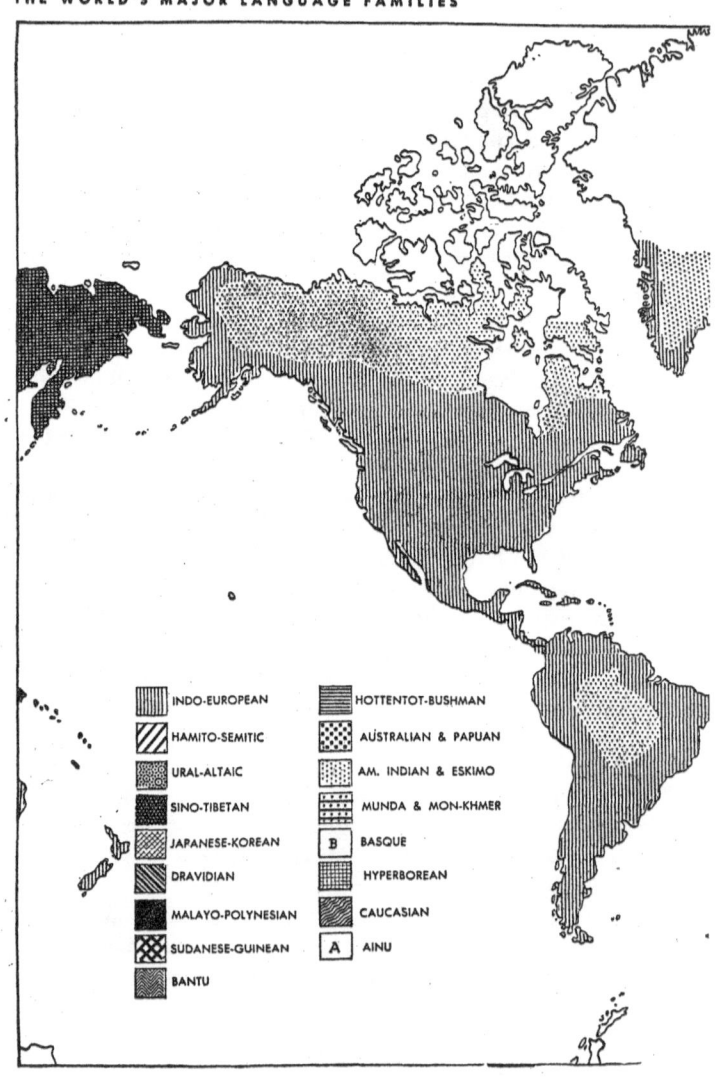

INDO-EUROPEAN

HAMITO-SEMITIC

URAL-ALTAIC

SINO-TIBETAN

JAPANESE-KOREAN

DRAVIDIAN

MALAYO-POLYNESIAN

SUDANESE-GUINEAN

BANTU

HOTTENTOT-BUSHMAN

AUSTRALIAN & PAPUAN

AM. INDIAN & ESKIMO

MUNDA & MON-KHMER

B   BASQUE

HYPERBOREAN

CAUCASIAN

A   AINU

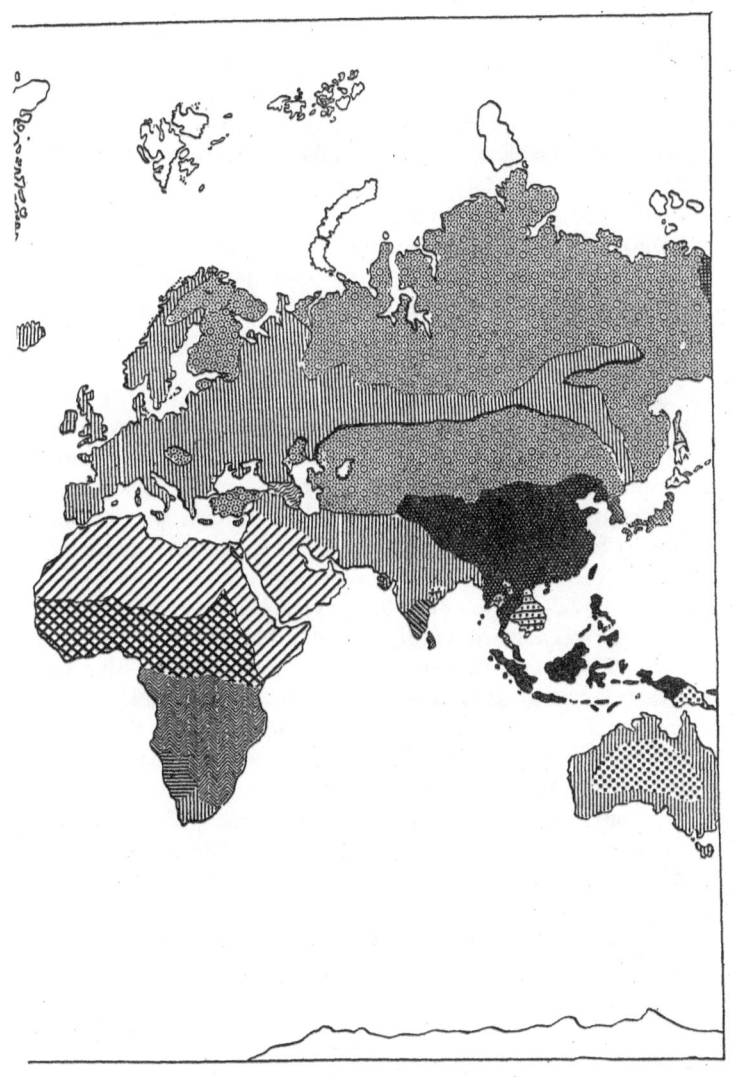

the coming of the Indo-European speakers who now occupy the northern portion of the Indian peninsula. Among the chief languages of the Dravidian group are Tamil and Telugu.

The Malayo-Polynesian family occupies the Malay Peninsula but is otherwise insular, covering Indonesia, the Philippines, Madagascar, New Zealand, and practically all the islands of the Pacific with the exception of Australia, Tasmania, and the interior of New Guinea. The speakers number between 100 and 120 million. The branches, which are named perhaps more on a geographical than a linguistic basis, are Indonesian, Melanesian, Micronesian, and Polynesian.

In Africa south of the Sahara and west of Ethiopia and Somaliland, our yet imperfect information indicates the existence of at least three separate language families, whose ultimate kinship is doubtful. The Sudano-Guinean languages run in a broad band from the southern edge of the Sahara to the point where the continent narrows south of the Gulf of Guinea. The narrower portion of Africa is occupied by languages of the Bantu group, save that in southwest Africa a third family, the Hottentot-Bushman, appears. The total number of speakers of these three African Negro language groups is in the vicinity of 130 million.

Classification becomes extremely difficult when we come to the native languages of the American and Australian continents. For the former, estimates vary from about 70 to about 120 different language families, while for Australia, Tasmania, and the interior of New Guinea the most reliable estimates (by languages rather than by families) indicate over 230.

Smaller groups for which no affiliation can be found are the Caucasian family of the Soviet Union, with two or

NUMBER OF EXISTING SPOKEN LANGUAGES IN EACH LANGUAGE FAMILY

Indo-European	132	Eskimo-Aleut	24
Semito-Hamitic	46	Caucasian	26
Ural-Altaic	66	Near-Eastern or Asianic	29
Japanese-Korean	2	Hyperborean or	
Sino-Tibetan	115	Paleo-Asiatic	12
Malayo-Polynesian	263	Burushaskī	1
Dravidian	26	Andamanese	12
Sudanese-Guinean	435	La-Ti	1
Bantu	83	Austroasiatic	
Hottentot-Bushman	6	(Mon-Khmer, Anna-	
American Indian	1230	mese, Munda)	52
(351 in North America; 96		Papuan	132
in Mexico and Central		Australian	96
America; 783 in Antilles		Tasmanian	5
and South America)		Ibero-Basque	2

TOTAL 2796

three million speakers and about 26 separate tongues; the Basque of the Pyrenees, with approximately one million speakers; the Ainu of the Japanese island of Hokkaido, with a few thousand speakers belonging to a mysterious white race; the Mon-Khmer of Cambodia and nearby regions; the Munda of India and Baluchistan; the so-called Hyperborean or Paleo-Asiatic tongues of Kamchatka, which may or may not be linked with the Eskimo-Aleut languages of Alaska, northern Canada, and Greenland.

The two factors that show extreme variation are the number of speakers of each family and group, and the

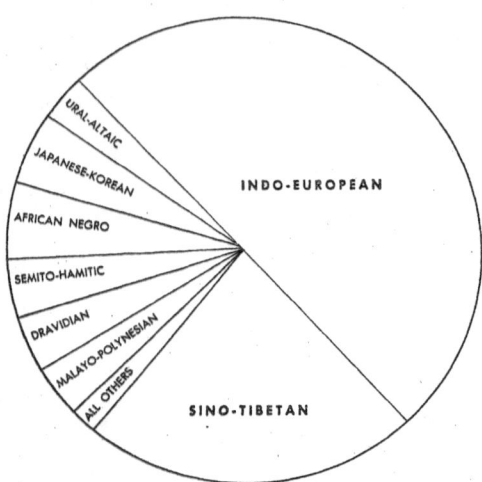

The pie chart shows segments labeled:
URAL-ALTAIC, JAPANESE-KOREAN, AFRICAN NEGRO, SEMITO-HAMITIC, DRAVIDIAN, MALAYO-POLYNESIAN, ALL OTHERS, INDO-EUROPEAN, SINO-TIBETAN

NUMERICAL DISTRIBUTION OF WORLD POPULATION AMONG LANGUAGE FAMILIES

	MILLIONS OF SPEAKERS		MILLIONS OF SPEAKERS
Indo-European	1300	Malayo-Polynesian	100
Sino-Tibetan	600	Ural-Altaic	90
Japanese-Korean	130	Annamese,	
African Negro (includ-		Mon-Khmer,	
ing Bantu, Sudano-		Munda	30
Guinean, Hottentot-		American Indian	15
Bushman)	130	Caucasian	2
Semito-Hamitic	100	Basque	1
Dravidian	100	Others	2

		Total	2600

("All others" in chart total 50 and are: Annamese, etc., American Indian, Caucasian, Basque, others.)

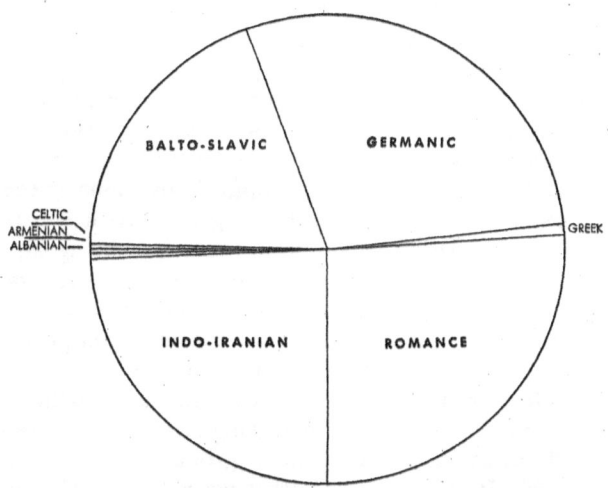

NUMERICAL DISTRIBUTION OF INDO-EUROPEAN SPEAKERS

	MILLIONS OF SPEAKERS		MILLIONS OF SPEAKERS
Germanic	380	Greek	10
Romance	340	Celtic	4
Indo-Iranian	310	Armenian	4
Balto-Slavic	250	Albanian	2
		Total	1300

amount of historical and other information available to us in connection with each group. This information is fairly satisfactory for Indo-European and Semito-Hamitic, less so for Ural-Altaic, Sino-Tibetan, Japanese-Korean, and Dravidian, quite scant for Malayo-Polynesian and the African Negro and American Indian groups, almost nonexistent for the Australian and Papuan languages. While it is true that more information of a descriptive type is being supplied to us all the time through the efforts of linguists, explorers and missionaries, the lack of historical records concerning the past state of many of these languages proves a mighty barrier to classification. It is quite possible that if such information were available all around, we might be able to reduce the thousand or so languages of the American Indians to half a dozen main groups, or even to a single stock. It is also possible that we would be able to establish definitely the links, now tantalizingly envisaged, between some of our best-known families, and thereby re-establish the Biblical dream of the time when all men were of one language and one speech.

But this is not very likely to happen, and the chances are that we must rest content with the knowledge now at our disposal, eked out, perhaps, by further research which is bound continually to run into the law of diminishing returns.

Indo-European languages, in their early stages, are universally flexional; this means that they work on a system of roots, which are more or less fixed, and endings, which are added to the roots to convey additional notions, like the English plural -*s*, but are not separate words in themselves. In addition to endings, there may also be pre-fixes, as when we speak of "de-hydration" or "un-becoming." The root, which may assume different patterns, very often runs consonant-vowel-consonant or consonant group-vowel-consonant. While the consonants of the root do not usually change, a change in the vowel is possible (English "sing-sang-sung"). Because of the fact that endings are used, and that there is a separate pattern of endings for various parts of speech, it is easy to divide up words of an Indo-European language into parts of speech: nouns, adjectives, pronouns, verbs, adverbs. To put it another way, the parts of speech reveal themselves by their behavior and the sort of endings and other changes they take on. In nouns, adjectives, and pronouns, the endings and internal vowel changes also indicate number (singular or plural), gender (masculine, feminine, or neuter), and case (nominative or subject, genitive or possessive, dative or indirect object, accusative or direct object, etc.). In verbs the endings show number, person (first or speaker, second or person addressed, third or someone else), tense (present, past, future, etc.), mood (real or indicative, hypothetical or subjunctive, direct command, or imperative, etc.), voice (active, where the subject performs the action; passive, where the subject receives the action, etc.).

This basic grammatical structure appears in all Indo-European languages to some extent, and the farther back we go in history the more clear and unmistakable it becomes. The earliest Indo-European languages on record—Sanskrit, which appears around 2000 B.C., Greek, from about 800 B.C., and Latin, from around 500 B.C.—all display it clearly. So do other early languages of the group, like Gothic (400 A.D.), Old Slavonic (900 A.D.), Anglo-Saxon, Old High German, Old Irish.

A relatively modern tendency that appears in some but not all Indo-European languages is to discard or reduce part of the flexional apparatus and rely instead upon word order and auxiliaries to make meanings clear. This process has gone a long way in English, where we are left with relatively few of the endings of ancestral Anglo-Saxon. The Romance languages have done the same to quite a degree for what concerns nouns and adjectives, but comparatively little for what concerns pronouns and verbs. The Slavic languages, except for Bulgarian, have had very little to do with this form of change.

If we examine the structure of a Semitic language, like Hebrew or Arabic, we find that it resembles Indo-European in some respects. It divides up its parts of speech into recognizable nouns, adjectives, verbs, and it has the concepts of number, person, gender, and case. (The genders, however, are only masculine and feminine, and the cases are only three instead of the eight that are clearly identifiable in early Indo-European.) The functioning of Semitic roots and endings is different. Instead of consisting of both consonants and vowels, the Semitic root has three consonants and no vowels. The three consonants are unchanging, while vowels may arrange themselves before the first consonant, between the first and second, or the second and third, or after the third, to provide all the accessory notions of gender, number, case, etc. which may be required. If we take the Arabic root KTB, which conveys the basic notion of "write," we find *KaTaBa* meaning "he has written," *KuTiBa* meaning "it has been written," *yaKTuBu* meaning "he will write," *'aKTaBa* meaning "he has made someone write," *KiTaBun* meaning "book" or "writing," *KāTiBun* meaning "writer." A better comparison than with English will appear if we take Latin: *SCRIB-ere*, "to write," *SCRIP-sit*, "he has written," *SCRIB-tum*, "written," *SCRIB-et*, "he will write," *SCRIB-itur*, "it is written," *SCRIP-tor*, "writer." The Latin root *SCRIB-* or *SCRIP-* (depending on the sound that follows) does not change but takes on endings; the Arabic KTB takes on not only endings but also vowel infixes and prefixes.

Uralic and Altaic languages such as Finnish, Hungarian, and Turkish have invariable roots which take no prefixes but to which a long string of suffixes may be added to convey all sorts of side notions, as in Turkish *AT*, "horse," *AT-ım*, "my horse," *AT-larım*, "my horses" (literally "horse-s-my"). From a verb root like *SEV*, "love," Turkish can go on to long combinations like *SEV-dir-eme-mek*, "not to cause to love." Hungarian *HÁZ*, "house," leads to *HAZ-ak-ban*, "in the houses" (literally "house-s-in").

The languages of these groups also show a principle called vowel harmony, whereby, if the root contains a vowel pronounced in the front of the mouth, like *i* or *e*, all suffixes must show a front vowel, while if the vowel of the root is pronounced in the back of the mouth, like *a, o,* or *u*, the suffixes must all bear back vowels. There are all sorts of modifications of this system, but basically it means

BASQUE: ILLUSTRATION OF POLYSYNTHETISM
ponet-ekila-ko-are-kin
cap   with the of with ("with the one who has the cap")
gizon (man)
gizona (man-the)
gizonagandik (man-the-for: for the man)
gizonak (man-the-s: the men)
gizonakaz (man-the-s-with: with the men)

MALAY: PLURAL BY REPETITION: SAMPLE OF WORD ORDER
orang (man)
orang orang (men)
Orang ini bukan raja kami.
Man this not king us. ("This man is not our king.")

---

that all suffixes must come in at least two shifts, to harmo-
nize with at least two possible classes of root vowels; the
Hungarian *HÁZ-ak-ban*, "in the houses," is paralleled by
KEZ-ek-ben, "in the hands." It may also be noted that these
languages, while they have concepts of grammatical number, case, and person, have no concept of grammatical gender, so that a distinction of masculine, feminine, and
neuter is meaningless. Japanese and Korean have at times
been suspected of being linked with Uralic and Altaic.
Since a brief description of Japanese appears in the next
chapter, this point may be held in abeyance.

The languages of the Sino-Tibetan family, of which the
most important is Chinese. have in common an invariable

URAL-ALTAIC: ILLUSTRATION OF VOWEL HARMONY

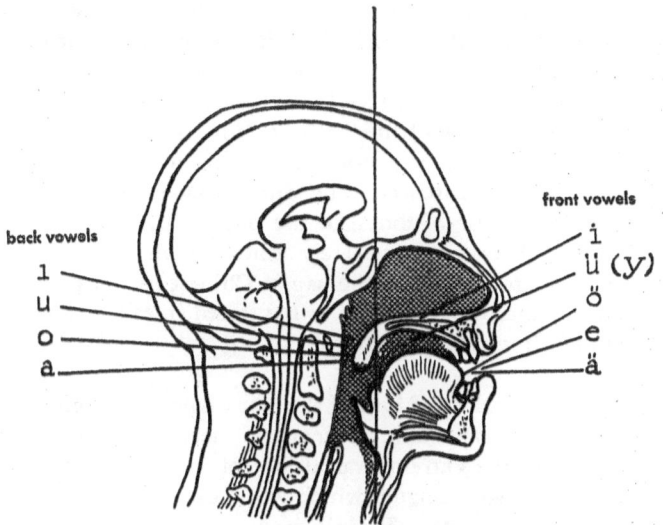

back vowels

ı
u
o
a

front vowels

i
ü (y)
ö
e
ä

Hungarian: A tarkatollú madarak holnaputàn | mind seregestül dél felé repülnek. ("The birds of motley-colored feathers will fly, tomorrow, all in a group, toward the south.")

Finnish: Antakaa ruokaa | tälle köyhälle miehelle. ("Give food to this poor man.")

Turkish: Odaları bana | gösteriniz. ("Let me see the rooms.") Paramı | nerede değiştire bilirim? ("Where can I get my money changed?")

root of one syllable (though there seems to be evidence that this was not always so). No endings can be added to this root, and no changes can be made in it (this is true of Chinese, but not altogether true of other members of the group). The words are not divided into easily identifiable parts of speech, as they are, by reason of their flexions, in Indo-European, Semitic, or Ural-Altaic; rather they assume the same unchanging form which appears in some English words ("*mail* this letter," where "mail" is a verb; "put this letter in the *mail*," where it is a noun; "put it in the *mail*box," where it is an adjective; or "I am getting *up*"; "I am going *up* the river"; "I'll *up* you five dollars"; "the *ups* and downs of life," where "up" is an adverb, a preposition, a verb, or a noun, according to its use and position in the sentence). The Sino-Tibetan languages, however, make use of tones, or the pitch of the voice, to distinguish between completely different meanings of words that are otherwise the same. Chinese *fu* may, according to the tone in which it is uttered, mean "man," "fortune," "prefecture," or "rich."

These illustrations of four of the many language families and language structures in existence will serve to give some indication of the extreme variability of language. There are African Negro tongues which work almost exclusively with prefixes (compare Swahili *m-thu m-zuri*, "handsome man," *wa-thu wa-zuri*, "handsome men," with Spanish *hombre hermoso, hombres hermosos*). Some American Indian and Eskimo languages combine what to us would be half a dozen different words into a single word-sentence, in which separate elements are identifiable to some extent but could not be used in isolation (Oneida *g-nagla-sl-i-zak-s*, "I am looking for a village," where *g-* conveys the idea of "I," *nagla* means "living," *sl* adds the force of a noun to *nagla*, thereby giving it the notion of "village," *i* is a verbal prefix indicating that *zak* conveys a verbal idea, "to look for," and *s* is the sign of continued action).

There is enormous range in the field of what individual languages consider essential for the expression of thought, and we are still in the process of discovering new language forms and language groupings. The main, significant language families, however, are by now known. It is interesting to note that of the world's thirteen languages with over fifty million speakers, no fewer than nine belong to the Indo-European classification (English, French, Spanish, German, Italian, Portuguese, Russian, Hindustani, Bengali). The Semito-Hamitic, Sino-Tibetan, Japanese-Korean, and Malayo-Polynesian families have one such language apiece (Arabic, Chinese, Japanese, Indonesian).

some typical language structures

Latin

Latin is a typical Indo-European language of the older, more archaic type. The parts of speech are carefully distinguished in Latin. Nouns, pronouns, adjectives, verbs, and adverbs are characterized by unmistakable endings. The nouns, divided into different declensional types, are masculine, feminine, or neuter. Six cases appear out of the eight that seem to have been original with Indo-European: nominative, genitive, dative, accusative, vocative (the case of direct address; but this has almost everywhere the same form as the nominative), and ablative, a case that is normally translated by "in," "by," "from," "with," and various other prepositions. Prepositions appear in Latin to a lesser degree than in English, since several of them are replaced by the mere case ending, and they may be used only with the accusative and ablative cases. (An older stage of Indo-European is shown by Sanskrit, which has eight cases, including instrumental, or by-with case, locative, or place-in-which case, and ablative, or place-from-which or separation case; in Sanskrit, the words that later appear as prepositions are used generally only as prefixes of verbs.)

Latin adjectives, appearing in two major declensional schemes, agree. with the noun and show number, gender, and case. The pronouns, by their form, indicate number, person, case, and occasionally gender. The verbs are divided into four major conjugations, with six indicative and four subjunctive tenses, a present and a future imperative, and numerous participles and kindred forms, which partake of the nature of both verb and adjective, or both verb and noun. Two voices, active and passive, appear. While person, number, tense, mood, and voice are normally shown by endings, there is in the passive a beginning of the system of auxiliaries which later becomes so common in the modern languages. Adjectives and adverbs show degree by means of endings.

The word order of Latin is rather loose, being designed to show emphasis rather than the relation between words. As Latin veers toward the Romance languages in the centuries following the fall of the Roman Empire, the word order becomes more and more fixed, while the system of case endings dwindles down in the direction of the single case now used by the major Romance languages. At the same time, there is an increasing use of prepositions, along with a growing use of auxiliaries in connection with verbs. Adjectives and adverbs show degree by the use of separate words rather than by endings.

The oldest sample of Latin, from the 5th century B.C., is the Praenestine Fibula. The inscription means: "Manius made me for Numerius."

Manios med fhefhaked Numasioi.

Manius me fecit Numerio.   (*This is how the same sentence would have appeared in classical Latin, about the time of Christ.*)

Maniu me fece per Numeriu.   (*Reconstructed Vulgar Latin of Italy, 7th century* A.D.)

Manio mi fece per Numerio. (*Modern Italian.*)

Another inscription, this from the year 746 A.D., when Vulgar Latin was beginning to turn into Italian, means: "On one side runs public highway number fifteen."

Ab uno latere decurrit via publica decima quinta. (*Reconstruction in classical Latin.*)

De uno latum decorre via publica nomero quindeci. (*Actual 746 inscription.*)

Da un lato corre la via pubblica numero quindici. (*Modern Italian.*)

Pater et filius mortui sunt. (*Classical Latin;* "The father and son died.")

Illu patre et illu filiu sun morti. (*Vulgar Latin of Italy, reconstructed.*)
Il padre ed il figlio sono morti. (*Modern Italian.*)

Illu patre et illu filiu sun mortos. (*Vulgar Latin of Spain, reconstructed.*)
El padre y el fijo son muertos. (*12th-century Spanish.*)
El padre y el hijo han muerto. (*Modern Spanish.*)
O pai e o filho têm morrido. (*Modern Portuguese.*)

Illi pater et illi filius sunt morti. (*Vulgar Latin of Gaul, reconstructed.*)
Li pedre(s) et li fils sunt mort. (*12th-century French.*)
Le père et le fils sont morts. (*Modern French.*)

Fratres non habeo. (*Classical Latin;* "I have no brothers.")
Non aio fratelli. (*Vulgar Latin of Italy, reconstructed.*)
Non ho (aggio) fratelli. (*Modern Italian.*)

Non aio germanos. (*Vulgar Latin of Spain, reconstructed.*)
Non he iermanos. (*12th-century Spanish.*)
No tengo hermanos. (*Modern Spanish.*)
Não tenho irmãos. (*Modern Portuguese.*)

Non aio fratres. (*Vulgar Latin of Gaul, reconstructed.*)
Nen ai fredres. (*12th-century French.*)
Je n'ai pas de frères. (*Modern French.*)

Fortior est bos equo. (*Classical Latin;* "The ox is stronger than the horse.")

Bovis est plus (magis) fortis quam caballus. *(Slangy Latin of classical period.)*

Illu bove e plu forte ca illu cavallu. *(Vulgar Latin of Italy, reconstructed.)*

Il bove è più forte che il cavallo. *(Modern Italian.)*

Illu boe es mais forte ke illu caballu. *(Vulgar Latin of Spain, reconstructed.)*

El buey es más fuerte que el caballo. *(Modern Spanish.)*

Illi bos est plus fortis ka illi caballus. *(Vulgar Latin of Gaul, reconstructed.)*

Li bues est plus forz que li chevalz. *(12th-century French.)*

Le boeuf est plus fort que le cheval. *(Modern French.)*

Bovis ille est magis talis de quantum caballus ille.
(Vulgar Latin of Dacia, the modern Rumania, reconstructed.)

Boul este mai tare de cât calul. *(Modern Rumanian.)*

Russian

Russian is a modern Indo-European language that still shows a great deal of the original Indo-European structure. As in Latin, there are no articles. Nouns, adjectives, and pronouns show gender, number, and case to approximately the same degree as in Latin, with separate declensional schemes for the nouns, and agreement of the adjective with the noun. Of the eight original Indo-European cases, Russian discards the ablative but retains instrumental and locative. Prepositions may appear with all the cases except nominative and vocative, and are abundantly used to reinforce the meaning of the case endings. The verb shows poverty of tenses (only present, past, and future appear) but retains the feature of aspect, which marks the action of the verb as complete or incomplete. Person and number are indicated by the verb ending, but the subject pronoun is generally used as well, something that does not normally occur in Latin or the older languages. There is a wealth of participial forms which often replace subordinate clauses.

The word order of Russian is not as free as that of Latin, but is somewhat freer than that of English.

SAMPLES OF RUSSIAN STRUCTURE

ЕСТЬ ЛИ У ВАС РУБЛЬ? (*Yest' li u Vas rubl'?*)
Is ? by you ruble? (Do you have a ruble?)

ОН УМНЕЕ МЕНЯ. (*On umnyeye menya.*)
He intelligenter of-me. (He is more intelligent than I.)

МНЕ ХОЧЕТСЯ ПИТЬ. (*Mnye khochetsya pit'.*)
To-me wants-itself to-drink. (I am thirsty.)

IMPERFECTIVE VERB	PERFECTIVE VERB
ПИСАТЬ (*pisat'*), "to be writing."	НАПИСАТЬ (*napisat'*), "to write" (once, and be through).
Я ПИШУ (*ya pishu*), "I am writing."	Я НАПИШУ (*ya napishu*), "I shall write" (once, and be through).
Я ПИСАЛ (*ya pisal*), "I was writing."	Я НАПИСАЛ (*ya napisal*), "I wrote" (and got through).

Я БУДУ ПИСАТЬ *(ya budu pisat')*, "I shall be writing." The perfective form of the verb has a tense which is present in form but future in meaning; see above.

Я ГОВОРЮ *(ya govoryu)*, "I am speaking."

Я ГОВОРИЛ *(ya govoril)*, "I was speaking"; literally, "I spoken"; the past tense is merely a past participle, declined like an adjective and agreeing with the subject; a woman would say ГОВОРИЛА *(govorila)*.

Я БУДУ ГОВОРИТЬ *(ya budu govorit')*, "I shall be speaking"; literally, "I shall-be to-speak"; the future tense consists of a form derived from "to be" plus the infinitive.

USE OF CASES

ОФИЦЕР ЗДЕСЬ *(ofitsyer zdyes')*, "The officer is here." Nominative case; note omission of "the" and "is."

Я ВИЖУ КАРАНДАШ ОФИЦЕРА *(ya vizhu karandash ofitsyera)*, "I see the pencil of the officer." Genitive case.

Я ВИЖУ ОФИЦЕРА *(ya vizhu ofitsyera)*, "I see the officer." Accusative case has same form as genitive for animate nouns, same form as nominative for inanimate; an independent accusative form appears only for feminine singular nouns.

Я ДАЛ КАРАНДАШ ОФИЦЕРУ *(ya dal karandash ofitsyeru)*, "I was giving the pencil to the officer." Dative case.

Я ИДУ С ОФИЦЕРОМ *(ya idu s ofitsyerom)*, "I am going with the officer." Instrumental case, required by preposition С (s), "with."

Я ГОВОРИЛ ОБ ОФИЦЕРЕ *(ya govoril ob ofitsyere)*, "I was talking about the officer." Locative case, required by preposition ОБ (ob), "about."

English

English is quite typical of those Indo-European
languages which have discarded a large part of their ancient structure and have gone over to what may be described as an analytical or broken-up system, in which
grammatical and other relationships are indicated by word
order and auxiliaries rather than by endings.

The Anglo-Saxon noun had, like the Latin or Russian,
several declensions and four full-fledged cases (nominative,
genitive, dative, accusative), with traces of a locative. The
modern English noun, having lost all endings save the *'s*
of the genitive and the *-s* of the plural, shows only number
and one separate case relation. Gender appears in theory
and by virtue of tradition, since it is not indicated by the
form of either noun or adjective; but the tradition is
maintained by the pronoun, with its separate "he," "she,"
"it" (which, however, merge into "they" in the plural).
Prepositions are used to indicate case relations, but the
two most common prepositions, "of," and "to," are frequently avoided by the use, respectively, of the genitive in
's and of position before the direct object. The present-
day adjective is completely invariable, whereas in Anglo-
Saxon it had an elaborate series of endings and agreed with
the noun. The adjective and adverb, however, retain the
old suffixes of degree, *-er*, and *-est*. The English verb has
only three separate endings, the *-s* of the third person
singular present, the *-ing* of the present participle, and the
-d or *-ed* of the past and past participle, plus a number of
vowel changes which appear in the past and participle of
strong verbs, and an occasional *-en* in the participle of the
same verbs. Verbs normally indicate person, number, tense,
mood, and voice by an elaborate array of auxiliaries.

The word order of English is quite rigidly fixed. The subject-verb-indirect object-direct object arrangement predominates, the adjective regularly precedes the noun, the adverb precedes the word it modifies. Some linguists choose to view English as in the transitional stage from the original Indo-European flexional system, in which endings predominate, to the isolating system of languages like Chinese, in which all endings are lost, the word becomes invariable and monosyllabic, and all relationships are shown by auxiliary words and word order.

EVOLUTION OF ENGLISH SENTENCE

ANGLO-SAXON: Him þuhte þæt his heorte wolde brecan.
MIDDLE ENGLISH: Him thoughte that his herte wolde breke.
MODERN ENGLISH: He thought (that) his heart would break.

Arabic

Here we have a typical language of the Semitic family. Besides what has been said in the preceding chapter (see page 268), we may note that in addition to singular and plural there is also a dual number, denoting two, used for objects that ordinarily go in pairs, like hands or eyes (the dual number also appears in early Indo-European languages, notably Sanskrit and Greek). Feminine nouns form their plural by adding an ending, but masculine nouns usually form their plural by change of the internal vowels. Adjectives regularly follow the noun and agree with it. The Arabic verb, conjugated by internal flexion (that is, change or addition of vowels before, after, and between the three consonants of the root), indicates person, number, and frequently gender. The basic tenses, imperfect and perfect, serve to indicate completion or incompleteness of the action rather than time, but there is the possibility of indicating tense by the use of prefixes and auxiliaries.

The word order of Arabic is fairly well fixed and serves to indicate significant relationships.

Bēt ir rāgil, "house the man" ("the man's house").

Rāgilēn kuwayyisīn, "men-two" (dual number) "good" (plural), ("two good men").

BROKEN PLURALS BY VOWEL CHANGE
kalb, dog   *kilāb,* "dogs."

bint, girl   *banāt,* "girls."

il kitāb kibīr, "the book big" ("the big book").

il kutub kubār, "the books bigs" ("the big books").

Chinese

In addition to what has been said before (see pages 270-272), Chinese, which rejects the Indo-European and Semitic concept of parts of speech, makes use exclusively of word order to indicate grammatical relations. The modifier regularly precedes the modified word; the order subject-verb-object is rigidly adhered to. There is no grammatical gender. Plurality may be indicated by means of a suffix but is more frequently left undenoted. Words used as nouns are often preceded by other words called classifiers, which place the classified noun in a certain unmistakable category and eliminate the possibility of misunderstanding (English "five *head* of cattle," pidgin "three *fellow* man," "five *piecee* shirt" for "three men," "five shirts," are similar in nature). The Chinese verb is absolutely invariable but may be given tense value by additional words ("I past day write," "I write finish" both indicate "I wrote").

SAMPLES OF CHINESE STRUCTURE

/jên -ti /fang ⌄tzŭ, "man of house the" ("the man's house").

\chê /jên \k'an \chien /hai ⌄tzŭ, "this man look see child the" ("this man sees the child").

⌄hao /jên, "good man."   /jên ⌄hao, "man (is) good."

-san \ko \jên, "three human-being man" ("three men").

/wo ⌄hsiě, "I write."

/wo ⌄hsiě \liao, "I write finish" ("I wrote").

⌄wo /tso -t'ien ⌄hsiě, "I past day write" ("I wrote yesterday").

⌄wo /ming -t'ien ⌄hsiě, "I bright day write" ("I shall write tomorrow").

⌄ni \k'an \chien \k'an /pu \chien, "you look see look not see" ("do you see?" with added implication "or don't you?").

Japanese

Japanese nouns are invariable, but to them are added suffixes which indicate case relations. Gender and number normally go unmarked but may be denoted by special endings if desired. Personal pronouns are handled exactly like nouns, taking the same case suffixes. They are usually omitted with verbs, which have endings that denote tense (present, past, future), something akin to mood (indicative, conditional, or subjunctive), degree of politeness toward the person you are addressing, but not person or number. Hence the Japanese verb is said to be "impersonal" and would literally be translated by some such expression as "there is a going," "there was a going," "there will be a going"; "who" does the going is left to the intelligence of the listener (notice that something similar appears in Latin, where *itur in silvas* means "there is a going into the woods"). The adjective, which normally precedes the noun, is often conjugated like a verb (here again there is an Indo-European parallel in such verbs formed from adjectives as the Italian *biancheggiare*, "to gleam white"). Many special honorific words appear, contrasting with "humble" words, which refer to what is owned by the speaker (*chichi*, "my father," *otōsama*, "your honorable father"). Classifiers appear, as in Chinese; they are regularly used with numerals.

Latin, Russian, and English all display Indo-European structure, but in various historical stages. The structural similarities between Indo-European and Semitic are brought out by Arabic, but there also appear basic differences. Japanese is sometimes said to be linked to Uralic and Altaic, but again seemingly basic differences appear. Chinese, completely different in structure from Indo-

Koko ni o kake kudasai, "Here at honor sitting please" ("Please sit here").

Kore wa nihongo de nan to iimasu ka, "This as-for Japanese-language in name as is-called?" ("What do you call this in Japanese?").

Myōnichi o uchi ni irasshaimasu ka, "Tomorrow honorable house in honorable-be?" ("Will you be at home tomorrow?").

Eigo ga dekimasu ka, "English-language subject-sign is-know-how?" ("Do you speak English?").

(NOTE: *ka* is like a spoken question mark at the end of a sentence.)

Dekimasen, "Is-know-how-not" ("I don't").
(Change from *-su* to *-sen* ending makes verb negative.)

European, yet shows similarity to certain Indo-European trends betokened by English. Other language families show still different peculiarities, but the entire gamut of linguistic structure seems to range between the two extremes of synthesis (putting together different concepts into one word or word-sentence) and analysis (breaking up concepts into individual word units).

6

SOME PRACTICAL LANGUAGE HINTS

what language is that?

During World War II, the Censorship Bureau had to examine for security reasons hundreds of thousands of letters exchanged between foreigners residing in the United States and relatives and friends abroad. The Bureau had a large and competent staff of translators in all the languages that were likely to come up. But one major hitch developed at the outset of the Bureau's work. As the letters came in, it was not always easy to determine in what language they were written. The foreign postmark or address did not always supply a clue, for a letter composed in Estonian might be addressed to a correspondent in Paris. At first, the letters were simply passed from desk to desk until they finally hit the appropriate interpreter. But this was a slow and time-consuming process. It was found far more expedient to delegate one employee, who had a bare smattering of numerous languages in their written forms, to act as a clearinghouse, glance at the letters, determine in what language they were written, and drop them into separate baskets that ultimately went to the right translators.

Most people are acquainted with the foreign-accent effect that is obtained by certain actors on the stage or screen, usually for purposes of humor. Even though you speak no word of French, you know the actor is impersonating a Frenchman trying to speak English. If you were asked how you know, you would be stumped. Yet the answer is simple. You have been exposed to enough spoken French in the course of your life to be able to recognize some of the specific sounds of the language and identify either the language itself or an accent from it that is reflected in the speaker's English (actually, this art of mimicry, depending upon the hearer's unconscious recognition, can be carried much farther, as shown by comedians who imitate the speaking mannerisms of some prominent person and thereby get a laugh from their audience).

In the newspaper, you come across an account of crimes perpetrated by people whose names are given. Their nationality is not stated, yet you shake your head and groan: "Why must we admit so many Ruritanians to this country?" Here the form of the names, or a characteristic ending that has registered in your subconscious mind, is at work.

All this may seem to be a sort of game, and it can be. In wartime, the game can be rather grim, with counterintel-

By endings, Latin first names frequently end in -us, -o, -a; Greek first names in -os, -a, -e, -ses, -des, -cles; Hebrew first names in -el; Italian, Spanish, and Portuguese frequently have -o for the masculine, -a for the feminine; French and German first names often have -e for the feminine; Japanese feminine first names often end in -ko.

FORMS TAKEN BY COMMON FIRST NAMES

JOHN: *German* Johannes, Johann, Hans; *French* Jean; *Spanish* Juan; *Portuguese* João; *Italian* Giovanni, Gianni; *Russian* Ivan; *Serbo-Croatian* Jovan; *Irish* Sean; *Finnish* Juhana.

JOSEPH: *French* same; *German, Russian* Josef; *Spanish* José; *Italian* Giuseppe; *Serbo-Croatian* Josip; *Hungarian* Jozsef; *Irish* Seosmh.

STEPHEN: *German* Stefan; *French* Etienne; *Spanish* Esteban; *Italian* Stefano; *Russian* Stepan; *Hungarian* Istvan; *Irish* Stiobhan.

IDENTIFICATION OF FAMILY NAMES

English: -son, -s
German, Yiddish: -sohn, -stein, -berg, -burg, von
French: du, de la, des (Duhamel, Desmoulins)
Italian: -i, di, da, de -is (De Gubernatis)
Spanish: -ez, del, de la, de los, de las (Gutiérrez, de los Ríos)
Portuguese: -es, do, da, dos, das (Nunes, Davega, Dos Passos)

Scandinavian: -quist, -rup, -holm, -strom, -dahl, -gren, -sen, -son

Dutch: van (den), ten, de, -en (Vandenberg, Ten Eyck, de Groote)

Irish: Mc, Mac, O', Fitz- (Mac is preferred for Scots Gaelic)

Welsh: Ap, P- (Apjones, Pritchard, Pugh, from Aphugh)

Rumanian: -escu (Enescu, Negulescu)

Russian: -ov (-off), -sky (change -ov to -ova, -sky to -skaya, in feminine); -itch or -vitch (feminine -vna) is a patronymic, used as middle name to indicate the father.

Ukrainian: -enko

Czech: -ek, -ak, -ik, -sky (Mladek, Novak)

Polish: -wicz, -ski (Sienkiewicz); change -ski to -ska in feminine.

Serbo-Croatian: -ić

Bulgarian: -ev (-eff)

Hungarian: -i (Perényi, Rákosi)

Finnish: -en (Kaikkonen)

Armenian: -ian (Guderian)

Greek: -poulos, -polis (Stavropoulos)

Turkish: -oğlu (Kadoğlu)

Hebrew: ben (ben Gurion; patronymic: means "son of")

Arabic: ibn (as in Hebrew)

In *Chinese, Japanese, Hungarian,* family name comes first: Chou En-lai = En-lai of the Chou family; Kossuth Lájos = Louis Kossuth

---

ligence recognizing a spy who otherwise speaks perfect English by just one little quirk in his pronunciation or use of a word. Censorship, OWI, OSS, Military and Naval Intelligence, even the city police, have often had to turn into linguistic detectives.

But there are plenty of peacetime applications of the science of language identification. Library workers, for instance, must have a smattering of many languages to be able to decipher the titles and authors and general topics of the numerous foreign books they handle. In human relations, it is sometimes very much worth while knowing what is the language of origin of the person you are dealing with, for it gives you an insight into his background and probable habits. If you recognize his name as Finnish, you will see to it that in the course of your conversation you don't say something derogatory about the Finns. If he speaks with a Southern accent, it will be wise to forbear from unfavorable comments about the South. If the accent is British, and you recognize it as such, you may be saved from stating in his presence that you don't care much for Britain's present policy.

On one occasion, I was very curious to know the na-

IDENTIFICATION OF GEOGRAPHICAL NAMES

TOWN, CITY: *German* -burg, -dorf, -stadt; *Dutch* -stad; *Scandinavian* -by; *French* -ville; *Italian* città, civita; *Spanish* ciudad; *Portuguese* cidade; *Russian* -gorod; *Serbo-Croatian* -grad; *Czech* -hrad; *Chinese* chow, fu

ISLAND: *German* Insel; *Dutch* eiland; *Scandinavian* ö, öy, holm; *Italian* isola; *Spanish* isla; *Portuguese* ilha; *French* île; *Russian* ostrov; *Japanese* jima, shima

RIVER, STREAM: *German* Fluss; *Swedish* å; *Italian* fiume; *Spanish* río; *French* fleuve, rivière; *Finnish* joki; *Russian* ryeka; *Arabic* bahr, wad, wadi; *Japanese* kawa, gawa; *Chinese* kiang, ho

MOUNTAIN: *German* Berg; *Scandinavian* fiäll, fiell; *French* mont, montagne; *Spanish, Portuguese, Italian* monte; *Russian* gora; *Turkish* dag; *Arabic* djebel; *Japanese* yama; *Chinese* ling, san; (MOUNTAIN CHAIN: *German* Gebirge, *Spanish* sierra; cordillera)

---

tionality and background of a man with whom I had dealings. He spoke with an obvious foreign accent, but it was difficult to place. But in the course of the conversation, he happened to mention "Limbaphone records." He meant "Linguaphone," and I corrected him. At the same time, I had an answer to my unspoken question. The only language where the *gu* of *lingua* turns into a *b* is Rumanian.

On another occasion, I was given a letter written in "Czech" to translate for a government bureau. I took one glance at it and said: "This is not Czech; it's Croatian." That put an entirely different light on the investigation, though I was never informed of its ins and outs.

Running across a quotation by an unknown author, I wondered whether he was British or American. I could have found out by consulting a card index in the library, but it wasn't necessary. In the three-line quote was the word "civilisation." Like "honour" and "defence," this is a British, not an American, spelling.

It is possible, without too great an effort, to get to identify the major languages of the world in their written form. If they use special systems of writing, it is not necessary to learn the system of writing to be able to identify them. If they use the Roman alphabet, there are individual marks, accents, letter combinations which can be learned without too much trouble, so that you know whether the written document you are faced with is composed in Polish or Czech, Swedish or Norwegian, Portuguese or Spanish. It is also possible to identify personal names, both first and family, so that you have a clue to the person's national origin. The same goes for place names that may stump you when you run across them in the press.

The identification of spoken languages is far more difficult and calls for a keen ear. Yet it is the sort of thing that we all do unconsciously when we identify a German, or

Italian, or French accent carried over into English. The foreigner is carrying over his own native sounds into his English speech, and those same native sounds will all the more frequently and clearly appear in his native speech. The peculiar lilt of Swedish and Norwegian, the relatively great range of pitch of French, the characteristic endings of a great many languages can be listened for and identified.

The purpose of playing linguistic detective may be mere amusement in the overwhelming majority of cases, but it may have extremely useful angles, ranging all the way from not offending people you may be in contact with to ferreting out a spy or saboteur. From the written-language standpoint, the ability to identify languages may save much time, enable you to go to the right person for a satisfactory translation, and bring abilities to light that you perhaps did not dream you possessed.

CLUES FOR LANGUAGE IDENTIFICATION

	SPOKEN	SPOKEN AND WRITTEN				WRITTEN
		"and"	"not"	"the"	Frequent endings	Letters and combinations
Swedish	musical pitch	och	inte icke	-en -et	-a -an	å, ä, ö
Norwegian	musical pitch	og	ikke	-en -et	-e -en	å, ae, ø
Danish	no musical pitch	og	ikke	-en -et	-e -en	aa, ae, ø
Icelandic	interrupted vowel (sje-tta)	og	ekki	-inn -i	-ur	þ, ð
Dutch	s followed by guttural ch; v intermediate between f and v	en	niet	de 't het	-ft -bt -ijn	no suprascripts; aai, ooi, oei, eeuw, uw, auw, ieuw, ij

	SPOKEN	SPOKEN AND WRITTEN				WRITTEN
		"and"	"not"	"the"	Frequent endings	Letters and combinations
German	tst (jetzt); ich-sound; glottal stop	und	nicht	der die das dem den	-en -er -em -es	script ä, ö, ü, äu schl-, schr-, schm-
Rumanian	ă-sound	și	nu	-ul -lui -lor	-esc	ş, ţ, ă, â, î pt, oa, ea, şt
French	middle vowels full nasals; intonation	et	ne-pas	le la l' les	-ez, -ons -ille -ment -eau -aux -eux	ç, é, è, ê, à, â, î, û, ô oi, ui, eu
Spanish	clear final vowels; j-sound; rr; final -s (apical and very strong, or weakened to h)	y	no	el la los las	-os -as -es -ado -ido	¿——? ¡——! sole accent mark: ' ie, ue ñ
Portuguese	unclear final vowels; final -s as -sh or -zh; nasals	e	não	o a os as	-inho -om -em -am	ão, ões, ã, õ, ç lh, nh three accent marks: ´ ` ^ ei, ou
Italian	clear final vowels; double consonants; vocalic endings	e	non	il la lo i, gli le, l'	-are -iamo -ato, -ata -ere -uto, -uta -ire -ito, -ita -i, -e	gl, gn sole accent mark: '

| | SPOKEN | SPOKEN AND WRITTEN | | | WRITTEN | |
		"and"	"not"	"the"	Frequent endings	Letters and combinations
Russian	no fixed accent; stressed syllable drawled; unstressed vowels unclear	i	nye	—	-il, -ila -al, -ala -ovo -omu -ov, -yev -aya, -oye	Cyrillic script: distinguishing characters: э,ы
Ukrainian	as in Russian	i	nye	—	-iv, -av -ib	Cyrillic script: distinguishing characters: ї, є,г
Polish	accent on penult; unstressed vowels clear; palatal combinations	i, a	nie	—	-ał, -ego -ać, -ieć	ą, ę, ć, ł, ń, ś, w, ź, ż cz, dz, sz, rz, szcz
Czech	initial stress; long unstressed vowels; clear unstressed vowels; sound of ř	i, a	ne	‿	-ého, -ý -ím, -íte -ti, áti	č, ď, ě, ň, š, ť, ž, ř, ů, v hl-, hr-, tř-, ml- (Slovak—ä, ľ, ô, no ř)
Croatian	no final stress; musical pitch; clear unstressed vowels	i, a	ne	‿	-oga, -ao, -og, -ar, -ati, -iti	dj, ž, lj, nj, ć, č, dž, š Serbian, using Cyrillic alphabet, has following distinctive letters: j ђ,ћ,љ,њ,џ
Bulgarian	stress not predictable	i, a	ne	-t -ta -to -tye	-iya, -aya	Cyrillic script; distinctive characters: ѫ,ъ,ѣ (but last two may also appear in pre-Soviet Russian)

	SPOKEN	SPOKEN AND WRITTEN				WRITTEN
		"and"	"not"	"the"	*Frequent endings*	*Letters and combinations*
Greek	sharp, apical sound of *s*; words having counterpart in learned English vocabulary	kai	ou mē den	o, ē, to oi ai ta tou tēs ton tois tais tous tas	-os, -on, -ēs, -ēn, -as, -mai -ein, -tai	Greek alphabet
Finnish	initial stress; clear long vowels and double consonants	ja	ei	—	-en, -aa, -ää, -mme, -tte, -lle -lta	ä, ö, y, aa, ää, ee, ii, oo, uu *No* b, c, f, q, x, z
Hungarian	initial stress; long, clear unstressed vowels; double consonants; middle vowels	és	nem	a	-ak, -ok -ek, -ök -ünk, -em -om, -es -et	á, é, í, ó, ú, ö, ő, ü, ű, cs, cz, gy, sz, zs
Turkish	usually final stress	ve	-ma- -me- (in verb)	—	-ar, -er -mak -mek -dan -den -im, -iniz -unuz	ç, ğ, ş, ı
Arabic	sounds of ', q, ḥ	wa	mush la	il	-āb, -īn -ēn, -ak, -ik, -kum -ān	Arabic script

Albanian: look for ë, shq, sht, dhj, q
Lithuanian: look for ñ, m̃, ĺ, ŕ, i̯, u̯
Lettish: look for ǧ, ķ, ļ, n, ŗ
Irish: Irish script; if in transcription, look for bh, mh, dh, mb, gc
Welsh: Look for y and w used as vowels (shwd, yr); ll, dd, rh
Indonesian: Frequent ě

To distinguish in written form *Chinese* from *Japanese:* if you see tiny characters to the right of the main character, along with frequent recurrence of the syllabic symbol *no* ("of"), ʂ, in main column of characters, the script is Japanese:

人	人ʔ	天	天ۥ
Chinese	*Japanese*	*Chinese*	*Japanese*

人 　人ﾟ
ʂ　or　ʂ

Chinese　*Japanese*

how to learn a spoken language

The acquisition of a spoken language depends on two things: the ability to understand the speech of a native speaker of the tongue *speaking at normal or near-normal rate of speed,* and the ability to express your own thoughts in the foreign tongue, at a rate of speed which, without necessarily being normal, is fast enough to keep your interlocutor from breaking in and trying to express your thoughts for you. Your accent, without necessarily being that of a native, should be close enough to it to prevent misunderstanding.

Speaking and understanding are faculties which are related in some ways, unrelated in others. The first involves your brain and speech organs, while the second involves your ears and your brain. It is generally believed that one learns to understand before one learns to express oneself, because that is the way a child does it. But a child is not an adult, and the adult will often be able to put together passable sentences in the foreign tongue and yet be unable to understand the native's rapid-fire reply. This is particularly likely to happen when the adult has learned the foreign language by the reading-and-grammar method, which means that he has memorized lots of words, phrases, and sentences but has not had much practice listening to the natives as they speak their language.

No better technique has been devised for the two spoken aspects of language than the one that consists of listening, repeating, and imitating. For this, a native speaker, or one who has practically the equivalent in the way of control of the language, is the best teacher. The instructor should, preferably, be a cultured speaker of the standard language rather than an illiterate or a speaker of a minor dialect. He should be made to repeat, as many times as necessary, words, phrases, and sentences the meaning of which is known or stated, and the learner should endeavor to mimic him as closely as possible, until he is satisfied that he can do no better.

Attention should be paid not merely to the sounds but also to the intonation of the voice and the syllable division of the words. For the intonation, a small four-tone xylophone is occasionally used to illustrate the "music" of the language and the tone pattern of various phrases and sentences. For the syllable division, it may be necessary to have the speaker slow down until he puts a pause between each syllable of his speech, imitating the language at first in slow motion, then speeding up on further repetitions until the normal rate of speech is attained. If these two items are properly handled, there will be real imitation of the native pattern; if they are not, there will certainly remain a trace of foreign accent.

What to do if native speakers and teachers are not available? For this contingency, numerous language recordings have been devised and are sold by various firms. Most of them are excellent and usually spoken by cultured native speakers of the standard language. There are two types of recordings. One runs right through, with no allowance made for repetition by the learner; it is claimed by the producers of these recordings that better results are obtained if the learner listens to the entire recording at least ten or a dozen times before he makes any attempt at repetition or imitation. The other type of recording has a pause of silence after the utterance of each word, phrase, or sentence by the native speaker, and this is to be utilized for immediate repetition by the learner. The claim here is that immediate and constant repetition is needed to give you the feel of the language from the outset. It is probable that each method works best with a certain type of learner. If a tape or wire recorder is available to the learner, he can record his own voice for purposes of comparison with the actual or recorded voice of the native speaker. This permits self-correction by listening for errors.

It is a statistically proved fact that while a language may consist of hundreds of thousands of words and millions of possible combinations of those words, the pattern of all ordinary conversation falls within ranges of high-frequency words and sentences, which occur over and over again. These observations form the basis of frequency lists used in educational institutions, for purposes of intensive study. Not only the words that occur most frequently in actual speech, but the phrase and sentence types of the same description should by all means be learned first, since the possibility of using them is so much greater.

Furthermore, familiarity with and easy use of certain high-frequency expressions has definite psychological values. In the first place, it gives the learner a feeling, erroneous perhaps, but nevertheless actual, that he is using the foreign language and to a certain degree controls it; this builds up his confidence and breaks down his inhibitions. Secondly, it gives the foreigner to whom he is speaking the feeling that he is deferring to his language and is making an effort to use it, instead of depending on the foreigner to use English. This builds up better public relations and makes for a friendly attitude on both sides, which in turn is reflected in broader opportunities to use the foreign tongue.

What sort of words and expressions should be learned

first and used at every opportunity? Common forms of greeting, expressions of politeness, inquiries about directions and purchases, numerals (these are important for use in pricing), friendly remarks about the state of the weather. In all these, be sure to learn not only the formula for the original statement or question, but also the formula for the expected reply, so that some semblance of a two-way conversation may take place. One or two hundred high-frequency phrases and sentences, coupled with a few hundred key words, will take care of at least half of all foreseeable situations. Special vocabularies and sets of phrases should, of course, be memorized for special purposes.

One point above all should be kept in mind. As a learner, you must overcome your natural fear, reluctance, timidity, and bashfulness, and plunge into the foreign spoken language in the same way that a swimmer plunges into the water. Of course you will make mistakes. But never mind the mistakes: go ahead and speak. Mistakes will be expected of you, and the kindly foreigners stand ready to correct you and set you right. If you put off speaking until you can speak perfectly, you will never speak; you won't even speak your own language, in which you, and all other speakers with you, make mistakes.

On one occasion, during World War II, I was asked to take over a second-year college class in French whose regular instructor had been drafted. Instead of following the program, which called for reading, grammar, and translation, I told the students, who were all boys rapidly approaching military age: "We are going to play a game: You are a detachment of paratroopers, who have just landed in southern France. I am a French peasant, the first living person you meet on French soil. You want lots of information from me: where the nearest town is, how many Germans hold it, where telephone and telegraph lines are located, and anything else that comes into your minds. I am sympathetic to your cause and ready and willing to answer your questions to the best of my ability. But I don't speak or understand a word of English. You may consult one another, use pocket dictionaries, help yourselves out with sign language, get your questions across to me in any way you can. Then you must interpret my answers, which will be given to you in good standard French. Let's see how much information you can get out of me. You will not be corrected or interfered with by me, save by accident, or when I rephrase a question that I don't fully understand."

It worked like a charm, and many were the lessons we spent imitating real-life situations. Sometimes I was the mayor of a town where they were trying to find billets, sometimes an innkeeper from whom they sought food and drink, sometimes a shopkeeper from whom they wanted to buy necessities. They learned more spoken French that way than they would have learned in years of ordinary grammatical study. Their inhibitions were broken down completely. They were being neither corrected nor marked, and the sole criterion of the lesson was understanding and making themselves understood. Language was linked with life, not with a grammar book.

Try this system if you can, or something similar to it. Conversing naturally with someone who is a native speaker of the language you are learning is probably the best way to acquire a foreign tongue.

In imitating and repeating the sounds of the foreign language, you may sound silly to yourself and fear that you may sound silly to your listeners. Get rid of this feeling, and remember that you sound much sillier when you try to avoid the strange sound of the foreign language by sub-stituting a sound from your own language. The immense advantage that children have over adults in learning spoken languages is that they are never bothered by inhibitions or worries about sounding strange or funny. So go ahead and speak. You don't learn to swim or drive by forever watching others. Sooner or later you must plunge, or take the steering wheel. Sooner or later, you must speak.

At the same time, do your best to imitate the sounds, intonations, accents of the native speaker's voice. Avoid facile substitutions on the ground that "it's very close, anyway." Remember that the foreign language is a law unto itself and does not have to defer to English or borrow from English, particularly for what concerns its sounds and tones. If the native voice sounds too high-pitched, or seems to have too great fluctuations of tone, don't assume that you can improve on it by making it lower or giving it less variety. But if you actually find it impossible to imitate it to perfection, go ahead and do the best you can rather than give up and lapse into English.

If you find it difficult to remember the words and phrases you want in the script or spelling of the foreign language, note them down in your own transcription, by ear. This practice is not recommended if you can do equally well by referring to the actual writing of the foreign tongue, since it puts a double strain on the memory; but for those who are better at learning through the ear than through the eye it may prove a satisfactory temporary crutch.

Americans have often been accused of inability to learn foreign languages, particularly in spoken form. This is simply not true, and thousands of native-born Americans who are excellent speakers of foreign tongues stand ready to disprove it. The real fault lies with our schools, which think they can do in two years what other countries accomplish in six or eight. A language takes time, work and patience, but so does everything else that is worth acquiring.

In transcription, pronounce Ü, Ö like *ee, eh,* but with rounded lips; for any vowel bearing ~ over it (AW̃, Ẽ), pronounce with closed-off nose, as though you had a head cold.

	"GOOD MORNING"	"THANK YOU"	"HOW MUCH?"
German	Guten Morgen (GOOT-en MOHR-gen)	Danke schön (DAHN-kuh SHÖN)	Wieviel? (vee-FEEL)
Dutch	Goeden Morgen (HOO-yeh MOR-heh)	Dank U wel (DAHNK Ü VEL)	Wat kost 't? (VAT KOST 'T)
Swedish	God morgon (GODE MOR-guhn)	Tack (TAHK)	Hur mycket kostar det? (HÜR MIK-et KOST-ehr DET)
Norwegian and *Danish*	God morgen (GODE MOR-guhn)	Takk (TAHK)	Hvor meget koster det? (VORE MAY-get KOST-ehr DET)
Icelandic	Góðan daginn (GO-thahn DAH-ghin)	þakka yður fyrir (THA-ka EE-thoor FEER-ir)	Hvað kostar það? (HVÁTH KOST= ahr THATH)
French	Bonjour (baw̃-ZHOOR)	Merci bien (MEHR-see BYẼ)	Combien? (kaw̃-BYẼ)
Spanish	Buenos días (BWAY-nos DEE-ahs)	Gracias (GRAH-thyahs)	¿Cuánto cuesta? (KWAHN-toe KWES-tah)
Portuguese	Bons dias (BÕSH JEE-ahsh)	Obrigado (oo-bree-GAH-doo)	Quanto custa? (KWAHN-too KOOSH-tah)

Italian	Buongiorno (BWOHN JOHR-no)	Grazie (GRAH-tsyeh)	Quanto costa? (KWAHN-toe KOS-tah)
Rumanian	Bună ziua (BOO-nuh ZEE-wah)	Mulţumesc (mool-tsoo-MESK)	Cât costă? (KUT KOST-uh)
Russian	Zdravstvuyte (ZDRAHV-stvooy-tyeh)	Spasibo (spuh-SEE-buh)	Skol'ko eto stoit? (SKUL'kuh ETuh STAW-eet)
Polish	Dzień dobry (JEN DAW-bree)	Dziękuję (jen-KOO-yen)	Ile to kosztuje? (EE-leh TAW kawsh-TOO-yeh)
Serbo-Croat	Dobar dan (DAW-bahr DAHN)	Hvala (HVAH-lah)	Koliko ovo iznosi? (KAW-lee-ko AW-vo eez-NAW-see)
Finnish	Hyvää huomenta (HÜ-vaa HWO-men-tah)	Kiitoksia (KEE-tok-syah)	Kuinka paljon? (KOO-in-kah PAH-lyohn)
Hungarian	Jó reggelt (YO REG-gelt)	Köszönöm (KÖ-sö-nöm)	Mennyibe kerül? (MEN-ee-beh KEHR-ül)
Turkish	Gün aydın (GÜN aye-DUN)	Teşekkür ederim (teh-sheh-KÜR EH-deh-reem)	Fiyatı kaça? (FEE-yah-tuh KAH-shah)
Japanese	Ohayŏ (oh-hah-YO)	Arigatŏ (ah-ring-ah-TO)	Ikura desu ka? (EE-koo-rah DES KAH)
Indonesian	Tabek (TAH-bek)	Terima kaseh (TREE-mah KAH-seh)	Berapa harga? (BRAH-pah HAR-gah)
Arabic	Şabāḥ il khēr (suh-BAHH il KHEHR)	kattar khērak (KAT-tar KHEHR-ak)	Bi kām da? (bee KAHM dah)
Chinese	╱ni╱hao	╲hsiĕ ╲hsiĕ	-dwo ╲shew ╱chyan

SAMPLE OF HIGH-FREQUENCY WORDS

ENGLISH	GERMAN	FRENCH	SPANISH	ITALIAN	LATIN	RUSSIAN
the	der, etc.	le, etc.	el, etc.	il, etc.	—	—
a, an	ein, etc.	un, une	un, una	un, una	—	—
of	(gen. case)	de	de	di	(gen. case)	(gen. case)
to	(dat. case)	à	a	a	(dat. case)	(dat. case)
with	mit	avec	con	con	cum	s
yes	ja	oui	sí	sì	ita	da
no	nein	non	no	no	non	nyet
one	ein, eine	un, une	un, una	un, una	unus, una	odin, odna
two	zwei	deux	dos	due	duo, duae	dva
three	drei	trois	tres	tre	tres	tri
ten	zehn	dix	diez	dieci	decem	desyat'
hundred	hundert	cent	cien(to)	cento	centum	sto
thousand	tausend	mille	mil	mille	mille	tysyach
water	Wasser	eau	agua	acqua	aqua	voda
man	Mann	homme	hombre	uomo	homo, vir	chelovyek
woman	Frau	femme	mujer	donna	mulier	zhenshchina
money	Geld	argent	dinero	danaro	nummi, pecunia	dyenghi
doctor	Arzt	médecin	médico	medico	medicus	vrach
I	ich	je	yo	io	ego	ya
you	Sie	vous	Usted	Lei	tu	Vy
he	er	il, lui	él	egli, lui	ille, is	on
she	sie	elle	ella	essa, lei	illa, ea	ona
we	wir	nous	nosotros	noi	nos	my
they	sie	ils, elles	ellos ellas	essi, esse loro	illi illae	oni onye
small	klein	petit	pequeño	piccolo	parvus	maly
large	gross	grand	grande	grande	magnus	bolshoi

The spoken language is a symbol of thoughts and ideas, just as money is a symbol of purchasing power. The written language is usually a symbol of a symbol, just as a check is a symbol of money.

In the languages that use alphabets, the written language attempts to portray, in visual form, the sound of the spoken language. There are languages, like the Chinese, which make use of pictograms and ideograms that stand not for sounds but for ideas.

The sounds of any language are quite limited in number. This means that alphabets, however complicated they may be, are relatively simple to learn, for the number of their symbols is limited by the sounds they portray. Objects and ideas, however, are practically unlimited, and this means that writing systems using pictograms and ideograms may get to be so complicated as to require a lifelong study.

For this reason many people study languages like Chinese and Japanese in spoken form alone, with Roman-alphabet transcriptions which indicate the sounds. This is a practical compromise between time limitations and the desire to acquire the language, but it leaves the learner in the position of an illiterate in the language he is learning.

In the overwhelming majority of cases, it is desirable to acquire the written as well as the spoken form of the language. But, in addition, there are special cases in which the learner has little use for the spoken tongue but finds it necessary to gain command over the written form.

The technique for acquiring a language in written form

is scorned by some, who claim that since language is primarily a speech activity, the one and only way to go about learning it in any phase is through the ear and the vocal organs. But even outside of the cases described above, which are more numerous than one might think (scientists who want to read books and tracts in foreign languages, publishers, editors, librarians, and others whose work deals primarily with written forms), it must also be remembered that there is a type of mind which is visual rather than auditory, and for this type of mind the oral-aural technique is the hard way to go about it.

There is not too much difference between the old-fashioned language teaching of the days before spoken-language techniques became fashionable, and the best method of learning a written language today. The primary appeal is to the eye and the brain. First comes a basic grammatical approach, with stress on those features of structure which are of the recurring variety. Here, perhaps, is where the old grammars blundered. Their main concern was with a symmetrical presentation of the facts of grammar, the basic rules, the exceptions, particularly the last named, because these supplied good quiz questions for final examinations.

There is nothing wrong with tackling language learning as a quiz game, provided it is really done in the spirit of fun, not in the spirit of trapping the unwary. But if we are to go about it in a practical way, for practical purposes, it may be as well to omit game features and concentrate on the subject on hand.

A truly up-to-date grammar of a foreign language will not attempt to present the language symmetrically—declension by declension, conjugation by conjugation, each with neatly labeled exceptions, and exceptions to the exceptions. It will start out with those forms which have the highest frequency of occurrence. To exemplify: in French you have three "regular" conjugations of verbs, which logically should be presented first, and several classes of irregular verbs, which, as exceptions, should follow. But it happens that many of the irregular verbs far outstrip in frequency of occurrence, both in spoken and written form, all the verbs of the "regular" conjugations. These high-frequency irregular verbs should, in a practical grammar, be offered first, regardless of whether this is or is not "logical." Logic would require that the possessive adjective and the possessive pronoun be presented together, or at least in quick succession, since there is an intimate logical connection between "I see my house" and "I see mine." In actual practice, the first type of sentence occurs far more frequently than the second and may actually be substituted for the second in case of need. The first should therefore be imparted early in the game, while the second may be relegated to the rear of the grammar. Words appearing in the vocabularies and used for examples and exercises should be the highest-frequency words in the language, and be employed in sentences of high frequency. When this is the case, you get away from the type of sentence that makes people laugh every time foreign languages are mentioned ("Have you seen my grandmother's hat lying on the bench in the garden beside the gardener's shears?"; but nobody will object to "Are you coming with me to the movies tonight?"). High frequency of both vocabulary and grammar are basic to good language learning, while perfectionism is no asset.

In acquiring a written language, it is important to get to the reading stage as quickly as possible. The type of material used for reading depends on the tastes and needs of the learner. One who is inclined toward literature should select literary works, but one inclined toward medicine or science will do well to concentrate on works in his field. For a general reading knowledge that is not specialized, the best materials are newspapers and magazines, which give the current language in its most current form and yet avoid glaring vulgarisms. One error made by old-line language teachers was to suppose that everybody was interested in the highest type of cultural literature. This definitely is not so, and a learner should not be discouraged from French merely because he does not properly appreciate Molière and La Fontaine.

Grammar and reading supply an excellent background for a later conversational knowledge of the language. One who has gotten a real grounding in the way the language is structured and in its basic words and expressions will often find that when he is exposed to the spoken language later on, he gets around to speaking and understanding it in a couple of weeks, as soon as his ears are attuned to the sounds and intonations.

All language is primarily memory work. If one does not memorize words and phrases from frequent repetition, one may memorize them from frequent reading or frequent writing. One excellent mnemonic device is to write, over and over again, words and phrases we wish to retain, pronouncing them as we write. In this fashion, a third type of memory, the sensory-motor, or kinesthetic, is added to the visual and the auditory.

Controversies sometimes arise over the use of subsidiary material. Should you concentrate merely *on* the language, or learn something *about* the language as well? How much time and effort should be devoted to what the schools call "culture" material—learning about the customs and habits and points of view and institutions of the country whose language you are learning? How much philological and historical material should enter language learning?

There is basically nothing wrong with learning interesting things about the language and its speakers. In some cases, that is the main point really desired by the learner. It certainly lends interest and removes some of the dryness inherent in grammatical forms, words, and sounds. At the same time, some discretion should be used. If the learner's primary aim is to learn the language, concentration should be on the language, even if side excursions are permitted. In all cases, particularly at the adult level, the learner's basic aims and interests should be kept in view. History and development of the language, literature, national institutions, geography and history of the speakers are all secondary when the primary aim is language learning.

Is it possible to attain a balanced diet which will include the aims of speaking the language moderately well, understanding all or most of what the natives say, being able to read the language, and being able to compose written messages in it which are fairly correct, though not necessarily literary? It undoubtedly is, and most of our schools and colleges today have this balanced diet as the chief aim in their language courses. For the person who has to learn a language without benefit of a school, a judicious combination of spoken-language records, a good up-to-date grammar which stresses high-frequency features, and the reading material suitable to his purposes will yield approximately the same result.

French

NOTE: Remember that any English transcription of a foreign sound is only a very rough approximation. In the transcription of French used here, *zh* represents the sound of *s* in "pleasure"; ü and ö represent the sounds of *ee* and *e* of "met," respectively, pronounced with lips rounded as for *oo;* nasal sounds are indicated by ã, ẽ, aw̃, ũh; they are pronounced, respectively, like *ah, eh, aw* and *uh,* but with passage between mouth and nose completely shut off, as by a head cold.

To avoid complicated verb tenses in French, use infinitive preceded by *je suis en train de* (zhuh SÜEE zã TRẼ duh, "I am in the act of") as a present; by *je viens de* (zhuh VYẼ duh, "I have just") as a past; by *je vais* (zhuh VEH, "I am going to") or *je veux* (zhuh VÖ, "I want to") as a future.

Je suis en train de parler (zhuh SÜEE zã TRẼ duh pahr-LAY), I am in the act of speaking, I am speaking.

Je viens de travailler (zhuh VYẼ duh tra-va-YAY), I have just worked, I worked.

Je vais donner (zhuh VEH daw-NAY), I am going to give, I shall give.

Je veux prendre (zhuh VÖ PRÃ-druh), I want to take, I shall take.

Conjugate the four main verbs as follows:

je suis	*viens*	*vais*	*veux*	("I")
(zhuh SÜEE)	(VYẼ)	(VEH)	(VÖ)	
tu es	*viens*	*vas*	*veux*	("you," familiar
(tü EH)	(VYẼ)	(VAH)	(VÖ)	singular)

il est	vient	va	veut	("he"; use *elle*
(ee-LEH)	(VYẼ)	(VAH)	(VÖ)	for "she")
nous sommes	venons	allons	voulons	("we")
(noo SAWM)	(vuh-NAW̃)	(zal-LÃW)	(voo-LÃW)	
vous êtes	venez	allez	voulez	("you," plural
(voo-ZEHT)	(vuh-NAY)	(zal-LAY)	(voo-LAY)	or polite)
ils sont	viennent	vont	veulent	("they"; if all
(eel SÃW)	(VYEN)	(VAW̃)	(VÖL)	are women, use
				elles)

Use these forms with the four infinitives given above; also with
faire (FEHR), do, make; *payer* (pa-YAY), pay; *manger*
(mã-ZHAY), eat; *boire* (BWAHR), drink. The infinitives of the
four key verbs are: *être* (EH-truh), be; *venir* (vuh-NEER), *come;*
aller (a-LAY), go; *vouloir* (voo-LWAHR), want.

Each sentence can be turned into a question by prefixing *est-ce*
que (ES-kuh):

Est-ce que vous êtes en train de manger? (ES-kuh voo-ZEHT ã
    TRẼ duh mã-ZHAY), Are you (in the act of) eating?
Est-ce qu'ils vont venir ici? (ES-keel VAW̃ vuh-NEER ee-SEE),
    Are they going to come here?
Est-ce qu'il vient de prendre le livre? (ES-keel VYẼ duh PRÃ-
    druh luh LEE-vruh), Has he just taken the book?, Did he take
    the book?
Est-ce que nous voulons payer? (ES-kuh noo voo-LÃW pa-YAY),
    Do we want to pay?

Each sentence can be made negative by putting *ne* (nuh) before
the main verb, and *pas* (PAH) after it:

Je ne suis pas en train de boire (zhuh nuh SÜEE pah zã TRẼ
    duh BWAHR), I am not (in the act of) drinking.

Il ne vient pas de travailler (eel nuh VYẼ pah duh tra-va-YAY),
He has not just worked, He did not work.

Est-ce que vous ne voulez pas donner le livre au garçon? (ES-kuh
voo nuh voo-LAY pah daw-NAY luh LEE-vruh oh gar-SỐ),
Don't you want to give the book to the boy?

Note that *ne* and *que* drop their final *e* before a vowel in the
next word.

Spanish (See pronunciation note on page 318.)

In Spanish, replace the present by *estoy* (es-TOY) with the
gerund. To obtain the gerund from the infinitive, change *-ar*
of the infinitive to *-ando,* and *-er* or *-ir* of the infinitive to
-iendo: comprar (kohm-PRAHR), *comprando* (kohm-PRAHN-
doh); *hacer* (ah-THEHR), *haciendo* (ah-THYEN-doh). This
gives you, literally, "I am buying," "I am doing." For the past,
use *acabo de* (ah-KAH-voh deh), "I have just," with the infinitive; for the future, use *voy a* (BOY ah), "I am going to," or
quiero (KYEH-roh), "I want," both with the infinitive.

Estoy hablando (es-TOY ah-VLAHN-doh), I am speaking.
Acabo de trabajar (ah-KAH-voh deh trah-vah-KHAHR), I
have just worked.
Voy a pagar (BOY ah pah-GAHR), I am going to pay.
Quiero tomar (KYEH-roh toh-MAHR), I want to take.

Conjugate the four key verbs as follows:

estoy (es-TOY)	*acabo* (ah-KAH-voh)	*voy* (BOY)	*quiero* (KYEH-roh)	("I"; use *yo* if you wish, but it may be omitted)
estás (es-TAHS)	*acabas* (ah-KAH-vahs)	*vas* (BAHS)	*quieres* (KYEH-rehs)	("you," familiar singular; *tú* may be used or omitted)
está (es-TAH)	*acaba* (ah-KAH-vah)	*va* (BAH)	*quiere* (KYEH-reh)	("he," "she," "you" polite singular; you may use *él, ella, Usted* [ehl, EH-lya, oos-TEHD]; the latter is more often used than omitted)
estamos (ehs-TAH-mohs)	*acabamos* (ah-kah-VAH-mohs)	*vamos* (BAH-mohs)	*queremos* (keh-REH-mohs)	("we"; use *nosotros* [noh-SOH-trohs] if you wish)
estáis (ehs-TAH-ees)	*acabáis* (ah-kah-VAH-ees)	*vais* (BAH-ees)	*queréis* (keh-REH-ees)	(little-used familiar plural; use *vosotros* if you wish)
están (ehs-TAHN)	*acaban* (ah-KAH-vahn)	*van* (BAHN)	*quieren* (KYEH-rehn)	("they," "you," polite plural; use, if you wish, *ellos, ellas, Ustedes* [EH-lyohs, EH-lyahs, oos-TEH-dehs])

Use these verbs with *hablar* (ah-VLAHR), speak; *trabajar* (trah-vah-KHAHR, work; *dar* (DAHR), give; *tomar* (toh-MAHR), take; *hacer* (ah-THEHR), do, make; *pagar* (pah-GAHR), pay; *comer* (koh-MEHR), eat; *beber* (beh-VEHR), drink; *venir* (beh-NEER), come. The infinitives of the four key verbs are *estar* (es-TAHR), *acabar* (ah-kah-VAHR), *ir* (EER), *querer* (keh-REHR).

To turn your sentence into a question, use question marks at the beginning and the end. To make it negative, use *no* before the verb.

No estoy comiendo (noh es-TOY koh-MYEHN-doh), I am not eating.

¿Quiere Usted hablar? (KYEH-reh oos-TEHD ah-VLAHR), Do you want to speak?

No vamos a trabajar hoy (noh VAH-mohs ah trah-vah-KHAHR OY), We are not going to work today.

¿No quieren beber? (noh KYEH-rehn beh-VEHR), Don't they want to drink?

No está tomando el libro (noh es-TAH toh-MAHN-doh ehl LEE-vroh), He is not taking the book.

Él está haciendo su trabajo, pero ella no está haciendo nada (EHL es-TAH ah-THYEHN-doh soo trah-VAH-khoh, PEH-roh EH-lya noh es-TAH ah-THYEHN-doh NAH-dah) , He is doing his work, but she is not doing anything.

PRONUNCIATION NOTE: The written letter *j* (also *g* when it appears before *e* or *i*) has the sound of a rasped guttural *h;* it is rendered by *kh* in transcription; *b* and *v* both have the sound of English *b* if they are initial or after a consonant; if they come between vowels, they are sounded like a *v* pronounced with both lips instead of with the lower lip and upper teeth, as in

English; the latter pronunciation applies even if the preceding vowel belongs to another word in the same sentence; thus *voy*, "I am going," is pronounced BOY; but *no voy*, "I am not going," is pronounced noh VOY.

---

how to improve your own language

The problem of what to do about your own language is not too different from that involving a foreign tongue. The question is how to speak better, get a better understanding of what is said by others, do more extensive and more profitable reading, and be more effective in your own writing.

Speaking is learned, as we have seen, by imitation. Better and more effective speaking is to be acquired by the imitation of the right kind of models. Who shall these models be? The choice is up to the individual and should depend, as always, upon his particular requirements and needs. If one is going to work among manual workers, it may perhaps be best not to use the language of literary or art experts. If one works among scientists, one should speak up to their level. This is merely a practical question of understanding and being understood.

Along with this, however, is the question of general propriety and effectiveness. Proper expressiveness and understanding do not require the slavish aping of every fashion of speech that may be current in a given group. Soldiers have been known to go through two years of army life without once using any of the profanities or obscenities common to large segments of their comrades, and without this trait of theirs ever being noticed. By using a natural, unaffected, straightforward type of speech, including vocabulary, grammar, intonation, and features of stress, you can generally reach all with whom you come in contact, offend no one, either by grossness or over-refinement, and make yourself perfectly understood. The avoidance of localisms and class features of speech is to be actively sought in the majority of instances, since such features add little or nothing to expressiveness and are breeders of wrong impressions.

Some people, afraid of "slumming," never use bright colloquialisms; others, afraid of being high-falutin, shy from using the best word in the right place. Good speech consists of combining satisfactory standard grammar with colorful, expressive words and word combinations; a controlled peppering with colloquialisms and even slang; articulation that is always clear; a good range of modulation, neither monotone nor exaggerated inflection. One should avoid jargon talk (as is so frequent today with psychoanalytic terms) and strive so to master vocabulary as to be able to talk with anyone on his own level.

The matter of a speaking vocabulary requires special attention. The more words you have at your disposal, the more effective your speech will be, provided you do not allow the overspecialized elements of your vocabulary to get into your everyday language. But within the everyday language of each and every speaker are thousands of words which can be used effectively. It will pay to learn the precise use and meaning of those words.

There was a time when one actively had to seek models for one's spoken language. Today, with all the forms of canned speech at our disposal, radio, TV, spoken films, the models are imposed upon us from above or, at least, from the outside. By and large, they are not bad models, since professional radio and TV men consciously strive for a form of speech that will be universally accepted throughout the country, while the spoken films, which offer a more diversified linguistic fare, have at least the merit of giving us a broad cross section of regional accents and class jargons, with which we may as well become familiar.

It is a well-established psychological fact that we tend to imitate those we admire. This brings a conscious element into our choice of speech and gives us freedom of the will in the matter of whom and what to admire, and therefore imitate. If our admiration runs along the line of Shakespearean actors, the chances are we shall eventually speak like Shakespearean actors; if we admire gangsters and their brand of talk, we are very likely to come out with that kind of speech. Let us therefore guard our admiration, and save it for the models our brain tells us are really worth while.

Should speech be a conscious or an unconscious process? Should there or should there not be awareness of choice of words and forms? Should enunciation be guided by the brain, or left to the reflexes?

Generally, the speaking process ought to be, and is, as unconscious as the handling of a car in motion by a good, experienced driver. Yet good drivers know that they can often anticipate certain situations and forestall certain unpleasant contingencies by the use of their conscious minds.

They can often realize that the driver ahead of them is about to do something foolish, and can exercise extra conscious caution, instead of waiting to slam on the brakes by sheer instinct when the emergency rushes upon them.

In like manner, we can guard our speech and actively direct it when circumstances call for it. We can "pick" the right word, the right form, the right intonation. We can make sure that our enunciation is not sloppy or hard to understand.

A man who is professor of English at one of our leading universities and a thoroughgoing scholar besides, mumbles in such fashion that he can hardly be understood. Does he realize it? Has he ever been told? Has he ever inquired?

The phrase "Your best friend won't tell you" goes for language at least as much as it does for halitosis. Therefore it will not be amiss if we occasionally inquire of people in whom we have confidence: "Do I speak clearly? Do you understand all I say, or do I force you to strain your ears and guess at my meaning?" The results of a few such inquiries may be vastly surprising.

When we come to reading, newspapers and magazines are able to supply a great deal of background. Books, however, should not be overlooked, because they contain the more permanent portion of our reading material. If you are fond of fiction, literature, and poetry, you should try to read the best of both the old and the new authors, within your own range of taste and preference. Do not persist in trying to read authors who bore you, but remember that tastes and interests change from one age level to the next. Give the "boring" authors another try a few years later. If you prefer nonfiction and the factual, remember that a balanced diet of history, biography, religion and philosophy, political and economic topics, popular discussions of the arts and sciences will have a broadening effect upon any individual, no matter what educational level he starts from.

One piece of advice can be universally handed out, and it applies equally to speaking, understanding, reading, and writing. If in the course of any of these language activities, you run across words whose meaning or use baffles you, don't by-pass them. Look them up in the dictionary and familiarize yourself with them. Each person has an active vocabulary, which he uses in his own speech or writing; he also has a passive, or recognition, vocabulary, usually many times the extent of the other, consisting of words he does not normally use but recognizes when he sees or hears them. Adding to both these vocabularies means enriching our life experience and extending our powers. The dictionary is the tool that enables us to do this. If you don't know the word, look it up and find out what it means and how it's used. Even such elementary pastimes as crossword puzzles and games of scrabble can be used to good advantage for this purpose.

More has been said, perhaps, on the subject of how to write than on anything else in the language line. We have been burdened with advice from schools of writing and journalism, from books and articles, as to just how to make our writing readable, interesting, fascinating, absorbing and, above all, salable. The gist of most of this advice is to the effect that we should avoid long words and long sentences and long paragraphs, use monosyllables, preferably of Anglo-Saxon origin, with no more than six or seven words to the sentence, three or four lines to the paragraph, putting the burden of our message at the very beginning, then retelling the story at leisure later on.

All this may be very good, and certainly it is accepted

newspaper practice. At the same time, one wonders whether newspaper reporting is the best possible of all styles, for all purposes. By all means say what you have to say, simply, in easily understood language, and in as few words as possible. But say it all, and say it clearly. If the meaning you want to convey is better rendered by a word of three syllables of Latin origin than by an Anglo-Saxon monosyllable, use the longer word. There is such a thing as sacrificing your real meaning to economy of space and time. Also, a distinction must be made between mere word padding and the legitimate elaboration of a thought or a point of view.

What literary models should you follow? By all means the ones you admire the most and think most effective. They may range all the way from Shakespeare to Mickey Spillane and from Dylan Thomas to Red Barber. But, here again, let your brain direct your admiration. Shakespeare and Dickens were and still are literary models. One wonders how far they would get today if they had to write for a living. Styles and points of view change, and the language changes with them.

In addition to the question of what one should read, the problem of how one should read often comes up for discussion. The present-day emphasis seems to be on speed of reading. This may be desirable in certain specialized occupations, where people have to scan large numbers of newspapers and magazines or skim through many books in a short time. The trouble is that it is applied to the ordinary reader, who is given the advice: "Read fast, cover a lot of ground, get the gist of what you are reading, and never mind the form or the details." One wonders whether a great deal is not lost by this method. What we read in leisurely fashion usually sinks in better than what we skim over, and if it is worth while, it should be allowed to sink in. The rapid-reading method for the ordinary reader is somewhat on a par with dashing through a countryside on a superhighway at seventy miles an hour. We may get to our destination fast, but we shall have missed a great deal of the scenery on the way. If viewing the scenery happened to be our primary purpose in making the trip, we shall have lost out almost completely, though we get to the end of the journey.

Language is the tool that has been given us to express our thoughts to others and to receive the thoughts of others. Whether it comes in spoken or written form, whether it is literary or colloquial, literal or symbolic, it is one of our most precious heritages. It is the means by which the accumulated experience of the human race may be passed on from generation to generation, instead of having to be repeated by each individual member. It definitely deserves some conscious thought and attention. Let us use it to the best possible advantage.

SAMPLE OF DICTIONARY USE

Suppose you are concerned with the word "post," in its various meanings and uses. Webster's *Collegiate Dictionary* will reveal, s. v. (this stands for *sub verbo,* "under the word"), that "post" has four primary meanings, each with a separate derivation.

The first general meaning is that of "pillar, prop, upright piece of timber or metal"; this comes from a word *post* which was used in both Anglo-Saxon and Old French, coming from the Latin *postis.* As a verb, it means to affix, announce, forbid (as to trespassers), enter a name upon. The most important of its derivatives is *poster.*

Meaning number two is "place where a soldier or soldiers are stationed." This comes from French *poste,* Italian *posto,* Low Latin *postum,* from classical Latin *positum,* "that which has been placed or set." It has a local American use in "veterans' post," a local British use as one of the bugle calls at tattoo. Its side meanings are "post of duty," "post of public service," "trading post." As a verb it means "to station." A military derivative is "post exchange," or PX.

The third "post" has to do with the mails. It comes from French *poste,* Italian *posta,* Latin *posita,* again "that which has been placed," but in a special connection. Among the meanings are "messenger," "one of a series of stations," the British "mailing," "post office," or "letter-box"; there is also a size of paper, so called because its watermark is a postman's horn. As a verb it means "to travel with haste," or "send by mail." Colloquially, to post is to inform, and well posted is well informed. In bookkeeping jargon, it means "to carry or enter an item." Among the many derivatives are postage, postal, post boy, post card, post chaise, post-free, post haste, postman, postmark, postmaster, post office, postpaid, and post road.

The last "post" comes from the Latin preposition *post,* "after," "behind," and retains that meaning in English, along with "subsequent to." Anatomically it means "behind a part of the body" (postrenal); medically, it means "after," as in "postoperative." Among its many derivatives are post-axial, post bellum, postdate, postscript, post-pone, postgraduate, post meridiem (or P. M.), post-mortem, as well as posterior and posthumous.

The story of "post" is now complete. You know its meanings and how to use it.

---

selective bibliography

(This bibliography is in no way meant to be complete or exhaustive. It lists only a few significant works which are in English and within the grasp of the lay reader. Works marked with one * are suitable for high school students; those marked with ** are at the level of college students and educated adults; those marked with *** are indicated for people who have a deep or semi-professional interest in the subject.)

GENERAL DISCUSSIONS OF LANGUAGE

***Bloomfield, L., *Language,* Holt, N.Y., 1933
**Bodmer, F., *The Loom of Language,* Norton, N.Y., 1943
***Entwistle, W. J., *Aspects of Language,* Macmillan, N.Y., 1953
**Graff, W., *Language and Languages,* Appleton, N.Y., 1932
***Gray, L., *Foundations of Language,* Macmillan, N.Y., 1939
**Hall, R. A., Jr., *Leave Your Language Alone,* Linguistica, Ithaca, 1950
**Jespersen, O., *Language,* Macmillan, N.Y., 1954
**Laird, C., *Miracle of Language,* World, 1953.
*Pei, M., *All About Language,* Lippincott, Philadelphia, 1954
**Pei, M., *The Story of Language,* Lippincott, Philadelphia, 1949

**Sapir, E., *Language,* Harcourt, Brace, N.Y., 1921

**Schlauch, M., *The Gift of Language,* Dover Publications, New York, 1955

***Sturtevant, E., *Introduction to Linguistic Science,* Yale University Press, New Haven, 1947

***Whatmough, J., *Language: A Modern Synthesis,* St. Martin's Press, N.Y., 1956

ENGLISH AND AMERICAN GRAMMAR, USAGE, AND HISTORICAL DEVELOPMENT

**Baugh, A., *History of the English Language,* Appleton, N.Y., 1935

**Fowler, H., *Dictionary of Modern English Usage,* Clarendon, Oxford, 1926

***Fries, C., *American and English Grammar,* Appleton, N.Y., 1940

**Horwill, H. W., *An Anglo-American Interpreter,* Clarendon, Oxford, 1939

**Jespersen, O., *Growth and Structure of the English Language,* Blackwell, Oxford, 1948

*Lambert, E., *Our Language: the Story of the Words We Use,* Lothrop, Lee & Shepard, N.Y., 1955

**Mencken, H. L., *The American Language,* Knopf, N.Y., 1938 (Supplement I, 1945; Supplement II, 1948)

**Partridge, E., *The Concise Usage and Abusage,* Philosophical Library, N.Y., 1954

**Partridge, E., & Clark, J. W., *British and American English Since 1900,* Philosophical Library, N.Y., 1951

**Pei, M., *The Story of English,* Lippincott, Philadelphia, 1952

**Potter, S., *Our Language,* Pelican-Penguin, Harmondsworth, 1950

**Robertson, S., *Development of Modern English,* Prentice-Hall, N.Y., 1938

**Weekley, E., *The English Language,* Deutsch, London, 1952

**Whitford, R. C., & Foster, J. R., *Concise Dictionary of American Grammar*, Philosophical Library, N.Y., 1955

SEMANTICS

**Chase, S., *The Power of Words*, Harcourt, Brace, N.Y., 1954
**Chase, S., *The Tyranny of Words*, Harcourt, Brace, N.Y., 1938
**Hayakawa, S. I., *Language and Thought in Action*, Harcourt, Brace, N.Y., 1949
**Hayakawa, S. I., *Language in Action*, Harcourt, Brace, N.Y., 1941
***Ogden, C. K., & Richards, I. A., *The Meaning of Meaning*, Harcourt, Brace, N.Y., 1952
***Korzybski, A., *Science and Sanity*, Science Press, Lancaster, 1933

WRITING SYSTEMS

*Irwin, K. G., *The Romance of Writing*, Viking Press, N.Y., 1956
***Diringer, D., *The Alphabet*, Philosophical Library, N.Y., 1948

LANGUAGE LEARNING METHODOLOGY

***Carroll, J. B., *The Study of Language*, Harvard University Press, Cambridge, 1953
***Gleason, H. A., *An Introduction to Descriptive Linguistics*, Holt, N.Y., 1955
*Huebener, T., *Vocational Opportunities for Foreign Language Students*, Modern Language Journal, Supplement Series No. 1, 1949
***Méras, E., *The Language Teacher's Guide*, Harper, N.Y., 1954
*Parker, W. R., *National Interest and Foreign Languages*, UNESCO, N.Y., 1954

***The Use of the Vernacular Languages in Education, UNESCO, Paris, 1953

INTERNATIONAL LANGUAGES

**Guérard, A. L., *A Short History of the International Language Movement,* Boni & Liveright, N.Y., 1922

LINGUISTIC GEOGRAPHY AND LANGUAGE SAMPLES

***Kurath, H., *Word Geography of the Eastern United States,* University of Michigan Press, Ann Arbor, 1949
**MacDougald, D., Jr., *The Languages and Press of Africa,* University of Pennsylvania Press, Philadelphia, 1944
**North, E., *The Book of a Thousand Tongues,* Harper, N.Y., 1938
**Pei, M., *The World's Chief Languages,* Vanni, N.Y., 1946 (distributed by Devin-Adair)
**Sayer, E. S., *Pidgin English,* published by the author, Toronto, 1944

DICTIONARIES

**Hulbert, J. R., *Dictionaries, British and American,* Philosophical Library, N.Y., 1955
**Mathews, M. M., *Dictionary of Americanisms,* University of Chicago Press, Chicago, 1951
**Partridge, E., *Dictionary of Slang,* Routledge & Kegan Paul, London, 1949
**Partridge, E., *Dictionary of the Underworld, British and American,* Routledge, London, 1950
**Reifer, M., *Dictionary of New Words,* Philosophical Library, N.Y., 1955
**Shipley, J., *Dictionary of Word Origins,* Philosophical Library, N.Y., 1945

index

Abbreviations, 167
Abstract words, 95
Accent, 97–114, 297 (see Pitch; Stress); foreign, 79–82, 290, 294–5, 300–1; marks, 294, 296
Adjective, 85–97, 267–75, 277, 279–81, 284, 311
Adverb, 93–6, 273–5, 280–1
Affiliation (see Classification; Families)
Affricates, 76
Afghan (see Pushtu)
Afghanistan, 40, 155, 180, 224, 254
Africa, 27–9, 36–7, 39, 137, 139–40, 154
African Negro languages, 33, 97, 153, 158–61, 175, 221, 224, 226, 247, 260–4, 266, 272
Afrikaans, 33, 159, 175, 223
Agreement, 274, 280–1
Ainu, 260–1, 263–4
Akkadian, 43, 122–3, 127, 177, 189–90, 192
Alaska, 27–8, 263
Albanian, 56–7, 127, 140, 180, 206, 224, 250, 254–6, 265, 299
Aleut, 263
Algeria, 36, 39, 156, 158–9, 161, 199
Alphabet, 22–5, 79, 109, 178–85, 231, 294, 309
Altaic, 126, 137, 139–40, 259–61, 263–4, 266, 269–71, 284 (see Ural-Altaic)
Alveolars, 74–6, 83
American English, 31–2, 51–8, 62, 100–1, 116, 130, 135, 162–5, 169–71, 194, 232–3, 293–4, 326 (see Eastern U.S. dialect; Midwestern; Southern U.S. dialect; U.S. English)
American Indian Languages, 33, 97, 132, 135, 137–9, 149–50, 152, 170, 193, 212, 226, 253, 260, 262–4, 266, 272
Amharic, 140, 224, 258
Analysis, 280, 285
Andalusian, 233
Andaman Islands, 137, 139, 263
Anglo-Saxon, 43, 47–9, 54, 78, 85–7, 96, 100, 134, 144, 146, 148–50,
152, 168, 193, 249, 251–2, 255–7, 268, 280–1, 323–5
Angola, 161
Annamese, 224, 259, 263–4 (see Vietnamese)
Antilles, 27–8, 136, 141–2, 146, 263
Apical s, 296, 298
Arabic, 15, 40, 34–5, 39–42, 45, 123–7, 135, 140, 149, 152, 156, 158, 161, 167, 175, 180–5, 193, 197, 209, 215–8, 223, 228–30, 233, 241, 251–2, 254, 258, 268–9, 273, 281–2, 284, 292–3, 298, 307; alphabet, 180–5
Aragonese, 126, 232–4
Aramaic, 43, 123, 127, 134, 151, 178, 181, 192–3
Archaism, 12–3, 131, 172, 177, 181
Argentina, 37–8, 40, 169, 171, 174, 202, 226
Argot, 60
Armenian, 126–7, 140, 180–1, 209, 224, 254–6, 265, 292
Article, definite, 87–8, 93–6, 277, 305; indefinite, 88, 93–6, 277
Articulation, point of, 75
Asia, 27–9, 33, 36, 39, 123, 139–40, 160, 215–8, 226, 259–62
Asia Minor, 44, 124, 126, 141, 144
Asianic languages, 123, 263
Aspect, 278–9, 282
Assamese, 224
Assyrian, 43, 122–3, 192 (see Akkadian)
Attic, 126
Australia, 26–9, 136–7, 141–3, 153, 226, 258; English, 32–3, 62, 135; native languages, 132, 137, 139, 260–4, 266
Austro-Asiatic languages, 263
Austro-Hungarian Empire, 37, 201
Auxiliaries, 89–90, 269, 274–5, 280, 282
Avestan, 178, 255–6
Aymará, 224, 226
Azerbaijani, 224
Aztec, 193, 226

Babylonian, 43, 60, 114, 122–3, 192 (see Akkadian)

Bahasa Indonesia (*see* Indonesian;
  Malay)
Balinese, 225
Balkan languages, 40, 44, 135, 141,
  254
Baltic languages, 127, 140, 169, 254–
  5, 258 (*see* Estonian; Lettish;
  Lithuanian)
Balto-Slavic, 140, 254–5, 265
Baluchistan, 254, 263 (*see* Beluchi)
Bantu, 137, 139, 158, 175, 260–4
Basic English, 238
Basque, 126–7, 135, 141, 173, 195,
  197, 205–6, 225, 233–4, 250, 260–1,
  263–4, 270
Belgium, 36, 195, 199–201, 207
Beluchi, 155 (*see* Baluchistan)
Bengali, 34–5, 39–42, 155–6, 193,
  223, 241, 250, 255, 273
Berber, 127, 224, 259
Bible, 122, 174–6, 178–82, 248, 266
Bicol, 225
Bihari, 155, 223
Bilingual world, 239
Bilingualism, 195, 223
Bisaya, 224
Boers, 33
Bolivia, 202, 226
Borrowed words (*see* Loan words)
Brahui, 155
Brazil, 37–8, 40, 141–2, 150, 169, 171,
  222
Breton, 126–7, 195, 197, 205–6, 225.
  234, 255, 257
British English, 26, 31–3, 54, 58, 62,
  100–1, 135, 163, 167, 194, 206, 293–
  4, 326
Brittany, 195
Brooklyn dialect, 31, 173
Brythonic, 255 (*see* Breton; Cor-
  nish; Welsh)
Bulgarian, 126–7, 181–5, 206, 224,
  250, 255, 257, 268, 292, 297
Burma, 27–9, 154, 161, 183; lan-
  guage, 224, 251, 259
Burushaski, 263
Byelorussian, 35, 127, 224

Cambodia, 224, 251, 263
Canada and Canadian English, 26–
  8, 31, 36, 38, 136, 141–2, 170–1,
  198, 207, 263; Canadian French,
  170–1, 198, 207
Canarese, 155, 223
Canary Islands, 203
Cant, 51, 59–66

Carthage, 124–5, 127, 194 (*see*
  Punic)
Case, 85–97, 104, 267–74, 277–80,
  284
Castilian, 126, 170, 232–4 (*see*
  Spanish)
Catalan, 56–7, 126, 195, 197, 205–6,
  224, 232–4, 255
Catholic Church, 43, 45, 179–81
Caucasian languages, 126–7, 158,
  225, 260–4
Celtic, 47–9, 124–7, 134, 140–1, 144,
  146, 148, 151–2, 192, 255–7, 265
Central America, 27–8, 136–8, 141–2,
  149, 226, 263
Central Italian dialects, 56–7, 232
  (*see* Rome; Tuscany; Umbria)
Centrifugal and centripetal forces
  in language, 108–9, 160, 169–70,
  174, 196, 233–5
Ceylon, 27–9, 154–5, 161, 175, 183,
  224
Chaldean, 192 (*see* Aramaic; Syriac)
Change, 10–11, 58, 78, 104, 108–9,
  129–36, 169–76, 324
Chile, 37–8, 202
Chinese, 15, 23, 25–6, 34–5, 39–42,
  54, 81, 89, 90, 94–6, 99, 101–2,
  123, 131–3, 137, 139–40, 144, 153,
  191–4, 209, 215–8, 223, 228–30,
  239, 241, 243, 251, 259, 270–3,
  281–2, 284, 292–3, 299, 307, 309
Christianity, 44, 178–85, 197
Class language, 6–7, 17, 51, 59–64,
  108, 320–1
Classical languages, 9, 17, 42–50,
  239 (*see* Greek; Latin)
Classification of languages, 42, 97,
  247–73
Classifiers, 283–4
Cockney, 33
Cocoliche, 174
Colloquialisms, 3–4, 11–3, 61, 65,
  312, 320, 326
Colombia, 202
Colonialism, 9, 27–30, 37–41, 153–
  161, 170–6, 195, 198–9, 202–3, 227,
  235–6, 258
Communications, 31, 58, 109, 132,
  191, 221
Community of speakers, 70, 77, 117,
  132, 177, 196–205
Congo, 199
Conjugation, 274, 284, 310–1 (*see*
  Verbs)

Conjunctions, 94–6
Conservative forces in language, 108–9, 171–2
Consonants, 74–6, 79, 82–3, 103, 105, 183, 268–72, 282, 295–8; clusters, 110–4; double, 99, 296, 298; voiced and unvoiced, 74–6, 83
Constructed languages, 9, 160, 236–43 (see International languages)
Coptic, 181, 259
Cords, vocal, 76
Cornish, 126, 255
Cornwall, 32, 146
Corsica, 124–7, 206; dialect, 56–7
Costa Rica, 202
Creole, 15, 175, 235
Cretan, 123, 192
Croatian, 126–7, 183, 201, 294, 297 (see Serbo-Croatian)
Cuba, 202
Cultural languages, 34, 37, 40, 45, 145, 149, 157, 211–8, 227–30, 235–6, 254
Cumberland dialect, 32
Cuneiform, 177
Curaçao, 175
Cyrillic alphabet, 180–5, 297
Czech, 99–100, 111–3, 127, 168, 193, 201, 209, 223–4, 234–5, 250, 255, 257, 292–4, 297
Czechoslovakia, 37, 39, 222

Dacia, 277; language, 141
Dalmatia, 57, 201; language, 56–7, 129, 255
Danish, 54, 126–7, 168, 224, 250–1, 255, 257, 295, 306
Danish invasions, 49, 54, 144, 149, 152
Declension, 86, 273–4, 277, 280, 310 (see Case)
Degree, 274–5, 280
Denmark, 37, 39
Dentals, 74–6, 83
Devanagari alphabet, 183–5
Devonshire dialect, 32
Dialects, 10, 12–3, 31–3, 51–8, 61–2, 64–5, 79, 82, 108, 116, 126, 150, 154, 180, 219–20, 223, 232–4, 310
Dictionary, 11–3, 46, 61–2, 219, 323–6
Diphthongs, 79, 82
Distortion of sound, 77
Distribution of languages, 33–42, 154, 220–5, 227–30, 263–4
Dominican Republic, 202

Doric, 126, 169
Double-talk, 66, 110–1
Dravidian, 141, 155–6, 250–1, 259–64, 266
Dutch, 33, 127, 135, 152, 156–7, 161, 166–7, 175, 193, 200, 208, 223, 234–5, 250, 253, 255, 257, 292–3, 295, 306

East Africa, 224, 226, 258
Eastern U.S. dialect, 31, 51–4, 232–3
Ecuador, 202, 226
Egypt, 29–30, 40, 180–1, 227
Egyptian, ancient, 22, 24–5, 43, 114, 123, 177, 181, 189–90, 192, 259
Elamite, 123, 192
Empty words, 95
Endings, 85–97, 104–5, 117, 132, 164, 243, 267–75, 278–81, 284–5, 291, 295–9
Engadine, 56–7
English, 15, 26–36, 38–45, 51–8, 74–6, 78–83, 85–98, 100–3, 105–6, 110–4, 123, 126–7, 130–6, 141–3, 149–53, 157, 159–61, 164–76, 181, 189, 193–4, 200, 209, 213–8, 223, 227–30, 234–41, 247, 249–57, 267–9, 273, 280–1, 284, 319–26 (see American English; Anglo-Saxon; British English; Middle English; U.S. English)
Eritrea, 39–40, 161
Eskimo, 22, 132, 260–4, 272
Esperanto, 9, 237–43, 250
Estonian, 126–7, 225, 234, 259, 289
Ethiopia, 39–40, 140, 181, 224, 227, 258–9, 262
Etruscan, 124–5, 127, 134, 141, 151, 167, 183, 189, 192, 231–2
Europe, 26, 37, 39, 44, 123, 126–7, 137, 139, 192–3, 205–8

Faliscan, 124–5, 255
Families of Language (see Classification)
Fanti, 224
Far East, 97, 192–3, 215–8, 239, 241
Finland, 137, 139
Finnish, 111, 126–7, 140, 180, 224, 237–8, 250, 259, 269, 271, 291–3, 298, 307
Finno-Ugric, 259
Flemish, 127, 195, 200, 223, 255
Flexions, 267–73, 281 (see Conjugation; Declension; Endings)
Florentine dialect, 220

Formosa, 137, 139
France, 36, 126-7, 144-5, 147, 195, 199, 205-6, 219-20, 225, 227, 232
Francien, 232
Franco-Provencal, 127
Franconian, 172, 176
Frankish, 165-6
French, 9, 15-6, 34-43, 47-9, 56-7, 75, 78, 89-91, 98, 100-1, 103, 105-6, 111-3, 126-8, 131-5, 141-3, 148-9, 151-2, 156-7, 159-61, 164-72, 174-5, 189, 193-5, 197-201, 209, 215-8, 220, 223, 227-30, 232, 235, 237-9, 241, 250-4, 255, 257, 273, 276-7, 290-1, 293, 295-6, 303-4, 306, 308, 311, 314-6, 325-6; Equatorial Africa, 36, 39, 199, 221; West Africa, 36, 39, 199, 221
Fricatives, 76, 83
Frisian, 224, 255
Friulian, 56-7, 225
Fula, 224
Full words, 94-5

Gaelic (see Irish; Scots)
Galician (Gallego), 126-7, 206, 232-3
Galla, 224, 259
Gallo-Italian dialects, 56-7
Gallurese, 56-7
Gaul, 147, 276-7
Gaulish, 124-5, 127-8, 148, 192, 255
Gauls, 50, 128, 169
Gender, 85, 90, 104, 267-74, 277, 280, 282-4
General American (see Midwestern; U.S. English)
Geography, 144, 191, 219-25, 293
Geolinguistics, 220
Georgian, 225
German, 9, 15-6, 34-6, 39-42, 55-7, 78, 89, 91, 98, 105-6, 111-4, 123, 126-7, 133-5, 145, 151-2, 159-60, 163, 166-8, 172-3, 175, 193, 195, 197, 200-1, 204, 206, 208-10, 215-8, 223, 227-30, 237-9, 241, 243, 248, 250, 253, 255, 257, 273, 291, 293, 296, 306, 308
Germanic, 113, 123, 127, 134-5, 140-1, 148-9, 165-6, 172, 179, 192-3, 200, 251, 253, 255-7, 265
Germany, 37, 39, 141, 144-5
Gestural language, 21, 24, 107, 121
G.I. English, 162-5
Glide sounds, 76

Glottal stop, 296
Glottals, 83
Gobbledegook, 64
Goidelic, 255 (see Irish; Manx; Scots)
Gondi, 155, 225
Gothic, 165-6, 179-80, 193, 255-7, 268
Grammarians, 116
Grammatical structure, 9-10, 84-97, 106, 108, 118, 129, 131, 150, 170, 212, 219, 251-4, 267-73, 275-8, 282-4, 312, 314-20
Greek, 9, 15, 22, 42-50, 84, 96, 98-9, 111-3, 124-7, 134-5, 140, 145, 151-2, 167, 178-85, 231, 239, 243, 251, 255-7, 268, 281; modern, 45, 56-7, 98-9, 127, 181, 193, 209, 215-8, 224, 250, 255, 257, 265, 291-2, 298; alphabet, 182-5; Byzantine, 140, 255
Greenland, 263
Grisons, 56-7
Guadeloupe, 36, 38, 198
Guaraní, 224 (see Tupi-Guaraní)
Guatemala, 202
Guiana, British, 27-8; French, 36, 38, 198
Guinea, Spanish, 202
Guinean, 247 (see Sudanese-Guinean)
Gujarati, 155, 223
Gutturals, 74-6

Haiti, 36, 39, 141-2, 175, 198, 235; Creole, 15, 175, 235
Hamitic, 123, 158, 258-61, 263-4, 266 (see Semito-Hamitic)
Hausa, 224, 226
Hawaii, 27-8, 137-8; language, 83, 110, 132
Hebrew, 22, 43-5, 123, 127, 134, 178, 182-5, 189-90, 192-4, 215-8, 224, 234, 248, 252, 254, 258, 268, 291-2
Hieroglyphs, 22, 43, 123, 177
High German, 55, 127, 255
Himyaritic, 140
Hindi, 41, 155-7, 183-5, 193, 223 (see Hindustani)
Hinduism, 178, 183
Hindustani, 15, 34-5, 39-42, 81, 193, 223, 228-30, 239, 241, 250, 255, 273 (see Hindi; Urdu)
Hittite, 123-4, 140, 192, 255
Hokkaido, 263
Holland, 37, 39, 200

Honduras, 202; British, 27–8
Honorifics, 284
Hottentot-Bushman, 158, 260–4
Huguenots, 200, 208
Hungarian, 90, 111, 126–7, 135, 140, 168, 201, 206, 209, 224, 250, 259, 269–71, 292, 307
Hungary, 37, 39, 137, 139, 222
Hyperborean, 260–1, 263–4

Iberian, 123–5, 127, 134, 141, 148, 192, 263
Ibo, 224
Icelandic, 127, 250, 255, 257, 295, 306
Identification of languages, 289–99
Ideographs, 22–3, 184, 299, 309
Ido, 242–3
Illyrian, 124–5, 140
Ilocano, 224
Immigrant languages, 32, 128, 135, 150, 172–6, 205, 208–10
Imperative, 267–274 (see Mood)
Imperialism, 235–6, 238–41 (see Colonialism)
Impersonal forms, 284
Incas, 226
India, 27–9, 37, 39–41, 123, 126, 137, 139, 141, 153–7, 161, 175, 177, 183–5, 218, 223–5, 241, 250, 254, 258–64, 274, 284
Indo-Aryan, 144, 155–6, 177, 254–5
Indochina, 36, 39–40, 156–7, 161, 199, 259
Indo-European, 43, 45–6, 59–60, 97, 123–7, 134, 137, 139–41, 158, 169, 180, 192, 249–50, 254–66, 267–8, 273–4, 277, 280–2, 284
Indo-Iranian, 140, 250, 254–5, 258, 260–1, 265
Indonesian, 15, 34–5, 39–42, 137, 139, 156–7, 161, 175, 184, 193, 218, 223–6, 228–30, 241, 251, 261–2, 273, 299, 307 (see Bahasa Indonesia; Malay)
Indo-Portuguese, 175
Infinitive, 86, 164, 279, 314–6
Infix, 269
Innovations, 11, 57, 63, 110–1, 169–72
Inscriptions, 126, 141, 275 (see Cuneiform; Hieroglyphs)
Intensity, 73, 116
Interglossa, 242–3
Interjections, 94–6

Interlingua, 9, 240–2
Internal flexion, 85, 87–8, 93, 96, 267–9, 281–2
International languages, 30, 44, 160, 179, 190, 229, 231–43
Interrogation, 278, 285, 315, 318
Intonation, 54, 97–114, 150, 296, 301, 312, 320
Iran, 40, 224, 254
Iranian (see Persian)
Iraq, 40, 122, 180, 224
Irish, 126–7, 206, 208–9, 225, 234, 248, 250, 255–7, 291–2, 299
Islam, 40, 140, 180–5, 197, 213, 215–8
Isogloss, 52–5
Isolating languages, 281
Isolation, 171–2
Israel, 43, 45, 178, 185, 194, 224
Istria, 57
Italian, 9, 15–6, 34–5, 39–43, 54, 56–7, 60, 91, 94, 98, 101, 103, 105–6, 110–4, 126–7, 130–1, 133–5, 148, 150–2, 159–61, 163–4, 167–8, 172–4, 181, 193, 195, 197, 200–1, 206, 208–10, 215–8, 223, 227–32, 241, 249–50, 252–3, 255, 257, 273, 275–7, 284, 291, 293, 296, 306, 308, 326
Italic, 124–5, 140, 192, 255, 257
Italy, 125–7, 141, 144–5, 220, 225, 275–7

Japanese, 15, 22, 34–5, 39–42, 99, 106, 111, 153, 160, 163–4, 193, 218, 223, 228–30, 241, 249–51, 259–61, 263–4, 266, 270, 273, 284–5, 291–3, 299, 307, 309
Jargon, 51, 59–66, 173, 320–1, 326
Javanese, 223
Jews, 44, 178, 185, 194, 208–9
Jobelyn, 60
Jordan, 40, 180
Judaism, 178
Judea, 194

Kabile, 259
Kalmuk, 127
Kanarese (see Canarese)
Karelian, 127
Kashmiri, 155, 225
Kherwari, 224
Khmer, 224, 250–1
Kirghiz, 127, 259
Korean, 15, 164, 218, 223, 250–1, 259–61, 263–4, 266, 270, 273

Kurdish, 224
Kurukh, 155
Kushitic, 123, 158, 259

La-Ti, 263
Labials, 74–6, 83
Labio-dentals, 76, 83
Ladin, 56–7 (see Rheto-Romansh; Romansh)
Lahnda, 155, 224
Lancashire dialect, 32
Lapp, 127, 259
Latin, 9, 11, 15, 22, 42–50, 57, 60, 89, 91, 95–9, 100, 104–6, 111, 116, 124–8, 130, 134–6, 141, 145, 148–9, 151–2, 165–8, 172, 178–85, 189–92, 215–8, 220, 231–2, 239, 243, 248, 252–7, 268–9, 273–8, 280, 284, 291, 308, 324–6; Archaic, 134, 172; Vulgar, 50, 60, 104, 134, 165–6, 220, 275–7, 326
Latin America, 36, 38, 149–50, 241
Latino Sine Flexione, 242–3
Latvia, 225, 254 (see Lettish)
Learned words, 113, 298
Learning of languages, 114–8, 300–19
Lebanon, 40, 180
Leonese, 126, 232–4
Lettish, 127, 225, 234, 254–5, 299
Liaison (see Linking)
Libya, 39–40, 161
Libyco-Berber, 123, 258–9 (see Berber)
Ligurian, 124–5, 127
Lingua Franca, 30, 226
Linguals, 76, 83
Linguistic atlas, 219–20
Linguistic geography, 219–20
Linguistic islands, 56–7, 144
Linking, 106
Liquids, 76, 83
Literacy, 215, 228–30, 235, 309
Literature, 19, 21, 30, 43–4, 65, 109, 145, 175, 177, 190, 206, 215, 234, 311–2, 324
Lithuanian, 126–7, 209, 224, 234, 250, 254–5, 256, 299
Liturgical languages, 177–83, 259
Loan words, 110, 128, 132, 146, 150, 163–8, 181, 213–4, 249, 251–2, 256
Localisms, 10, 31, 51–8, 108, 220, 320–1
Logudorese, 56–7

Low German, 55, 126–7, 255
Luba, 224

Madagascar, 36, 39, 137, 139, 141, 143, 199, 224, 262
Madurese, 224
Magyar, 224 (see Hungarian)
Malagasy, 224
Malay, 156, 175, 223, 226, 270 (see Bahasa Indonesia; Indonesian)
Malaya, 27–9, 40, 175, 261–2
Malayalam, 155, 223
Malayo-Polynesian, 137–9, 250–1, 260–4, 266, 273
Malta, 27–9, 175
Maltese, 175
Manchu, 259
Mandingo, 224
Manhattan, 209
Manx, 255
Marathi, 155, 223, 255
Martinique, 36, 38, 198
Mayan, 192, 226
Meaning, 11, 21, 24, 46, 69, 80–1, 84–5, 92–3, 101, 107, 117–8, 249, 251, 269, 272, 326 (see Semantics)
Mediterranean languages, 134, 151, 192–3
Melanesia, 137–9, 175; language, 262; pidgin, 15, 235 (see Pidgin)
Messapian, 124–5, 127
Metalinguistics, 214–5
Methodology, 14, 17, 21, 300–19
Mexico, 136, 141–2, 149, 169, 202, 226, 263
Micronesia, 137–9; language, 262
Middle English, 49, 134, 281
Middle High German, 166
Middle vowels, 296, 306, 314–6 (see Vowels)
Midwestern American dialect, 31, 51–4, 62, 233 (see U. S. English)
Migrations, 37, 40–1, 128, 136–45, 150–1, 169–76, 258
Military influence, 109, 128, 161–8, 178, 229–30
Minoan, 126
Minorities, 205–10
Missionaries, 30, 40, 179, 221, 266
Modified languages, 238
Modulation, 100–2, 320
Mongolian, 248, 259
Mon-Khmer, 260–1, 263–4
Monogenesis, 248
Monosyllabic words, 102, 270–1, 281, 323–4

Mood, 267, 274, 281, 284
Moors, 149, 233
Mordvin, 225
Morocco, 36, 39–40, 156, 158–9, 199
Morpheme, 93
Morphology, 84–97, 132 (*see* Grammatical Structure)
Mossi, 224
Mozambique, 161
Mozarabic, 126, 233
Munda, 141, 155, 260–1, 263–4
Mycenean, 192

Names, family, 291–2, 294; personal, 291, 294; place, 144
Nasals, 76, 83, 296, 306, 314–6
Nationalism, 197–205, 234–41
Native words, 98, 151–2, 257
Naturalized words, 98, 151, 214
Near East, 39–40, 178, 180–1, 192–3, 227, 258
Negation, 285, 315, 318
Negro languages (*see* African Negro)
Neo-Melanesian, 235
Nepali, 224
Nepo, 242–3
New Caledonia, 198
New England, 53–4
New Guinea, 137, 139, 175, 226, 261–2
New Hebrides, 198
New York dialect, 32, 54, 65, 173–4, 200, 209
New Zealand, 26–8, 33, 62, 135–7, 226, 258, 262
Newspaper language, 63, 221, 322–4
Nicaragua, 202
Nigeria, 27–9, 226
Norfolk dialect, 32
Norman Conquest, 148, 152, 168
North Africa, 39–40, 141, 143, 156, 158–61, 180, 194, 227, 241, 258–61
North America, 26–8, 37–8, 40, 141–2, 153, 226, 263
North Italian dialects, 150, 220
North Semitic, 182–3
Northumberland dialect, 32
Norway, 37, 39
Norwegian, 126–7, 168, 224, 237, 250, 255, 257, 294–5, 306
Nouns, 85–97, 267–73, 277, 280, 283–4
Nubia, 181
Number, 84–5, 90, 104, 267–72; dual, 281

Number of speakers, 34–5, 130–3, 190–5, 220–5, 228–30, 254, 263, 274, 277–8, 281–4
Numerals, 211, 251, 284, 308

Object, 84–97, 267, 281
Obsolete forms, 12–3, 131, 231
Oceania, 160–1 (*see* Pacific Islands)
Occlusives, 74–6
Occupational language, 108 (*see* Jargon)
Official languages, 45, 58, 150, 153–61, 172, 174, 195, 198–9, 202–3, 226, 235, 258
Old Bulgarian, 180
Old Church Slavonic, 180–1, 183, 256–7, 268
Old English (*see* Anglo-Saxon)
Old French, 165–6, 168 (*see* French)
Old High German, 193, 256–7, 268
Old Irish, 256, 268
Old Norse, 165
Old Persian, 123, 255
Old Prussian, 126, 255
Organs of speech, 19, 21, 69–76, 79–80, 102, 121, 310
Origin of language, 121–9
Oriya, 155, 224, 255
Oscan, 124–5, 127, 134, 151, 192, 232, 255
Ostyak, 127

Pacific islands, 27–9, 33, 36–7, 39, 142–4, 226, 260–2
Pahari, 155, 224
Pakistan, 27–9, 39–41, 154–7, 161, 180, 183–5, 218, 241
Palatals, 76, 83, 297
Paleo-Asiatic, 263
Pali, 193
Papiamento, 175
Papuan, 137, 139, 260–1, 263–4, 266
Paraguay, 202, 226
Participles, 86, 274, 278–81
Particles, 95
Parts of speech, 92–7, 267–73, 282
Pasimology, 24 (*see* Gestural language)
Patois, 206
Pattern of speech sounds, 79, 110–3, 150–1, 212, 251
Pennsylvania, 53, 172; German, 172–3, 175, 200
Persian, 126–7, 153, 180, 183, 192–3, 224, 249, 254 (*see* Iran)
Persons, 92, 274, 278, 281–2, 284

Peru, 202, 226
Philippines, 27–9, 33, 36–7, 39, 142–4, 226, 260–2
Phoenician, 123, 127, 192, 194
Phoneme, 80–3, 117
Phonetic spelling, 3–4, 22–5, 219
Phrygian, 124, 141
Pictographs, 22–3, 299, 309
Picture writing, 22–5
Pidgin, 15, 30, 174–6; English, 175–6, 235
Pitch, 73, 99–101, 104, 116, 272, 295, 297 (see Accent)
Plosives, 74–6, 83
Plural, 84–97, 267–72; broken, 282; repetitive, 270 (see Number)
Poland, 37, 39, 201
Polish, 99, 126–7, 193, 209, 223, 234–5, 250, 254–5, 292, 294, 297, 307
Polite forms, 284, 306–7, 316
Polynesian, 137, 139, 262
Polysyllabic words, 102
Polysynthetism, 270, 272
Portugal, 37, 39
Portuguese, 15, 34–5, 37–9, 42–3, 98, 105, 126–7, 135–6, 141–3, 149–50, 152, 159–61, 169, 171–2, 175, 193, 206, 223, 228–30, 232–3, 241, 247, 250, 255, 257, 273, 276, 291, 293–4, 296, 306
Possession, 84–97
Praenestine Fibula, 275
Prakrits, 177, 193
Prefixes, 85, 98, 105, 267, 269, 272, 274, 282
Prepositions, 88, 93–6, 267, 274–5, 277–8, 280, 308
Pronouns, 87–8, 93–6, 212, 267–8, 273–4, 277–8, 280, 284, 308, 311, 316
Provençal, 126–7, 206, 255
Puerto Rico, 27–8, 202
Punic, 123–5, 127, 134, 192, 194 (see Carthage)
Punjabi, 155, 223
Purism, 60–1, 109, 190
Pushtu, 155, 180, 224, 254 (see Afghanistan)

Quichua, 224, 226

Radio, 63, 221, 233, 321
Rajasthani, 155, 223
Reading, 311–3, 322–6
Reception of sounds, 77–83

Recordings, 14, 114–8, 221, 312
Regional languages, 235–6, 238–41
Religion, 30, 43–4, 109, 122, 145, 149, 177–86, 196–7, 200, 204
Rhetian, 56–7, 127
Rhetic, 124–5, 127
Rheto-Romansh, 56–7, 255
Roman Empire, 148, 172, 178–9, 196, 274; Eastern, 140
Romanal, 242–3
Romance languages, 11, 42–3, 45, 60, 96, 103–4, 113–4, 124–7, 134–5, 145, 148–52, 165–8, 172, 180–1, 243, 250–5, 257, 265, 269, 274–7
Romans, 60, 114–6, 127–8, 141, 147–8, 169, 191
Romansh, 56–7, 200, 225
Rome, 44, 172, 231–2; dialect, 220
Roots, 105, 243, 256–7, 267–73, 282
Ruanda, 224
Rumanian, 126–7, 135, 172, 181, 201, 206, 223, 250, 255, 257, 277, 292, 294, 296, 307
Russian, 15–6, 34–5, 37–42, 45, 91, 95–6, 99, 100, 106, 110–4, 126–7, 131–3, 135, 141, 144–5, 181–5, 193–4, 209, 214–8, 222–4, 227–30, 234–6, 237–9, 241, 249–50, 254–5, 257, 273, 277–80, 284, 291–3, 297, 307–8

Sabine, 232
Salvador, 202
Samoa, 137, 139
Sanskrit, 43, 59, 99, 123, 126, 177–8, 183, 192–3, 215–8, 250, 255–7, 268, 274, 281
Sardinia, 124–5; language, 56–7, 127, 225, 255
Sassarese, 56–7
Scandinavian, 47–9, 54, 135, 152, 173, 193, 208–9, 234–5, 250–3, 255, 257, 292–3 (see Danish; Icelandic; Norwegian; Old Norse; Swedish)
Scientific language, 30, 43–4, 46, 64, 114–8, 157, 215, 227–30, 240, 312
Scots, 206, 225, 234
Scottish English, 33, 49–50, 65, 78
Semanteme, 93
Semantics, 24, 69 (see Meaning)
Semiconsonants, 76, 82–3
Semitic, 22, 45, 97, 122–5, 127, 158, 180–5, 249–51, 258, 260–1, 263–4, 266, 268–9, 271–2, 281–2, 284

Semito-Hamitic, 258–61, 263–4, 266, 273
Semivowels, 76, 82–3
Sentence, 93, 272, 281; stress, 99–101 (see Intonation)
Serbian, 56–7, 126–7, 181–5, 297
Serbo-Croatian, 130, 168, 193, 224, 250, 255, 257, 291–3, 297, 307
Shilh, 259
Siamese, 224, 251 (see also Thai)
Siberia, 139–40, 259–61
Sibilants, 76
Sicel, 124–5, 127, 151, 167
Sicilian, 56–7, 150, 220
Sicily, 124–5, 150
Sindhi, 155, 224
Singhalese, 155, 224
Sino-Tibetan, 155, 250–1, 259–61, 263–4, 266, 270–3
Slang, 3–4, 6–7, 10–3, 51, 59–66, 172, 277, 312, 320
Slavic, 46, 56–7, 100, 113–4, 124–7, 135, 141, 144, 152, 167, 173, 180–5, 192–4, 208–9, 243, 254–8
Slovak, 127, 201, 209, 224, 255, 257, 297
Slovene, 127, 224, 255
Somali, 224, 259
Somaliland, 258, 262; British, 27–9; French, 199
Somerset dialect, 32
Sonants, 74–6
Sound, 19, 21, 51, 69–83, 85, 108, 117, 122, 129, 131, 150, 219, 309, 312, 318; shifts, 116, 252; waves, 69–77
South Africa, 27–9, 141, 143, 175, 224; English, 32–3, 62, 135, 258
South America, 27–8, 37–8, 40, 136–7, 141–2, 149, 171, 202–4, 224, 226, 263
South Arabic, 123
Southern Italian dialects, 56–7
Southern U.S. dialect, 31–2, 51–4, 116, 232–3, 293
Southwest Africa, 27–9, 261–2
Soviet Union, 37, 39–40, 215–8, 224–5, 227, 234–6, 239, 241, 258–61
Spain, 37, 39, 126–7, 141, 144–5, 147, 149, 203, 206, 232–4, 276–7
Spanish, 9, 15–6, 34–7, 40–3, 80, 89–91, 98, 101, 103, 105, 111–3, 127, 133–6, 141–3, 148–52, 159–61, 164, 166, 169–72, 174–5, 181, 193–4, 202–4, 207–9, 215–8, 222–3, 228–30, 232–3, 241, 250, 252, 255, 257, 272–3, 276–7, 291, 293–4, 296, 306, 308, 316–9
Speech, 24–5, 41, 51–8, 69–83, 93, 107, 109, 122, 295–8, 300–10, 319–21
Speed rate of language, 300
Spelin, 242–3
Spelling, 10, 58, 109, 294 (see Phonetic spelling)
Spirants, 76
Standard language, 6–7, 10, 58–60, 65, 108–9, 115, 174, 196, 232, 301, 320
Stratification of language, 65–6, 108
Stress, 99–101, 104, 297–8, 320 (see Accent)
Structure (see Grammatical structure)
Subject, 84–97
Substitution of sounds, 77, 79, 83, 295, 305
Sudan, 181, 227
Sudanese-Guinean, 158, 260–4
Suffixes, 269–70, 283–4 (see Endings)
Sumerian, 60, 122–3, 177, 189–90, 192
Sundanese, 224
Suprascripts, 295
Surds, 74–6
Swahili, 224, 226, 272
Sweden, 37, 39
Swedish, 41, 126–7, 168, 200, 208, 224, 238, 250, 255, 257, 293, 295, 306
Switzerland, 36–7, 39, 56–7, 195, 199–201, 204, 207, 225
Syllabary, 109, 299
Syllabic pattern, 83, 97–114, 301
Symbolism, 5–7, 21–5, 70, 92, 107, 109, 309
Syntax, 44, 84–97, 243 (see Word order)
Synthesis, 285
Syria, 40
Syriac, 181 (see Aramaic; Chaldean)

Tagalog, 156, 224
Tahiti, 137, 139, 198
Tamil, 155, 223, 251, 262
Tasmanian, 261–3
Tatar, 259
Technological language, 44, 47, 160, 215, 228–30
Telugu, 155, 223, 251, 262
Tense, 86, 89–90, 92, 214, 267–72, 274, 278–84, 314, 316

Teutonic, 141 (see Germanic)
Thai, 224, 259 (see Siamese)
Thailand, 40, 183
Tibetan, 144, 224, 251, 259
Tokharian, 140, 255
Toltec, 226
Tones, 101, 272
Trade, 30, 34, 109, 128, 145, 161-8, 228-30
Trade languages (see Jargon; Lingua Franca)
Transcriptions, 306-7, 309, 314-8
Translation, 8, 117, 179-83
Transylvania, 201
Trentino, 56-7, 201
Tuareg, 259
Tungus, 259
Tunisia, 36, 39, 156, 158-9, 199
Tupi-Guaraní, 226 (see Guaraní)
Turcoman, 127, 259
Turkey, 40, 137, 139, 184, 224
Turkish, 124-7, 135, 140, 167, 193, 224, 250, 259, 269, 271, 292-3, 298, 307
Tuscany, 232

Ukrainian, 55, 126-7, 183-5, 193, 223, 254-5, 292, 297
Umbria, 56-7, 232
Umbrian, 124-5, 127, 134, 151, 192, 255
United Nations, 194, 240
United States English, 26, 31, 37-8, 40, 207-10, 219, 232-3 (see American English; Eastern U.S. dialect; Midwestern American dialect; Southern U. S. dialect)
Ural-Altaic, 126-7, 137, 139, 155, 158, 249-50, 259-61, 263-4, 266, 269-71
Uralic, 137, 139-40, 259-61, 263-4, 266, 269-71, 284
Urdu, 41, 155-7, 183-5, 193, 223 (see Hindustani)
Uruguay, 40, 202
USSR (see Soviet Union)
Uzbek, 224

Vedic, 177, 192
Vegliote, 56-7, 129-30, 190

Velars, 74-5, 83
Venetian, 56-7, 220
Venetic, 124-5, 127, 151
Venezuela, 202
Verbs, 86-97, 214, 267-75, 278, 280-3, 314, 316; irregular, 311; strong and weak, 281
Vietnamese, 15, 156-7, 223, 259 (see Annamese)
Vocabulary, 9, 44, 59, 92-7, 108, 129, 131-2, 150, 162, 170-1, 181, 190, 212, 219, 249, 251, 303, 311, 320, 323-6; active and passive, 323
Vocal organs (see Organs of speech)
Voice, 92, 267, 274, 281
Volapük, 9, 237-43
Votyak, 127
Vowel harmony, 269-71
Vowels, 74, 79, 82-3, 103-6, 183, 267-72, 282, 295-8; front and back, 82-3, 269-71; long and short, 99, 297; middle, 296, 306, 314-6

Walloon, 200
Welsh, 126-7, 206, 225, 234, 250, 255, 257, 292, 299
West Africa, 221, 223, 247
West Germanic, 134, 255
Western Hemisphere, 36-8, 192-3, 258
White Russian (see Byelorussian)
Word order, 84-97, 268, 270, 274, 278, 281-3 (see Syntax)
Writing, 13-4, 21, 24-5, 31, 41, 45, 79, 93, 102, 107, 109, 122, 126, 178-85, 190-1, 294-9, 309-13

Xhosa, 224

Yiddish, 110, 173, 208-10, 224, 291
Yorkshire dialect, 32
Yoruba, 224
Yugoslavia, 37, 39, 56-7, 183, 206, 224 (see Serbo-Croatian; Slovene)

Zonal languages (see Regional languages)
Zulu, 224